HOTELS,
HOSPITALS,
AND JAILS

HOTELS, HOSPITALS, AND JAILS

A MEMOIR

ANTHONY SWOFFORD

TWELVE

NEW YORK   BOSTON

Twelve

Hachette Book Group

237 Park Avenue

New York, NY 10017

www.HachetteBookGroup.com

Printed in the United States of America

RRD-C

First Edition: June 2012

Twelve is an imprint of Grand Central Publishing.
The Twelve name and logo are trademarks of Hachette Book Group, Inc.

The Hachette Speakers Bureau provides a wide range of authors for speaking events. To find out more, go to www.hachettespeakersbureau.com or call (866) 376-6591.

The publisher is not responsible for websites (or their content) that are not owned by the publisher.

10 9 8 7 6 5 4 3 2 1

Library of Congress Cataloging-in-Publication Data
Swofford, Anthony.
    Hotels, hospitals, and jails : a memoir / Anthony Swofford. — 1st ed.
        p. cm.
    ISBN 978-1-4555-0673-6 (regular) — ISBN 978-1-4555-1351-2 (large print)
1. Swofford, Anthony.   2. Swofford, Anthony—Relations with women.
3. Swofford, Anthony—Family.   4. Swofford, Anthony—Drug use.
5. Authors, American—Biography.   6. Persian Gulf War, 1991—
Veterans—United States—Biography.   7. Veterans—Mental health—
United States.   8. Veterans—Family relationships—United States.
9. Veterans—Drug use—United States.   10. Fathers and sons—United
States—Biography.   I. Title.
    PS3619.W64A3 2012
    818'.603—dc23
    [B]
                        2012003936

This book is for my father,
John Howard Swofford
&
my love is for
Christa

HOTELS,
HOSPITALS,
AND JAILS

WAR IS THE POETRY OF MEN, BY WHICH THEY SEEK TO GAIN
ATTENTION AND RELIEF THROUGHOUT THEIR LIVES.

—THOMAS BERNHARD
GATHERING EVIDENCE

Prologue

There are days I still fantasize about combat, long nights when I wish I had rejoined the Marines as an infantry officer after September 11 and gone back over and got some war to score that kill I'd missed the first time. Most people don't understand that desire, but I was born a war baby: my father impregnated my mother while in Honolulu on R & R from Vietnam. And I believed that there existed no grander test for a man than combat. Every other pursuit was pure, unimportant leisure when compared to a firefight. I didn't know if another war would make me a better man, but it might. It certainly would have changed me. Or it might have killed me.

What did I do instead of heading back to war? My first book, *Jarhead*, was turned into a movie, and I wrote and published a novel. I divorced one woman, and I spent many years falling in love with various versions of the wrong woman and walking away from the right woman once. I bought two engagement rings. I bought a beautiful apartment on West Nineteenth Street in Manhattan. I taught at a few different colleges. I ate at some of the best restaurants in the world (in Paris, Madrid, Tokyo, Istanbul) and at some of the worst (in Ho Chi Minh City and Australia's Pilbara region). I spent an unconscionable amount of money on Burgundy wine and I drank most of it. I bought and used the occasional batch of recreational drugs. I nearly killed myself in a sixty-thousand-dollar sports car. I watched my father get sicker and sicker from a heinous disease that was possibly partially the result of his twenty-three years in the military and his exposure to Agent Orange. I thought about killing myself for months on end. A few times I fantasized about killing my father.

I flew women to London and Tokyo and Oakland and Seattle and other cities I've forgotten.

Once I slept in a hotel room in Shinjuku, Tokyo, with my girlfriend Ava. Staying in a room ten floors below us was a woman named Anya whom I had flown to Tokyo from Munich. A few Metro stops away in Roppongi was a Japanese girl I'd just spent a week with before my girlfriend Ava and my ex-girlfriend Anya arrived, a few hours apart. Somehow, I had sex with all of these women throughout the week and I did not get caught. This is to say, I took risks. And the meaning of the word *girlfriend* had a lot of elasticity. I thought I'd created a new language of lust, but really I spoke artifice and despair.

I told so many lies about my whereabouts late at night or early in the morning I'm certain I set a record for the audacity of my libido.

I believe that having been a marine and having gone to war helped me become a great liar. Growing up with a Vietnam War veteran for a father helped me become a liar, too. I learned this from my father: If the lie will not get you blown up, the lie is worth whatever the cost. My father excelled at deceit. He deceived his wife and children about what kind of husband and father he was, but mostly he deceived himself about how that little war in Southeast Asia had changed him.

Like many combat veterans I know, my father and I lived with the wickedly exciting and doggedly exhausting knowledge that we had once, for a short period of time, flirted with death, and won. This knowledge is like a drug, the purest cocaine or eighty-year-old Highland single malt scotch: once you have had some it alters your understanding of the world and of other people and of consequences.

If I lied to a lover about what neighborhood or city or country I'd slept in the night before, it didn't really matter: the relationship might sour but she would never *kill me*. Lying about sex became fun. It became a hobby. Manhattan bored me, drinking bored me, drugs bored me, but lying about sex never bored me.

Eventually I had wasted such a massive amount of money on women, wine, drugs, cars, and booze that my dissipation and deceit blew up in my face. I looked up one day and could no longer afford the mortgage on my apartment. I had to sell and became, in a way, homeless.

I would have liked to ask my father for advice but at the time our relationship was in complete disrepair.

But for some time my father had owned a Winnebago and a dream: that we two traverse the country and come to an understanding and discover a friendship. One trip wasn't enough. Neither was two. It took three.

I

Goodbye to All That

In February 2004, on the first night in the apartment I had bought on West Nineteenth Street in Manhattan, Ava and I slept downstairs. The mattress had been delivered that afternoon and I told the delivery guys to leave it in the living room. I liked the idea of the bare apartment, the walls freshly painted gallery white, nothing in the apartment but a new mattress, a bottle of champagne in the refrigerator. We brought in food from the Indian deli on Ninth Avenue. We drank the champagne and we made love.

My last night in the apartment, in May 2010, I dragged the mattress downstairs and splayed it on the bare living room floor. It was the last piece of furniture I needed to rid myself of.

Ava and I had been broken up for nearly three years but we habitually slept together every few months, whether or not one or both of us had a partner. Sometimes these evenings went well. Sometimes they did not.

I'd called her earlier in the week and asked if she wanted to say goodbye to the Mountain Lodge. The apartment invoked a Tahoe ski condo, with a two-story brick fireplace and a brick sitting window and dark wood spiral staircase.

Ava had been with me when I first saw the apartment and had somehow convinced me that I should make an offer on the most expensive property I'd looked at during my two-month, seventy-three-apartment search. That was the morning after the first night I had done cocaine with her, and only the second or third time in my life I had taken the drug.

(*Note to reader:* when purchasing an apartment, do not do so after a night of cocaine.)

Now we sat on the terrace and looked at the Empire State Building. We champagne-toasted the apartment. Six years earlier, at the age of twenty-eight, she had been beautiful. Now she was just pretty. I was six years older than she but her face held numerous and deeper lines. She'd spent her college years and her early thirties running around Manhattan doing cocaine and sleeping with many men, and smoking packs of cigarettes, and those men and that cocaine and those cigarettes had begun to take a toll.

She asked, "How many times do you think we had sex here?"

"Thousands."

We went inside. I had thrown a plain white sheet over the mattress.

Knowingly, playfully, she asked, "And why is this still here?"

"I thought you might want to say goodbye to the mattress."

"I thought that for once you might want to do this the right way," she said.

"What is the right way?"

"Marriage. Babies."

"We have never known the right way," I said.

We undressed ourselves and made love slowly and deliberately, as though defusing a bomb.

Afterward we walked around the corner to a new hip restaurant. We sat at the bar and drank gin martinis, hers dirty, mine with a twist.

After I paid the bill she said, "Once more."

We returned to the apartment. I felt as though we were entering a crime scene and the crime had been my life in New York City. We went straight to the mattress.

An hour later she dressed and we kissed at the door. She said, "Goodbye, Mountain Lodge. I'll miss you."

She did not say that she would miss me nor did I say I would miss her. I never saw her again.

I sat down on the mattress. I looked around the apartment. It had been the center of my life for many years: work, lovers, cooking. Writing. Sex. Eating.

I dragged the mattress three stories down and out of the building and threw it on the sidewalk. An old man I knew from the neighborhood passed by. He stopped and stared at the mattress, stared at me, pointed at the mattress with his cane.

He said, "You gettin' rid of that? It's a perfectly good mattress!"

I said, "That mattress should burn."

I hailed a cab to my girlfriend's house.

The next morning I moved alone to a cabin in Mount Tremper, in the Catskills.

MY NEW HOME sat on ten acres on the side of the mountain. From my former life in Manhattan I had brought with me two pieces of art, an abstract figurative painting and a drawing. The caption beneath the drawing—a dehumanized fool's version of tic-tac-toe—read: WHAT ARE YOU TRYING TO SAY TO ME? I DO NOT UNDERSTAND.

I'd bought the drawing five or six years earlier but the relevance of the artist's quotation to my life had in the prior six months reached its zenith. I understood no one. Others had difficulty understanding me.

I needed the solace of a cabin on the side of a mountain in order to redirect my life. But the cabin I found had thick beams and the forest around me was comprised of very tall old-growth pine trees, and thick beams and tall trees were an invitation to a self-hanging.

In addition to the artwork, I dragged to the mountain a few suitcases of clothes; a desk I'd had custom-made in Manhattan by a Japanese woodworker whose family had been creating beam-and-trestle furniture for five hundred years; a pair of handmade cowboy boots I'd had fashioned in Austin; ten cases of Burgundy, whites and reds; one hundred books from my library; two Turkish rugs I'd bought in Istanbul; a collection of family photographs; a wooden airplane that my paternal grandfather had constructed as a boy during the Depression; my maternal grandfather's baseball glove from the same poor period in American life; two jump ropes, one leather and one plastic; one Le Creuset Dutch oven, yellow; a large and perfectly seasoned cast-iron skillet; a memory foam pillow.

I decided that over this summer I would rid myself of the waste from a number of troubled romantic relationships. Recently there was the Bad Writer; the charming but sexually incapacitated ER Physician; the beautiful, dynamic, and sweet but troubled Dancer I almost married; the Rich Girl/Boho Artist I almost married; the Canadian Writer I should have married; another Canadian Writer I might have married.

But the grand master of my romantic ruin was Ava, the woman I'd moved to New York for in 2004.

I remember the temptation, the first kiss, and the moment when passion overrode and crushed common sense.

We met at a party in Topanga Canyon on the deck of a house with a Pacific Ocean view. We were both in town for the *Los Angeles Times* Festival of Books. She was twenty-eight and Cuban American. Her hair was black and long and straight. She had a wide girlish smile and a deep throaty laugh. She sold advertising for a New York art magazine and wanted to be a psychologist.

She said, "I have a live-in boyfriend in Brooklyn. He's lousy in bed and has a crap job in television. And he won't marry me. My father says 'Why buy the cow when the milk is free?'"

I knew that when preparing to cheat certain women malign the husband or boyfriend and invoke the folksy wisdom of the father.

I said, "I have a girlfriend who lives in SoHo and Victoria, BC. She's a wonder in bed and a great writer."

She stroked my beard and said, "I like your beard. My father has a beard."

She read aloud the time from my Rolex dive watch and said her father also wore one and that like all the old Cuban guys in Miami her father pretended to run a scuba diving company but was really still trying to assassinate Castro. She said her father was a friend of Luis Posada and had been in Caracas in September 1976 and after reading his journals she thought he might have been involved in the downing of Cuban Airlines Flight 455. I assumed that all the Cuban American girls from Miami made this boast. All of this is to say she was beautiful, dark-skinned, and possibly dangerous.

She looked at my watch again and said, "Let's get out of here."

I had no license but I drove her rental car down from Topanga to the beach at Malibu because we determined that I was less drunk. We walked toward the water and kicked our shoes off.

She said, "I want you to kiss me."

And I did.

Her shoes, stylish red Italian flats, were sucked out to sea in the wash and I broke the kiss and waded into the water to retrieve them. They were her favorite shoes and I had saved them and we returned to kissing. I don't know how long the kiss lasted, a few minutes, twenty, an hour, a month. I forgot about my girlfriend who was meeting me in Seattle the next day, I forgot about any woman I'd ever loved or kissed. We kissed more and I held her wet, red shoes in my hand.

We returned to the car and continued to kiss.

And then the Malibu cops rolled up and asked us both to get out of the car. The cop who interrogated me was Japanese American, about my age, compact and ripped, and fast-talking. I'd grown up with kids like him. My best friend from childhood was a cop in Sacramento. This guy in front of me, I knew exactly where he was coming from: he wanted to bust bad guys but didn't care too much what you did if you weren't an absolute menace.

He asked me for my license and I told him I didn't have one, that me and my girl were just sitting in the car, and that we were about to switch places so she could drive back to the hotel because I would never break the law and drive without a license.

He stared at me, as if to say *Are you kidding me, you expect me to believe that?* But he broke a half smile and said, "Quick thinking, smart-ass. Are you drunk or on drugs?"

And I said, "No." False.

He said, "If you don't have a license, who drove here?"

I said, "Her." False.

He said, "Why were you in the driver's seat?"

I said, "I wanted her to have more legroom." False.

He looked at me, either disgusted or impressed with my commitment to the lie. He walked over to her and asked, "Is your boyfriend on cocaine?"

She said, "No." True.

He asked, "Are you on cocaine?"

She said, "No." True.

He said, "There's a ten o'clock beach curfew in Malibu. If you move your car about twenty-five feet south, you can hang out on that beach or in your car and do whatever it is you need to do. I don't care. But get out of Malibu."

I don't know why the cop didn't press the issue. Maybe his shift was ending or maybe he didn't care what we were on as long as it wasn't cocaine.

Years later I would wish the cop had pushed the issue—after all, I had been sitting in the driver's seat, and any fool would have known that I'd intended to drive without a license. So what if the cop had pressed things, what if he'd checked my sobriety, what if he'd pulled me in for the night?

Ava and I wouldn't have gone back to my hotel room and been unfaithful to our partners. And I wouldn't have changed the course of my life for the next many years.

Ava studied for her PhD in psychology during our three years together. I paid for everything except her rent. I overheard her tell a friend that she was on the Swofford Stipend. Once I caught her stealing fifties from my wallet but I didn't confront her: if I had she might have left me. She introduced me to the regular recreational use of cocaine. I cheated and lied; she cheated and lied. We turned each other into animals.

*   *   *

I TOLD MYSELF that the side of the mountain would save me. Down the block from my cabin sat a Buddhist monastery, and while I didn't plan on attending meditation, I read my Shunryu Suzuki and felt that if I was close enough, it just might count as meditation. The mountains, they say, have magnetic forces, and the mountain magnetism would pull some of the good forces across the side of the mountain from those bald monks and into my cabin oasis. When it comes to spiritual health, propinquity is everything, right?

But the two six-by-sixteen-inch beams in my cabin were close, too, as well as that multitude of old-growth trees and a fittingly thick length of rope I'd been carrying around for a few years. I once wrote that the suicide is brave, which would make the rest of us cowards. I felt a coward. It would have been easy enough for me to drive down to Kingston and buy a shotgun and a single shell at Wal-Mart. I made the excuse that I didn't want to make a mess for my new landlords, a kindly hippie-ish string-instrument-playing couple in their mid-fifties with two liberally educated daughters and a happy plot of land with a very fine old mountain dog, and what a complete *dick* I'd be to blow my brains out all over their carefully constructed and manicured and maintained mountain ideal. Also, what would happen to all my stuff? My life was currently in storage on five pallets in East Williamsburg, Brooklyn. All my papers, and most of my books, and a few pieces of furniture, the few I hadn't given away while I prepared to leave Manhattan.

During the day I stayed on the mountain and I wrote. At nights I might drive to Phoenicia and drink beer and watch sports with construction workers. I walked to the top of Mount Tremper, three miles up and back, once a week.

On weekends a twenty-five-year-old hedge-funder from Manhattan would take the bus up after she got off work on Friday afternoons. We would drink and have sex, and sometimes do drugs, and watch sports until Monday morning, when she took the bus back to Manhattan. We did stupid things like buy scratcher lottery tickets, and drive forty-five miles for bad Mexican food and to get drunk with the locals. We'd flip a coin to see who got to drive home at two or three a.m.

But one weekend I'd had enough and I told her not to come up because I had a lot of work to do, and I never saw her again. She was a very pleasant girl and I am sorry that things ended abruptly. She sent me a few text messages accusing me of ruining her life, but I told her this was impossible, and that she was young and smart and pretty and by most measurements had a full and good life waiting in front of her.

I THOUGHT ABOUT suicide. I read Suzuki's *Zen Mind, Beginner's Mind* again and again.

I rewrote, thousands of times, this quote:

A good father is not a good father.

2

John Howard Swofford

My father sat in a chair in the corner of his hospital room, upper body hunched over a brand-new government-issued aluminum walker. This was December 1999. The last time I'd seen him, in August, he'd helped load my U-Haul for my move from Sacramento to Iowa City. He'd lifted boxes and furniture, and he'd bought the beers and pizza, and later he'd treated my friends to a strip club, lap dances for everyone. Now he could barely lift his head to greet me.

"Hey, Bubba," he said, deploying my least favorite of the multitude of nicknames he had for me: Tone. Old Tone. T-Bone. Pussy Hunter. Jarhead.

"Hey, Dad," I said. "What's the word? When can we wheel you out of this fleabag joint?"

"You ain't wheeling me nowheres. The doc says walk. I'm gonna walk."

"So let's hit it." I clapped my hands twice. I had a date that evening in San Francisco with my old college girlfriend.

A few days earlier I'd received a phone call from my sister Kim telling me that the Old Man had bit it hard in his living room—he'd collapsed, grasping for life, gasping for air. And whom did he call? Nine-one-one? No, he called a guy who performed menial labor for him. And the guy drove over in his pickup truck and heaped my father into the front seat, and here at the hospital his doctor told him to stop smoking or he would die soon.

When? he asked.

Now.

He'd smoked for forty-five years. He'd also spent twenty-two years in the Air Force, thirteen months in Vietnam, many of those months within the Agent Orange–tainted jungles and many other years breathing the fumes from the narcotics of war that drive the workings and skeletons of every military base.

Here we were on a military base, the same place I'd been born, Travis Air Force Base. In the late 1960s, while her husband fought in Vietnam, hippies spit at my mother's car as she entered the base to take her children to the hospital or to buy groceries.

My father pointed out the window. "You see that building, that short building over there? That's where you were born."

"You tell me that every time we're on base."

"Well, Bubba, maybe it's important to me."

It would be many years before I could understand the importance of such a building to a man.

Right now all I wanted was to wheel the Old Man out of here. Hell, I'd fireman's-carry him, if need be. I had a seven p.m. drinks date in San Francisco, forty-five miles away, and nothing would stop me from making it. I hadn't been laid since moving to Iowa City. My father was alive and breathing. I needed to get him home and I needed to hit the road.

"Have some patience with me, Son. I'll be slow a few days and pretty soon here I'll be back up to speed."

We stopped by the pharmacy and picked up a twelve-pack of meds. It took the pharmacist half an hour to explain the proper usage and the possible negative reactions and interactions. Other than to treat a bad batch of migraines in the 1970s, when he'd returned from Vietnam, my father had never been medicated.

He asked the pharmacist, "How the hell do you guys expect me to remember all of that?"

"We don't," he said. He handed my father a card with the pharmacy number on it. "Give us a call anytime."

I carried my father's meds and the overnight bag my sister had packed for him. My father slowly scooted along the corridors of the hospital—a working military hospital that also served the large retiree population in the area. Creaking GIs lurked everywhere. Many wore baseball caps from whatever unit they were most proud of serving with.

It took half an hour to get to the car.

He said, "Now, Tone, how about you take me grocery shopping? And I want to rent some movies. I think I'll be bed-resting for a week."

Within the confines of the hospital my father had not seemed out of place. Hobbling around were other addled men; whether it was from disease or old age or drink or smokes or government-sanctioned pesticide campaigns, the sick men belonged there in the massive sick bay of Travis Air Force Base. With a glance around I could easily find some guy worse off than my father: the blind, the amputee, the insane.

But in the parking lot of the strip mall near his house I registered just how incredibly sick he was. I knew this would only worsen. I removed his walker from the trunk and opened it at the passenger door. He needed help up. Hanging from the walker was a toy figurine of some cartoon character I vaguely recognized.

"What is this?" I asked my dad.

"The candy stripper gave me that, Tone."

"Candy striper. Not stripper. But they don't even use that term anymore."

"Oh, right. That was one of them, what do you educated people call it? Freudian trips?"

"Slips."

"Right. Freudian strip. Candy stripers. Well, they'd get more business if they hired some candy strippers, don't you think?"

"I suppose the dirty old GIs would like that."

"Who you calling dirty and old?"

"Who do you think?"

With his stripers and strippers and Freudian trippers, I could not tell if my father was playing with me. Probably so. But I did not have the patience for this. The time was now four forty-five p.m. and I had less than three hours before I needed to be seated at a bar with a girl, a girl who would definitely have sex with me.

"Dad, just tell me what groceries you need and what movies you want. I can do this in twenty minutes. We'll be out of here."

It was nearly the shortest day of the year and already getting dark.

Dad said, "Give me some patience, Tone. I want to be outside. I got stuck in that room a week."

And so we took our time. I walked slowly alongside my father. The severity of his disease began to register for me. I noticed how people looked at my father: the Man Lugging an Oxygen Tank. I knew the first thought that came to my mind when I saw a person using oxygen: poor white riverboat gamblers in the Midwest or South chain-smoking the Social Security Administration and Medicare into oblivion.

I wanted to say to the people who stared: *No, you've got it all wrong. He's a veteran. He was in Vietnam. It might have been Agent Orange.* But of course I knew it wasn't Agent Orange: it was forty-five years of Marlboros.

This was not my first experience with feeling humiliation because of someone else's dire medical condition: in 1997 and 1998 my brother, Jeff, slowly died of a cancer and I was always ashamed of his illness whenever we were in public.

Is this a moral weakness in me?

Perhaps, I thought, as a little girl stared at the cartoon toy hanging from my father's walker and then looked in horror at the oxygen tube shoved up his nostrils. With a shriek the girl recoiled into her mother's pants leg.

We bought groceries for one of my father's favorite one-pot meals, something he called goulash but that was really just a mash of over-boiled vegetables and meat in canned tomatoes, massively dosed with paprika.

We rented a stack of Clint Eastwood and Arnold Schwarzenegger movies.

Back in the car Dad said, "You know, I'd like to have dinner with Clint Eastwood someday. Jeff met him down in Carmel, didn't he say?"

"Jeff claimed a lot of things," I replied.

"Maybe when I'm catting around again I'll go down to Carmel and look old Clint up."

"You should do that."

"Other than Johnny Cash, Clint is my guy. When I was your

age they used to say I looked like Johnny Cash. That's what old Margarita in Texas used to say. 'Johnny, you look just like Señor Cash.' Damn that tickled me. Old Margarita. I'll have to visit her, too."

My father either did not grasp the immensity of the medical event he'd just survived, or he refused to recognize the totality of change it would bring to his life. This stubbornness or ignorance probably kept him alive for so many years while other patients might have just given up and died. His diagnosis was COPD, chronic obstructive pulmonary disorder. Others might call it emphysema. COPD sounds, I don't know, snappier? Less trashy? Emphysema connotes poor white riverboat gamblers in the Midwest or South chain-smoking the Social Security Administration and Medicare into oblivion. COPD? It's just an acronym. But the end result is the same: your lungs will quit working someday and you will die. The elasticity of the oxygen sacs in your lungs will eventually fail, the sacs will dry up and calcify, and eventually you will want to inhale but there will be no room. All around you, everywhere, there will be oxygen, but you will be allowed none of it.

When I thought of my father's lungs I thought of an old hunk of white coral that I'd had as a kid. I knew that it was bad to have a piece of coral. I knew that the coral reefs of the world were diminishing, but I liked having this strange piece of the ocean. The coral sat on my desk next to the piece of lava from Mount Fuji.

Brazenly, my father wanted to stop by one of his drinking holes just to say hello to the guys. It was now six-thirty. My date in San Francisco would never happen. I called the ex-girlfriend and she agreed to meet me in Fairfield later that night. I took my father to his bar.

I never understood it then, because he never articulated it, but I guess my father was proud of me. I was his son who had gone off and joined the Marines and served in a sniper platoon and gone to war and kicked Saddam's ass, and returned home and gone to college, and paid his way through it working in a warehouse and with a little help from the GI Bill. And now I was in graduate school in Iowa City.

He introduced me to the bartender, a woman in her fifties wearing ten pounds of makeup and thirty years of rough road. She looked as though she'd been drinking since the previous night's shift ended. "This is my son Tony. He's gonna be a famous writer someday. He's studying it in Iowa. The Writers' Warehouse, right, Tone?" He winked at the bartender.

"Something like that. Can I have a double shot of bourbon?" I asked the bartender.

"That all they teach you in writing college, how to drink?" he asked.

"That's one of the rumors about the place."

Writers' Warehouse. Freudian strip. If I had paid more attention, it was a funny skit my father performed: the father playing redneck to his smarty collegiate son. But the animosity that ran through his commentary was so obvious, or obvious to me. Anyone else would just see a charming older Southern gentleman who liked flirting with the ladies. Now he was not only old, but sick, too. His virility and vanity had taken a mortal blow. The handsome dark devil, the Johnny Cash look-alike, the wild man, the ravishing lover, his lungs had failed him and he was down for the count. Everyone knows the dick needs oxygen in order to perform. He did not want to admit it, but this was a major loss. This was *the* major loss. My father lived for good times and

he also lived for the ladies. My father took the ladies out dancing and drinking and he took them home. Good-Time Johnny.
Good-Time Johnny might have to take a final bow.

I drank my bourbon in silence while my father talked with
his bar friends. They were happy to have him back in the crowd.
Everyone always loved my father and his Southern charm. He
was a good fella, that John Howard Swofford.

I stepped out to make a call to the girl in San Francisco. Hell,
why not meet here at this divey little bar? I gave her directions.

My father asked me what all the commotion was on my
phone. "What are you planning? You got that look in your eye.
I know that look. That's the Pussy Hunter. Swofford libido. A
blessing and a curse. Who is it this time?"

Did I like this? Did I like my father calling me Pussy
Hunter? Yes.

"Marin County," I said. When I'd dated this girl in college
my father could never remember her name, only that she had
grown up in Marin County, and so that is what he called her.

"Goddamn, Tone. Pulling out the reserves? Marin County.
Nice girl."

"I was supposed to meet her in San Francisco. But she's coming here."

"Right here? To the bar? Hell, Tone. Don't do that. Take her
out somewhere nice. Take her to dinner. Take her out dancing."

Lessons from a pro.

He continued, "This must be a generational thing. You can
just meet a girl out for a few drinks and call it a night? Just like
that?"

"It depends on the girl and the night. We have known each
other awhile."

"I might know a woman awhile but still take her out on a Friday night. There's a good steak house downtown. Take her there, for Christ's sake."

"She's a vegetarian."

"Jesus, Tone. Jesus. My own son. Meeting a girl at a shitty bar and gonna try to get in her pants. You gonna get a hotel room?"

"Nope. I'm going to fuck her in your Cadillac."

"Goddamn, Son. You can't do that. You'll get you both arrested. And I'm not gonna bail your silly ass out. Fucking in a car. Jesus Christ."

Marin County never showed.

I helped my father settle into his home, into this new lifestyle of sickness.

I arranged his meds by day and dose. I plugged in the oxygen system that had been delivered to the front stoop that afternoon and cut a hundred-foot length of medical tube. I cut up the veggies and the meat and threw it all in a large pot with a few quarts of water, four chicken bouillon cubes, canned tomatoes, and a cup of paprika. We watched *Hang 'Em High* and my father fell asleep next to me on the couch. His oxygen tube hung from his nostrils like a clear snake and the oxygen machine howled.

The next afternoon a guy from the company that would service his oxygen came by. He was a big burly dude with a goatee. He said that his own father had succumbed to this disease.

"My old man," he said, "he did what most people do when they get the diagnosis. He sat on his ass and got fat and stayed lazy and he was dead in two years, right there in the chair he sat in when he got home from the hospital. I couldn't tell you if he ever moved once."

"I plan to stay active. I plan to keep my job. This thing won't take me down. Not soon, anyway," my father said.

"Sir, I can't say it's a pleasure to meet you. It's never a happy occasion when I meet a new customer. But I do hope we'll have your business for a very long time."

I couldn't help but think that someday this big burly dude with a goatee would show up to deliver my father his oxygen and instead find him dead.

I SPENT THE rest of my winter break from grad school kicking around Northern California, crashing on friends' couches or floors or in the bed of some former girlfriend or another. Every few days I'd drop in on my father and run errands for him or complete chores around his house.

One night Marin County met me at my dad's house.

"Good to see you, darling," my dad said, extending a hand and making a slight bow. "It seems like it's been years."

"Only months, Mr. Swofford. I saw you in August when we helped Tony load his truck for Iowa."

"Right, right."

I had not reminded my father of her name and I saw his brain working hard to retrieve it from his cloudy memory bank. And I knew he would not. Throughout my boyhood he never remembered my friends' names. He referred to them by the names of the streets they lived on: Boyd, Marconi, Walnut, Lillian Lane.

"Your folks still live over in Marin County?" he asked.

"They do. And my younger brother."

"Right. Right. Your father has a younger wife, and a son?"

My father could not remember this woman's name but he

recalled that her father, a man his own age, had a wife in her late thirties and a young son.

"So, Dad. How about I make dinner?" I offered.

"There's goulash in the fridge!"

"I'm not feeling the goulash. I picked up steaks. I'll throw them on the grill."

My father looked lewdly at Marin County off and on throughout the evening. She was seven years younger than I and possessed a freshness and innocence not yet fractured by the bigger world. She worked as an intern with a radical publishing company and her father paid her rent in the Mission. She made bad art with crushed eggshells, and she wanted to change the world. And she was gloriously open in bed, or wherever we had sex.

For a few months while we dated in college she had lived at home and I would drive to Marin from Sacramento. We'd head into San Francisco for a date and then later return to Marin. We'd drive to the top of Mount Tamalpais and have sex in my truck, and then I'd drive her home. I'd park my truck around the corner from her dad's house and sleep in the cab, and in the morning we'd reconvene. Sometimes I'd do this for three days straight without a shower.

I cleaned the dinner dishes while they watched a Clint Eastwood movie.

"Hey, Pops," I said, interrupting a gunfight. "We're going to head out for a drink. You mind if I take your car?"

"No problemo. Just don't drive her drunk."

"We'll only have a few. Back at your local."

"Tell them you are Alabama John's son."

We didn't make it to the bar. We didn't leave my dad's driveway.

We jumped in the backseat of his car and turned it into our own little sex dungeon.

During a break, Marin County said, "I like your dad. He's a sweet guy. I like his accent. Is he going to be OK?"

"I don't think that being on oxygen is OK. But he plans to stay active, and he seems to have a pretty good attitude right now. He's not overly depressed and he's not giving up; he's not talking about where he wants us to bury him, so maybe he'll hang on awhile."

"Will you tell him we screwed in his car?"

"He'll figure it out."

"You are so bad."

Later when I entered my dad's house he was asleep on the couch. I awoke him and helped him back to his room.

He said, "Goddamn, Tone. As soon as you walked out the door I remembered her name. And now I've forgotten it. You have a good time?"

"We didn't leave the driveway."

"Dang. Something wrong with the car?"

"Nothing wrong with the car. We sat and talked."

He looked at me with a sidelong glance.

"You're bullshitting me, Bubba. You had sex with that girl in my goddamn car! Jesus. You better pay to get that interior detailed tomorrow. God knows what you did in my goddamn brand-new car. Thank god it's leather seats."

Was it cruel of me to invite a young, beautiful woman into my father's house and parade her sexuality and her youth in front of the dying beast and then have sex with her in his car? Probably. But maybe it got him off.

The next day I mowed his lawn and made a few more pots of goulash before heading back to Iowa City. He stood in his driveway as my taxi backed away. He leaned on his walker. He hadn't dressed. He wore the uniform of old sick men: white T-shirt and briefs. His legs were pale as rice and his forearms deeply sunstained by decades of outdoor labor. The oxygen tube snaked down his body, a river, a story, a life. I waved to my father, not knowing when I'd see him again, or how long he might live.

3

Fairfield to Billings, the Joker Is Out of Breath, April 2009

One afternoon in April 2009, nearly a decade after his first collapse, I arrived at my father's house and he greeted me in his driveway wearing white briefs with a T-shirt tucked in so that the look approximated that of a onesie. These days he wore dentures, but he hadn't had a chance to put them in. He grinned at me, all gums, like a baby.

In the age-old tradition of crotchety and stubborn men, my father fought his diagnosis of COPD with abandon and verve. He held on to his job running a strip mall maintenance crew, even though a medical retirement coupled with his military retirement would have provided enough financial security for him to thrive and even head to Mexico for the winters.

I want to live, he screamed every morning as he cleared his lungs of muck and prepared for work.

Friends of his had gotten sick and died dozens of different ways, and the Old Man was still kicking. I'd been married and divorced, and the Old Man was still kicking. I'd lived in Iowa City, Portland, Oakland, and now Manhattan; I'd traveled around the world twice; I'd written and published two books; and the Old Man was still kicking. I'd been engaged and unengaged to two different women, and the Old Man was still kicking.

He did not say hello, he said, "Goddamn, Tone, we got a lot of work to do to get this rig road-ready!"

The next morning I'd enclose myself with my father in his forty-four-foot Winnebago to drive from Fairfield, California, to Billings, Montana, in order to attend my niece's college graduation. Over twenty-five hours, twenty-three minutes, and 53.7 seconds we'd carve our way through 1,100 miles of the western United States. The physical sensation of driving a Winnebago at high speeds approximates that of sitting in a Manhattan studio apartment while a 5.5-magnitude earthquake revs unabated within your four thin walls.

My father had prepared a twenty-five-point pre-trip checklist.

During my middle school and high school years my father dictated my daily routine with a checklist he prepared every Sunday evening for the following week:

Brush teeth. (Daily. AM, at school after lunch, PM)
Floss teeth. (Daily, PM)
Eat three pieces of fruit. (3x daily: breakfast, afternoon
    snack, dinner)
Feed and water dogs. (2x daily)
Shower. (Daily)
Wash cars with Dad. (Saturday or Sunday)
Pick up dog poop. (Saturday, regardless of weather)
Mow lawn. (Saturday, weather permitting, check with Dad)
Perform pool maintenance. (Chemicals, vacuum, maintain
    flower planters)
Dust, straighten, and vacuum bedroom. (Saturday)

*(All of these chores must be performed in order to receive the full allow-
ance. Deductions will be made for failures. It is possible to receive Zero
Allowance and to attain a Negative Balance. Further punishment is
also possible: groundings from: TV privileges, phone use, and friend
visitations.)*

The allowance of a few dollars fluctuated. I think I topped
out at $5.50 a week in 1986.

The reward for completing the Winnebago checklist remained
elusive. And how might my father punish me for failure?

In his kitchen I made a pot of goulash for the road. We'd
shopped earlier at the commissary on Travis Air Force Base. As
we passed the old hospital where I was born, now an adminis-
trative building, he'd pointed to it and said, once again, "Hey,
Bubba. That building there is where you were born."

I loaded the RV cabinets with bags of chips and crackers and
cookies. The goulash-filled Tupperware went in the refrigerator.
On the RV I checked the oil and transmission fluid and wiper
fluid levels. I checked the water level on the batteries. I checked
the oil level on the generator. I made sure the hydraulics worked.
I made sure that the slide-out bedroom and living room worked.
I popped a bag of popcorn in the microwave. I made certain the
refrigerator and freezer refrigerated and froze. I flushed the toilet.
I ran the shower and the sinks. I turned on the TV. I checked the
slide-out stairs. I tied down ten cylinders of my father's oxygen.
I climbed on the roof and had a peek around, and everything
looked attached. I stood tall on the roof. I looked up and down
my father's suburban street. I spread my arms wide. The sun beat
down on me heavy and bright. I wanted to ride all the way to
Montana on the roof.

*   *   *

BEFORE LEAVING NEW YORK for this trip I'd had a drink with my friend Oren, and he asked me, "What the hell are you going to talk to your father about for one thousand miles?"

I said, "He'll piss me off by spewing a bunch of garbage about Mexicans and Arabs and Asians, and I'll tell him he's a stupid old racist fuck. And then we'll drive for a few hundred miles in total silence. And simply to piss me off he'll spew more racist shit he doesn't even believe. And I'll call him a racist fuck. And he'll tell me that I'm young and stupid. And he'll tell a story about his best friend when he was a young boy, the black kid whose mom worked for his grandparents, and how he was banned from playing with this best buddy of his in the front yard, and he never understood why, and it hurt his feelings that he couldn't play with his best buddy in the front yard, so one day he just did it, he walked to the front yard with his best buddy, this black kid, and they played with their toys in the front yard, and it lasted a few minutes, until the black boy's mother came running around the corner and snatched the boy up by his arm and dragged him to the backyard. And then the lady grabbed John Howard by the arm and dragged him into the house through the front door, where he was yelled at by an old blind aunt, and he never saw the black boy again. And he will say that that is the reason he left the South when he was seventeen and never wanted to return. And somehow this will stand as his defense against the politically incorrect shit he says. He'll say that I know nothing about the South and nothing about race because I was raised in color-blind California, and that he went out of his way to raise me in an integrated and open community and that I had many black friends growing up and I should thank him for that. And I'll say, 'You are fucking crazy.'"

"Will you talk about your brother?" Oren asked.

"Only if I bring him up," I said.

"That's going to be a long one thousand miles."

WE CRESTED WELLS, Nevada, the Winnebago whined, and I pushed us east on Highway 50. Above my head a cupboard jutted open and a dozen CDs crashed to the floor and scattered like playing cards.

We were on our sixth time through Merle Haggard's *Greatest Hits* and our third stretch of total silence after a fight over some racist and politically incorrect garbage that had come out of his mouth.

But my father wanted to talk. He said, "This is just between you and me. You take everything so serious. So I say something about Koreans eating dogs, and your little sister is Korean? What does that mean? It's a joke from Vietnam."

"Vietnam? A joke? Kim is not a joke. She is your daughter, my sister, our family. You don't get it, man? It is not cool to say racist shit about Koreans eating dogs. Not. Fucking. Cool."

"You know the Vietnamese eat dog. You told me you ate dog sausage in Vietnam. So what's the difference?"

"It's not a joke. It's not funny. You sound totally ridiculous. Do you not understand that they are totally different countries?"

"We fought 'em both. It's all Orientals to me."

I deliberately swerved toward the right and hit the deep gashes in the pavement, which made a sound like a torso being beaten with a hose, and my father said, "Ho, Tone, keep her steady."

As we entered Wells my father said, "Wells, Nevada, home of the famous Cottontail Ranch. Wanna get some tail?"

My father is a self-proclaimed joker. I've used the word *antagonist* to describe him more than once. He likes to, as he puts it, "get under your skin." He likes to "stir the pot" and "keep it interesting." But maybe he's serious this time? And for a minute I thought about it. I thought about those stories of French fathers taking their sons to visit a prostitute when they turn sixteen or twelve or whenever it is that Frenchmen start frequenting brothels. We could swing in, just have a beer, and take a looksee at some girls. I thought, I admit, that it would make a good story, and I could write an essay about drinking beer in a Nevada whorehouse with my father, sell it to a slick magazine, pay for a trip somewhere.

But I said, "No, thanks."

At age eighteen while a marine in the Philippines it was one thing to walk into a bar and let a girl sit on your lap while listening to Duran Duran or New Order. But at age thirty-eight, outside the depressed town of Wells, Nevada, traveling at sixty-five miles per hour in a metal earthquake with my oxygen-depleted father, hanging out with prostitutes was an entirely different concept.

"Obscene," I said to my father. "That would be obscene."

He yelled, "It's legal!" And he laughed. "Hell, Tone, you've turned into a little pansy. Ain't you a marine? Don't marines live off beer and whores? I never met a marine didn't live off beer and whores."

If life were so simple as beer and whores we'd all be drunk and laid.

Silence.

Twenty miles later he said, "I guess that's what happens when you go big-time. Now you gotta be a gentleman."

I ignored him. It was midnight and I'd been driving for about eight hours. I'd stopped for gas and a candy bar in Winnemucca and otherwise I'd been at the wheel trying to keep this traveling earthquake between the lines.

I'd never been a headache man but my head throbbed; it felt as though power drills had split my temples open, the pain bled down into my jaw, into my teeth, so bad my tongue hurt and the roof of my mouth stung. I thought about calling the physician I was dating in New York and asking her to call in a prescription to a pharmacy in some shit town in the middle of nowhere in Nevada or Idaho, in the middle of the night, for something big, something strong to knock me out—an antipsychotic, that's what I needed. A buffalo tranquilizer. I needed to get so high that my father would have to drive the rest of the way and I could sit in the seat next to him, drooling, pain-free.

I THOUGHT OF how easy it would be to end this trip: first yank the oxygen tube out of his nose, then just keep driving. He'll wallow a bit in pain, he might grasp for me but I'll easily swat him away: if I must, I'll beat him away, I'll beat him with my closed fist; he's a small man now and I weigh two hundred pounds, my forearms are as muscled as his legs and I will crush him, I will watch him slowly expire. I'll drive all night in splendid silence and pull into a gas station, say in Whitehall, Montana, I think I have enough gas to get there, and I'll walk in and ask the nice lady behind the counter with feathered and unevenly bleached hair if she'll call the police because I think my father has died in his sleep in the passenger seat of his RV.

33

I'll walk outside and sit on the curb with my head in my hands, wait for the sheriff to arrive; the sheriff will be a real cowboy. He'll wear a sheepskin-lined denim vest with his badge pinned near his heart, he'll wear cowboy boots caked with horse shit and hay, he'll wear on his hip the biggest pistol east of Butte. And I'll tell the sheriff the story of how my father and I went to the Cottontail Ranch in Wells, Nevada, and how my father watched me fuck a prostitute and just after that said to me one of the last things I heard him say: *Tone, that sure was fun, we'll have to do it again someday.* And then he fell asleep and I kept driving and he seems to be out of breath.

"He's expired," the sheriff will confirm after a brief investigation. And he'll console me the way cowboy sheriffs do: squeeze my shoulder, say he's sorry for my loss, and tell me to keep on truckin'.

And when he realizes I don't understand, he'll say, "We don't got a morgue here, son. Whyn'cha take 'er on down the road."

And this is how I will come to drive around with my dead father next to me in his RV.

BACK IN THE RV, in the middle of the night, my father said, "Can't I joke a little? You sure are high-strung."

This is the most ironic statement in the history of spoken language. My father calling me high-strung. The man was so tense and angry when I was a kid that I cowered at the mere mention of his name.

"Just guy talk, Son. Don't be so goddamn serious. Locker-room talk." He said this as though I'd hurt his feelings. He stared out the window. Silence. The Joker was hurt.

*   *   *

AT A PARTY back in New York I told a friend the story about my father asking me to become a paying customer at the Cottontail Ranch. The friend was disappointed when I told him that I said no. He thought I'd ruined a perfectly good story.

I said, "Can't the story be *not* going?"

"That's no story," he said. "Writer doesn't go to whorehouse with father. That's no story!"

With a few keyboard strokes I discovered that the Cottontail Ranch had been closed since 2004. It was on the market. I found Web images of the old ranch. It looked like a bleak place where dark men did bad things to women. Though some women probably put themselves through college working weekends at the ranch, and some girl probably bought her daddy a gold Cadillac, and some girls probably raised a family and paid a mortgage, and some girls probably made a party out of loving.

AT TWIN FALLS we stopped to change drivers, not a simple matter of switching seats. Each time my father exerted himself he was challenged to fill his lungs with oxygen. The man wanted to breathe easily; he simply couldn't. The man wanted to live, he worked hard at it, but he didn't have long: eventually his lungs would simply quit. In the ten years since he'd collapsed his lung capacity had slowly diminished and the number of meds he was on had increased.

At the side of the road in Nevada he had to dope himself up. I realized that he'd been lying subtly to me for a few years. He'd always told me that there was a schedule for the inhalers, and that made sense to me and I paid no attention to his timing and it made me think that he was somewhat healthy, or healthy enough to be medicated on a schedule, but alongside the desert in Nevada I realized that he took the inhaler whenever he exerted himself and that at this point moving meant exertion.

He stood at the RV's kitchen sink and administered an inhaler. At some point in his treatment he'd discovered a system for the inhalers; a respiratory therapist had told him that he shouldn't immediately stack the meds but rather take a break between the two inhaled medicines in order to increase their efficacy, ten minutes—and so he took one and then he stood at the kitchen sink of his RV, and he breathed heavy for ten minutes, bent at the waist.

He set a kitchen timer shaped like an egg. He hadn't unwrapped the timer, it was still in its packaging just as it had been when he'd bought it, likely on a military base: in the store you'd give it a spin and see if the sound of the alarm agreed with you. Apparently it satisfied my father.

I walked outside. I pissed. I thought I saw the eyes of a coyote in the brush. The moon hung thin in the sky like a silver splinter in the universe's thumb. The desert smelled like my piss and dirt.

Back in the RV, on his second inhaler, my father gargled water and spit it out. I found this disgusting. I'd spent my childhood listening to my father, each morning, coughing the smoker's phlegm up from his lungs. I'd sit eating Wheat Chex and drinking Sunny Delight with my siblings, and down the hall he'd gag on the by-products of his own body. Gargling, spitting.

But now that he was sick the gargling and spitting were part of his treatment: the sick person must wash his mouth of the medicine after it has been inhaled—the remains of the medicine, for some reason my father can't articulate, must not stay in the mouth. And so he gargled and spit: and again my father disgusted me.

He took the wheel.

*　　*　　*

I USED TO say that my father was a builder. In reality he was a handyman. He fixed a fence, he threw up some Sheetrock, he fixed your plumbing, replaced your toilet, rewired your electricity, added a new living room, converted your garage into a place where your drug addict nephew could crash for a few months. If he needed to, he'd hire a guy or two for the serious labor, ripping up the earth or tearing down a wall, mixing and pouring concrete, hauling broken appliances out of a kitchen or mudroom.

But I never told anyone this. I wanted my father to be a master of the universe. This is the wish of every boy. But what I really wanted was for him to master love: I wanted my father to love and protect me forever, until the day I died: an impossibility.

THIS IS A story about my father almost getting his ass kicked in a dive bar in Fairfield, California, three days before Christmas in 1996. The next day I'd go hiking on the Lost Coast with my roommate, so I visited my father in Fairfield for an early Christmas. Since I'd returned from the Marine Corps four years earlier my father had insisted on being buddies. He called me "Bubba." He called me "Old Tone." He thought we should hang out and drink and talk about women. He liked talking about cars but he loved talking about women even more. He might be halfway through a story about the 1956 Thunderbird that he and my mother drove from Washington State to Georgia, and then he'd pause, thinking of all the women he might have had along the way had he only been single.

"That car," he'd say, "was a pussy magnet. I'd loan that to single guys on the weekends and they'd get so much tail."

The bar where we drank was just outside Travis Air Force

Base. When I was born it was called Cats. It was a strip club back then. I imagine that just prior to and shortly after my birth my father probably put in some quality time on tip row at Cats. Strip bars across the world are filled with men whose wives are heading to the delivery room.

I'm quite certain that this Christmas visit was the first time that my father told me about Margarita, his "Mexicana lover," as he referred to her. He'd once told me about going to a whorehouse in Juárez, and at first I thought he was conflating the stories, that the sad prostitute from Juárez was a stand-in for all the Mexican women he'd wanted to or had slept with. My father's storytelling is maddeningly circular and often devoid of proper pronouns and temporal markers, and back when he drank, this confusion-laced narrative style was even more pronounced. After half an hour of hearing about Margarita I realized that she was a real woman and that when they'd met she'd been married to another Air Force guy and had lived outside an Air Force base somewhere in Texas and that at this time I was seven years old.

I said, "So you cheated on Mom with a married woman?"

"Her old man was an asshole. He never fucked her. And what your mom never knew never hurt her."

I thought of my young mother: a woman who gave up college for life as a military wife. I see her drying dishes at the sink, apron tied in a bow at her waist. My father's poison, his lies and marital misdeeds, piles up in her bloodstream as she goes about the house. There she is: a happy wife and a generous and loving mother, there she is changing my diapers, tending my brother's bloody knees, dressing my older sister.

A photo: we are on the lawn of the Vacaville house, my mother, brother, sister, and me. My younger sister has not yet been adopted. It's Easter 1973, I'm two and a half years old. My mother is dying and the only person who knows this is my father, the man taking the picture, the man poisoning her blood and the blood of our family with his lies and misdeeds.

So we were at the bar that used to be a strip club, one of my father's locals, and the bartenders and other regulars knew him. They called him Alabama John. They talked about so-and-so, the Fuckup, and so-and-so, the Wife Beater, and so-and-so, the Drunk. I sensed that they envisioned themselves in a television show: as famous as all the famous drunks in television shows about bars, because in the television shows no one pukes in the bathroom and no one bangs up the family station wagon on the way home; in television shows the drunks are pretty and hand-some and witty and well-read and never too obviously drunk in public, the place where most drunks spend a lot of time drinking and embarrassing themselves.

The actual bar was shaped in a circle, with the liquor shrine in the middle. The liquors on offer were low- to middle-shelf. Beer came in the can. My father alternated between blended scotch and soda and beer. I guessed this was some old trick for getting less drunk. I'd always thought that the trick was alternat-ing water with drinks or not drinking alcohol at all.

"Look at that hot Mexican girl over there," he said. "Damn I love the Mexican girls. I bet her name is Margarita. She's with a fucking convict. Look at that piece of shit covered in tattoos."

Now I followed him: drunk in a bar sees a pretty Mexican woman, thinks of the Mexican woman he cheated on his wife with, tells his son the story of his infidelity so his son knows that he was once a virile man who could have any woman he wanted.

"Hey, Pops, maybe it's time to roll. I can drive."

"It's early. Let's have another."

I had a girlfriend at home in my bed in Sacramento. What was I doing out on a Friday night with my father in a shitty dive bar in Fairfield?

He got up to take a piss. He needed to navigate through the area with two pool tables in order to make it to and from the bathroom. On the way back from the bathroom he nudged the pool cue of the young ripped Latino guy who was with the pretty Mexican girl.

My father was fifty-six and still holding on to his good looks and dark hair. Despite decades of smoking, his skin was taut, and because of working outside he had a suntan that announced vitality. He had a bit of a beer belly because he'd never exercised. But he was a laborer from a long line of laborers. In the past two hundred years there had been a few businessmen, a lawyer or two, one professor, but otherwise the Swoffords had been farmers or laborers. His arms and shoulders were strong, the strength gained by humping ninety-pound bags of concrete and stacks of four-by-four studs, hanging Sheetrock, laying roofs, digging ditches.

He considered himself a pretty bad motherfucker, the kind of crazy bastard only a fool would mess with, the kind of crazy bastard who would challenge an ex-con on a Friday night in a seedy bar in Fairfield.

My father had his finger in the guy's face, the way he used to shove his finger in my face. I started across the bar. By the time I got there the ex-con had my father shoved against the wall with his pool cue crushing my dad's chest.

"Hey, brother," I said. "That's my pops. He's an old man. He's just drunk and talking shit. Let's walk it off, man. No one needs this. It's Friday night, no way to start the weekend."

40

"Your pops needs to watch where he's walking. He's been bumping into my cue all night, and looking at my girl like he's gonna try to fuck her. She don't fuck old men."

"You never know what she does when you're in jail," my father said.

"You're lucky I'm on parole. I'd break your face."

I peeled the cue out of his hand and pushed him a few feet back.

To my father, I said, "Go back to your seat," as though chastising a kindergartner.

The ex-con stared at me. He was a beast. He'd crush me.

I said, "Sorry, bro. He's being stupid. Holidays. Bad time of year."

We settled back into our seats. One of his drinking pals took a couple digs at my dad. He didn't appreciate it.

"This place is full of assholes," he said.

But we stayed for another.

It took him a few minutes to cool down.

"So, Bubba," he said. "Tell me about this little hiking trip you're doing with Mike."

My father rarely asked questions about my life. Mostly he talked, about cars and women and how the government was screwing him, the post office, the DMV, the IRS.

His question surprised and excited me. My father, interested in my life!

"It's going to be great," I said. "The Lost Coast. It's one of the most remote hiking areas on the West Coast. We're getting dropped off at the north trailhead and picked up three days later twenty-five miles south. We probably won't see more than two or three other people for the whole trip."

"Twenty-five miles?" he asked. "That's it? That's a little Boy Scout hike. I can hike that trail better than you young bucks. You think you're tough? You think you're hot shit? Why don't you do fifty, down and back?"

"I don't think I'm tough shit. That's the way people do the hike. It will be difficult in parts. We have to know the tides to navigate beaches. There might be intense weather. It's no Iron Man but it's not a Boy Scout hike either."

"Well, when you ladies want to do some serious hiking, when you want an old pro to teach you how to hike, like we did back in the jungle, give me a call."

I could only laugh. I laughed in his face, and said, "Dad, you couldn't hike two miles without having to stop and catch your breath. In my entire life I've never seen you exercise a day."

He got snarly. I remembered this nastiness from when I was a kid, a brand of anger and bravado and quick temper that constantly threatened to explode: a bucket of dynamite with a short fuse.

"OK, Tone. You think you can take your old man? You think you can hike farther than me? You think you're stronger than me? You want to take it outside, is that what you want?"

At this point in my life I was of out of shape. I'd rarely worked out since leaving the Marine Corps, but was still fairly solid; I hadn't lost much muscle, and I worked in a warehouse five nights a week, palletizing about a ton of groceries every night. I'd crush him.

"No, Dad. I don't think that's a good idea. Why don't we have another drink?"

At the time my father was living with a woman in a house they'd bought together, but for some reason he'd wanted to stay with me in a hotel, so we'd booked a room at a budget chain. After drinking a while longer we returned to the hotel and ate at the chain restaurant nearby, the kind of place where you can get pancakes, eggs, three kinds of sausage, and hash browns for five bucks.

I slept fitfully. I wanted to be back in Sacramento in my own bed with my girlfriend. But here I was in a roadside hotel with my drunken father. In the middle of the night he got up and puked all over the bathroom. I left at six a.m., without a shower, without saying goodbye.

I sat in my beat-up pickup truck in the parking lot for a while. It was a chilly Sacramento Delta morning, some drifting dense fog rolling in through my windows, the wetness of outside gathering on me and the interior of the vehicle. I thought I could sit there forever in my junker truck in the fog.

IN TWIN BRIDGES, Montana, I sat in the passenger seat of the RV in a massive truck stop parking lot. We'd pulled in at five a.m. when it was still dark outside but now it was beginning to be light. A heavy fog had descended on the mountains to the north and west. The truck stop overflowed with big trucks and cowboy pickups. I watched the cowboys and the truckers get out of their rigs and head toward the restaurant that promised "Eggs as Easy as You Want 'Em, All Day."

At the kitchen sink my father administered his inhalants, and he coughed and gagged, bent over barrel-chested at the waist.

"Breakfast, Pops?"

"Not for me, Tone. Not sure I can make it."

The restaurant was seventy-five feet away. He was in really bad shape.

I ate alone at the counter. The chatter behind me was about hay, and horses, and barns. I liked Montanans. Good people. I'd spent some time here over the years. My older sister had lived in Montana for more than a decade. And my ex-wife's parents had retired to a spread in Whitehall, thirty miles up the road. Sarah Freeman and I had divorced before I saw the finished place. I had not seen her parents in six years. They were two of the finest people I had ever met and I missed them immensely. It was difficult for me to think of Susan and Les without weeping. I recalled a mentor once telling me that it took a man ten years to get over a divorce.

AT THIS POINT I was pushing six years, a long recovery considering Sarah and I got married six weeks after we met.

After our first night of sex, over omelets at a crappy Iowa City diner, Sarah said, "Let's get married."

And I replied, "Yes. Let's."

It was March 27, 2000. We decided to marry on Friday, April 21. Sarah had her poetry workshop on Mondays and I had my fiction workshop on Tuesdays, so Friday would work. We were broke, so we couldn't do Vegas or Mexico, and her parents lived in Chicago, so we had to go west: destination Omaha. We swore silence; that we'd tell no one. At the Iowa Writers' Workshop, a fishbowl devoid of privacy, we would pull off a privacy coup.

On the drive to Omaha from Iowa City we stopped at a restaurant called The Machine Shed. I remember eating a massive breakfast. I had some second thoughts about marrying Sarah. There was plenty of reason for pause. We had only known each other for six weeks. We were both in graduate school. I'd met her parents but she'd not met mine. I ate my massive breakfast—three eggs, bacon, sausage, biscuits, and pancakes. Sarah ate a single poached egg. And neither of us brought up any of the reasonable objections to getting married so soon.

At that point in my life she was the most beautiful woman I had ever known and I still don't understand why she wanted to marry me. She came from a Hyde Park academic family. I came from a military family. She'd gone to Reed College out of high school; I'd joined the Marine Corps and then hit the Sacramento community college circuit, eventually transferring to a state university. When I talked to her about having been in the Marines I might as well have been telling her about the few years I worked in the carnival or the time I traveled in a flying saucer.

Judge Samuel V. Cooper married us. We paid his two clerks twenty bucks each to be our witnesses. I wore black loafers, gray slacks I'd bought at Nordstrom a few years before, and a blue long-sleeved shirt. She wore patent leather high heels that looked as if they might have cost a few hundred dollars but that she'd found at a discount store for seven bucks. She wore a black pencil skirt and a black blouse and her grandmother's pearl earrings.

Judge Samuel V. Cooper told us that he could give us the traditional municipal court vows but that he liked to personalize the affair, based on his Native American heritage. We agreed to follow his lead. He said something about the couple and the village and the village building shelter for the couple. He said some things about rain and lightning. It all seemed to make sense to us. We traded plain gold rings.

We walked outside, to a bright sunny Omaha day. An old couple nearby offered to take our picture in front of the courthouse. I felt certain that Sarah Freeman and I would remain married forever.

*   *   *

BACK IN THE RV my father and his lungs were up and running and he wanted to hit the road. The radio said we might hit snow on the other side of Bozeman. We needed to make it to Billings tonight, and a storm would stop us in our tracks.

We pushed along I-90 at a good pace. I was exhausted. I wanted to deliver my father to his RV park and check into my hotel. My girlfriend would already be there from Manhattan. She practiced emergency room medicine, and I knew she'd come prepared with pills for all that ailed us both: pain, anxiety, insomnia, malaise, and roadway ennui.

But for now the hills and farmland of central Montana ensorcelled me.

My father sat next to me in his tighty-whities. His handsomely silver Einsteinian hair looked as though it were going through a chain reaction. I wore a pair of yellow boxer shorts with black dachshunds on them, cowboy boots, and a green T-shirt that declared GETTIN' LUCKY IN KENTUCKY. Quite a sartorial sensation this morning, the Swofford men.

My father reached across the cab and grabbed my forearm, and said, "Tone, I think we need to get some things out in the open and clear the air. I think you need to get some venom out."

So this was the reason my father had asked me to fly to Fairfield and drive a thousand miles with him in his RV. It was a reconciliation ploy. I drove a few miles in silence. I popped my ears, stretched my neck, cleared my throat. I banged my left foot against the door. I felt a rage like none other come over my body. The rage burst at the top of my head and oozed down my body like lava. But the rage was good. I wanted the rage like I wanted those pills stowed in my girlfriend's carry-on. The pills were legal, prescribed by a doctor. The rage was legal, too.

"What makes you think I have venom?" I asked calmly.

"Look at you, Son. The steam is coming out of your body. I can feel your rage."

"Why do you think I have rage?"

"I don't know. Only you know what enrages you. But I can tell you it's not good for you. It'll kill you. And if I die before you get it out, it'll kill you even faster."

I drove a few more miles. Yes, I had rage. Yes, I had homicidal rage. Yes, I had fantasies about killing this man. Don't all sons fantasize about killing their fathers? But I suppose most sons get over it by their early twenties. Maybe I'm just a slow learner. After all, it had taken me six years to get a bachelor's degree.

I focused on the beautiful landscape. I stared at massive free-range cows.

"Do you really want to know what enrages me? Because I will tell you. But I don't think these are things that you are prepared to hear. They are not pretty things. They are not the kinds of things that families like to talk about at this point in the life of the family. By now everyone is supposed to be over their shit, they are supposed to have their own families, and they are supposed to move on and shut up so the older generation can look in the mirror and lie to themselves about what kind of parents they were. By parents, I mean you, Father. Mom is not a part of this conversation. Mom was a saint. All she did was try to protect us from you and your bullying ways."

"I don't need to talk about your mother."

"I don't care what you need to talk about. I spent my entire childhood being spoken to and being told what to do by you.

You never asked me questions. You told, you directed. You would have been a wonderful tyrannical film director. I remember that you liked to talk about Generalissimo Franco from your time in Spain. You admired the guy. You considered him a benevolent dictator. Do you know how many people he killed?"

"What does Franco have to do with this?"

"A man is the sum of the men he admires."

"Jesus, Tone. What kind of crazy talk is that? What is burning you up, Son?"

I liked the sound of the rush of the road beneath the RV. It was a humming, a mad march. I could take us over the cliff like a herd of bison. My father did not want to hear what I had to say. He considered the case closed on most of my grievances, the statute of limitations expired. I knew this much from a letter he had written me a few years earlier. He wanted me to tell him that I was over all those bad times from my childhood and now we could be friends. But my father failed to recognize that what I wanted and needed was a father, not a friend, not some old dude who would tell me stories about banging prostitutes in Juárez. I had plenty of lunatic friends who told better prostitute stories than he. What I needed was a father who would ask me questions about my life, ask me what I strived for, ask me how I'd failed, ask me why my marriage hadn't worked, tell me to give it another try with another woman, tell me that having a family was worth sleeping with only one woman for the rest of your life. Even if he didn't believe it.

I said, "Please never tell me another story about cheating on my mother. It doesn't make you cool. It simply makes you look like a jerk. Do you think I'm impressed? I'm not. I know about having a lot of women. I have done all of my screwing while unmarried. For every sex story you have, I have twenty. It's no big deal. Some men fuck a lot of women. Others don't."

"I'm not bragging, Tone. I thought I could talk to you like a man, I thought."

I interrupted him, "Do not tell me that when I was seven years old in Vacaville that you did not shove my face toward a pile of dog shit in the backyard. You did not put my face *in* the dog shit, I will concede that. But you dragged me across the yard by the back of my neck and you shoved my face within inches of the pile of dog shit that I had missed while performing my weekly chore. While doing so you yelled at me at the top of your lungs and accused me of being a liar. Tell me how you would feel right now if I grabbed you by the back of your neck and dragged you out of the RV and shoved your face in a pile of bison shit while yelling at you. I was seven years old. You were a thirty-six-year-old man. You had absolute physical power over me and you abused me. I will never forget that. On the day I die, in five or so decades, I will think of the day my father dragged me across the backyard to shove my face toward a pile of dog shit."

"We have different memories of that event," he said, obviously shaken. "You were a young boy and you needed to be taught how to properly perform your chores. I will admit that I did things then that today people would consider abusive. It was the way I was raised, it's what I knew."

"That's bullshit, and you know it. You had a wife who told you that was not the way to raise a family. Didn't you admire her parents? Did you not see that the way she was raised was superior to the backwoods Georgia way you were raised? I know you loved her father. Albert was the first grown man you admired and loved. You knew that he never abused his children. Why did you not use his model?"

"Things might have been different if Albert was still around when you kids came along. I loved him."

My father looked away from me and out at the prairie. He quietly cried.

After a few miles he cleared his throat and blew his nose into a handkerchief.

He said, "Albert Warner was a very fine man. It crushed your mother to lose her father at such a young age. Hell, it crushed me."

Road sign for a Vista Point Ahead. I needed to pull over and get some fresh air. Luckily there were no other vehicles stopped. I walked out in my cowboy boots and boxers. Snow had begun to fall. I felt the cold in my dick. I walked to the edge of the parking lot and pissed in the grass. I looked out across the prairie. I saw bison and a perfect red barn, a white farmhouse in the distance. I wondered who lived there and how dark their lives had ever become. I knew that my childhood could have been darker than it was. I thought of something good from my childhood. I couldn't keep beating my father up. I thought of the time we stopped in Yosemite and drank fresh water from a waterfall. I thought of spending summers driving through national parks. But then I thought of the time in the Grand Tetons when my father had reached through the doughnut hole that opened up the cab of the truck to the camper and grabbed me by the neck and bashed my head against the edge of the camper because I had asked a stupid question, probably about what time we were eating breakfast. It was on a cold morning just like this. I had to get that out of my head. I needed something good. I needed a happy memory. I loved my father, I knew this. And he must have known it, too. But there was so much dark shit. I was tired and strung out. I needed to settle down. I needed to exercise. I went into the RV and exchanged my cowboy boots and boxers for running shoes and a pair of sweats.

My father said, "What the hell is going on? We need to get to Billings. This thing ain't snow-safe. We'll skid off the road and kill ourselves or the highway patrol will turn us around, one or the other."

"Give me ten minutes. I need to clear my head."

"OK. I'll do an inhaler."

While my father administered his meds to his dying lungs I ran circles around the parking lot on the side of the prairie. I loved the man. I hated the man. I knew that he must love and hate me. I looked just like him. I wondered if that made it harder for the parent to separate from the child. It was impossible for him to look at me and not see his younger self. And for my father youth meant virility, Johnny Cash, the ladies. I was stealing his virility. Consumed by disease, he bequeathed to me all the power that had once been his. But he could not respect me because I had not yet fathered a child. He could not pass anything on to me because I had not yet had a child, but he *had* to pass it on to me because he had lost all his power and my older brother was dead. I ran for fifteen minutes and came down from my rage.

Back in the captain's chair I steered the beast toward the road.

My father said, "It's good for you to get this venom out. I don't know how I can help you. But I'll do whatever I can. I admire you, Son. I'd like to have a grown-up, adult relationship with you. I had problems with my own father. But in my twenties I realized the problems weren't going to be solved and it was time to be an adult and recognize that he'd done the best he could given the circumstances, and to hold on to my anger would do more harm than good."

"I don't understand what you mean by an 'adult relationship.'"

"Spend time together. Talk about life."

"Why suddenly do you want to talk about life? Why were you unable to talk to me about life when I was a boy? This inclination of yours would have come in handy for me when I was an awkward and lonely boy. I don't remember one incident during my teen years when you asked me how I was doing, or what I wanted, or needed."

"Damn, Son. Give me a break. I wasn't a great father. I should have been around more. I should have been more present in your life and asked you more questions."

"But you were too busy fucking your secretary, right?"

"I can't do this. Nothing will appease you. If you hate me, then you hate me. Why do you hate me?"

"I don't hate you for my childhood. I don't hate you for having a zipper problem. You are a pretty cool guy. People love your company, and I see why. You tell good stories. You've got a good and hearty laugh. I hate you because eleven years ago my brother died and you didn't go to his funeral. That is why I hate you. I hate you for that and for that alone. And I will never forgive you."

We drove in silence for about a hundred miles. They were good smooth road miles. The snow had stopped dropping and blew across the asphalt in psychedelic curlicues and paisleys of white. An SUV with Oregon plates, loaded down with ski gear, buzzed by and I was sure it was my friend Tom from Portland, but I called him on his cell and he said no, he wasn't in Montana, as far as he could tell he was doing bong hits in his basement.

Around Big Timber, my father said, in the quietest voice I'd ever heard from him, "I do not expect you to ever know what I felt when Jeff died. I hope you never experience anything like it. To lose my firstborn son was the most heart-wrenching thing that could ever happen to me. There is no other pain in the world that could ever compare. And I can't promise you that if you die tomorrow I will have the strength to make it to your funeral. I have no idea how I would react. No one ever does. Please do not hold that against me until the day I myself die."

"I can't promise you that."

AT BILLINGS I set my father up at the RV park and caught a cab to my hotel. My girlfriend was there, in bed, totally passed out at four p.m. after munching down three or four sleeping pills. We had a dinner for my niece that night, so I stayed away from the doctor's collection of pills. For the moment.

The dinner went well. It was the first time in five or six years that all five of us—me, my two sisters, and both parents—had been together. I largely ignored my father and mostly talked to my niece's dorky boyfriend. Dez is a tall girl and this short little guy came up to her armpits, at best. It was obvious that he did not like this height situation by the way he talked about the fast cars that his father owned.

I said, "Dude, someday you're gonna have to buy your own fast car."

The doctor passed me a pill under the table and I took it. A few minutes later everything began to float and I said I needed to get back to the room, that the drive from California had exhausted me.

But the doctor and I went to a bar downtown filled with a bunch of hard mothertruckers. I was completely doped out of my mind on whatever muscle relaxant she'd given me. While we sat drinking Budweiser for two hours there were at least five fistfights in the bar, two of them involving massive Native American lesbians.

Eventually we returned to our hotel room. The doctor and I had Ambien sex. I never loved her but I used those words when she did. Before I dated the doctor I had been engaged to a dancer who once threw away books from my bookshelves by female writers she suspected I might have slept with. I had in fact slept with only two of the ten accused. In contrast, the doctor, despite her pill use and urge to share, was a sea of total calm, the classic rebound after the chaos-producing dancer. The dancer had world-class beauty and a dancer's body; the doctor had plain looks and the body of an overworked ER physician who ate a lot of takeout from Staten Island Italian joints. The doctor ended our relationship after she had worked three straight overnighters and broke into my phone and read e-mails about me having sex in the women's bathroom at the Brooklyn Inn with a twenty-five-year-old hedge-funder while she saved lives in a crappy ER in Staten Island. There was also the e-mail about the one-night stand with the Australian academic.

But here now in Billings the Ambien sex satisfied me in the way that Ambien sex always satisfies: you are having sex while on Ambien so what can possibly be wrong with the sex? Nothing. And you wake up in the morning as though it never happened.

I was supposed to retrieve my father from his RV park at eleven in the morning in order to make certain that he made it to the graduation event, but he called me a few minutes before I planned to leave the hotel to tell me that there was no way he was going to make it, his lungs just weren't up to it.

I said, "Are you serious? I flew to Northern California from

New York to drive you a thousand miles in order to attend Dez's graduation and you can't make the ceremony?"

"I'll try to make it to the party," he said. I hung up.

The doctor gave me a few pills.

We made it to the massive sports complex for the graduation. I was sitting in the stands with my family when I realized that no one had any flowers for Dez.

I asked my sisters, "Do you have flowers somewhere? Dez needs flowers. Look around, everyone has flowers to give their kids!"

I panicked. A woman can't graduate from college without a bunch of flowers. What on Earth were we thinking?

I said to my mother and sisters and the doctor, "I'm going downtown to get some flowers. I'll be back before it's over."

In my pill-addled state I had trouble finding a florist. Eventually I did, after driving recklessly around Billings for half an hour or so. I made it back to the complex just as the show broke up. I'd procured two massive bouquets of flowers. I gave one to my sister and one to my mother in order that they could hand them to Dez. The photo session went off without a hitch. I'd saved the day!

My niece threw a party for a few dozen friends. We got some great family photos. I did not speak much with my father. The doctor chain-smoked cigarettes with my sister Tami's drug addict parolee girlfriend, and at some point the girlfriend took me to a country-and-western store and I bought a massive belt buckle with a steer on it. It never occurred to me how wrong it was that during my niece's graduation party I drove around town with her mother's parolee girlfriend, a stash of pills in my pocket. Eventually the girlfriend would rob my sister blind, steal a church van, and pawn all of Tami's jewelry in Spokane. We Swoffords have trouble finding the right women.

I went out dancing that night with my niece and her short boyfriend and their friends. The doctor slept. We went to the most cutting-edge club in Billings. It was way out in the industrial part of town. On one side was a good old cowboy honky-tonk bar, and on the other side something approximating a massive Chelsea dance club in miniature. Bottle service here meant a six-pack of Buds.

The doctor had loaded me up on pills and I was totally twitched out of my mind. But I could not betray this to my niece. Somehow I kept it together. I danced all night with her friends, all very nice young people. At some point, while on the honky-tonk side of the bar, and away from my niece and her friends, I kissed a cowgirl. Later I tangled limbs with the cowgirl in the cab of her boyfriend's pickup truck.

The next thing I knew I was back in Manhattan.

I talked to my father a few weeks later and we agreed that the RV trip had been a success and that we should hit the road again together soon.

4

Brother, to Thy Sad Graveside Am I Come

X-POP3-Rcpt: swoff@pop3
To: ahswofford@ucdavis.edu
Subject: Talk to me
X-Mailer: Juno 1.38
From: jswofford@juno.com (Jeff Swofford)
Date: Fri, 23 Jan 1998 13:54:47 EST

Dear Tony,
I left a message on your telephone today at about 12:30 to call me ASAP.
I'm planning a big party the end of next week and want you to be here.
You can get discounted tickets to visit relatives who are facing impending death. I can tell you on the phone how to show proof, if required. I can help with the money. I know you just started school and I'm sorry to die at such an inconvenient time, but I really need you here little

brother. There won't be any gloom out here, just guitars, singing and lots of partying. Call me soon.

Love,
Your Big Brother

Impending death. Upending death. How do you show proof to the airline that your brother is dying? Photographic evidence?

See here, Mr. Airline Representative, this is a photo of my brother a year ago, the picture of health, a thirty-four-year-old father of two: notice the shine and elasticity of his skin, the sheen and splendor of his red hair; notice the bulky forearms, the wide strong chest; notice the two radiant children, notice the smiling pretty wife.

Now, Mr. Airline Representative, here is a photo of my brother from last week: notice the sallow and hollow cheeks; notice the grayish pall of his skin; notice the hairless head; notice the thin weak body. Notice the children at the back of the frame, watching their father as death watches him, and notice the wife, turned away from the camera, eyes on the distance unknown.

May I have a discounted rate? Sacramento to Atlanta?

I don't recall if I received a discount or not. I wouldn't have asked of my own accord. There are those people you've just met who will give you their entire medical history along with the histories of their parents and lover and siblings: leukemia, heart murmur, childhood diabetes, heart failure, intubation, constipation, hernia, dementia, delirium tremens. I do not share such information with total strangers.

MY YOUNGER SISTER Kim picked me up at the airport. At the time she lived in Atlanta and during the past few years, when she and my brother both lived in the city, they had become very close. Twelve years separated them so Kim barely remembered Jeff from her childhood.

Over the last year while my brother was ill Kim had been a regular caretaker for the children and for my brother's family in general—staying with the kids when my brother was at chemo with his wife, driving them to school, doing the shopping, performing all manner of errands.

I jumped in the passenger seat and gave Kim a kiss on the cheek.

"How is he?" I asked.

"Dying," she said morbidly. "They're increasing the morphine. The hospice nurse is at the house now, with Mom and Melody. The kids are a mess."

She took us out to Camp Creek Parkway and drove the long, sloping road southwest toward Douglasville. As a kid I'd taken this route many times, always on happy occasions: a family reunion, my grandparents' wedding anniversary, a summer vacation trip to Six Flags.

We passed Six Flags, shuttered for the winter.

Kim said, "Iris wants to see you again."

Iris was her friend and whenever I was in town we flirted and drove around the rolling hills of West Georgia in her beat-up car listening to the Velvet Underground and talking about living someday in New York City.

We passed the chain stores and restaurants that signaled I was in another country: Piggly Wiggly, Chick-fil-A, Winn-Dixie.

MY BROTHER WAS the only true athlete in our family. When it came to sports, I was a dilettante: a few years of unimpressive football play; four years of wrestling in high school where I was known more for guts and conditioning than moves, with one strong season my junior year; two seasons of rugby during which I scored one tri, received a concussion, and split my face open twice—causing my mother to faint at least once.

Jeff ferociously played defensive back for the same school where later I'd founder. He received a small scholarship from Sacramento State College. He joined the Army, I'm still unsure why, halfway through his junior year of college.

In the Army he stayed ripped by spending hours at the gym. In Munich, in the mid-1980s, he competed in bodybuilding competitions. The photos of him from that era show a man with a deeply chiseled body and a confidence that could have been bottled, copyrighted, and sold.

In early 1997, at the age of thirty-four, Jeff still committed himself to tenacious workouts. Despite being married with two kids and attempting to start a new career after thirteen years in the Army, he always made time for exercise. Such was his dedication to the gym that I wondered if he might have a slight mental imbalance that manifested in manic fitness pursuits. Or, equally likely, he was simply vain.

I'd taken a trip to Atlanta during my winter break from college.

On this trip I'd mostly hung around with my brother and his family and Kim, visiting the outlying aunts and uncles occasionally or seeing them when they dropped by my brother's house.

Jeff relished being older and in better shape.

"Hey, kid, want to race three miles? I can still kill it in seventeen minutes, twenty seconds," he'd say with a big grin, or "Hey, kid, want to see how much you can deadlift? Bench-press? Squat?"

One afternoon I agreed to a session at the gym. He said his body had been aching, that he'd been going to a chiropractor. He chalked it up to "old age" and the rigors and stresses of raising children and starting a new career.

I expected that Jeff would kill me at the gym, beat me by a hundred pounds on squats and fifty or even seventy-five at bench.

We warmed up on bench with two plates, 135 pounds, merely feathers. I knocked out fifteen repetitions. I knew I'd hurt badly the next day, but I didn't want to look like a total wimp in front of my brother. We jacked it up to 185, then 205, then 225. I held my own with Jeff. We were both surprised. He complained about pain in his back. He stretched. He said the sauna would cure all that ailed him.

We set up the squat rack. Two hundred and twenty-five pounds. Three sets of fifteen repetitions was our plan. Jumped rope for two minutes to warm up. I was sweating. I liked this, I felt good and strong and able. Jeff blew out his first set without a problem, going way deep into the squat, his ass just inches from the ground. I knew that if I tried to go that deep I'd rip something—my shorts, my quadriceps, or my brain stem.

I barely completed a full squat and my brother heckled me. But I finished my reps.

"Dude," I said, "I haven't done squats in four years. I won't be able to walk for a week if I go as deep as you."

"You're weak, kid."

He slapped me on the ass, lovingly.

He blasted out another set. I watched my brother, a fine physical specimen, and I thought of the man inside the body—the mind, the heart—the father, husband, son, brother. I was a son and a brother but not yet a husband or a father. These two other, further dimensions made him seem, in some ways, deeply ancient and removed from the petty rush and tumble of my life: books, beer, girls, and moody rock music.

I wanted to know the man inside the body. I'd seen him with his children, patient and loving. He spoke to them in a calm and reassuring voice. I'd seen him discipline them occasionally, for minor childhood infractions: running inside, screaming at the top of their lungs, an innocent food fight at the table—flying orzo and broccoli.

These same kinds of crimes when we were children would have warranted major censure from our father: no television for the night; no phone for a week; occasionally, a spanking or the belt.

Jeff didn't have the best marriage. He and Melody mostly disagreed on child rearing: she approached the children as friends, colleagues, seeking their advice; Jeff thought that this was destructive to family cohesion and consistency and that being friends with your children was something best attempted when they were out of college or later.

They'd both had affairs a few years earlier, he first, then she. I never got the complete story, but he'd told me once about making love to a woman in the Arizona desert and that he'd paid dearly for the misdeed, a misdeed returned in kind. He'd deserved it, he said. Now back to the work of the marriage.

He was trying to start a new gig, as a physician headhunter for hospitals. He lacked eighteen credits for his bachelor's degree. He had plans to pull together his education and career and marriage.

I grunted out my next set. Jeff began limping around the squat rack.

He said, "I think that's it for me, little brother. My back is wrecked. I need to ice it tonight and see my chiropractor ASAP. I hate getting old."

To his chagrin I threw on another fifty pounds and pounded out a last set.

"Thirty-four is old," I said.

THAT NIGHT JEFF and I went out alone to dinner. We grabbed BBQ at a down-home place off the interstate.

"Look at these disgusting people," he said, gesturing around the restaurant. "You and I worked out today. We're in shape." He paused. "Well, I'm in shape and you're coming back. We can afford some ribs and a few beers. These people eat like this every day, go home and sit on their asses, and drink more beer and wake up tomorrow morning and do it again. I gotta get out of the South. I miss California. People are in shape, they care about what they eat, they exercise."

"Not everyone out there is in shape, bro. There are fat people everywhere."

I knew he harshly judged overweight people, a bias he'd inherited from our maternal grandmother, but tonight he was particularly critical. There were, in fact, a number of people in our own extended family who could stand to lose twenty pounds or more, and I didn't feel like condemning them.

"Not like this fat. This is pure obesity. This is gluttony." He spit the word *gluttony* out, condemning the entire South to heart disease, diabetes, sepsis, and a well-deserved early grave.

He went into his story about lifting weights one weekend at Venice Beach, way back in the eighties. I'd heard it dozens of times and I tuned him out, gazing at the mountains of discarded pork ribs and the empty sweet tea glasses and beer bottles that littered the tables. Gluttony, indeed, a very fine portrait of.

I thought I knew the source of his agitation. During my shower I'd heard him and Melody fighting, in the closed-lip, low-boil way that couples practice when other adults are in the house—or at a nearby table if they're dining out. I chose not to bring it up. Really, I didn't care why they had been fighting. I was enjoying my ribs and my beer.

And my little sister had set me up on a date later that night with one of her friends and I looked forward to meeting the girl.

"Listen, bro," he said, pulling me out of my fantasy about Iris.

He paused and his face hardened; he worked his jaw, and his deep blue eyes darkened and his mood went from sun-bright baby oil muscle beach revelry to deep South thunderstorm: hail, flooding.

"I might need to come out and live with you for a while. We're talking about splitting up. For a trial. Melody will take Kelley back to her mom's in Minnesota. And I'll take Christian with me. I want to come back to Sacramento. I'll bang out three quarters at UC–Davis, finish my degree, and start grad school. I'm thinking physician's assistant."

I had no idea how to respond. Did my older brother just say he wanted to come live with me, his five-year-old son in tow? How could he possibly have just said that?

"Of course," I said. "Whatever you need. I've got a roommate right now, but I think he's moving out soon. If you need it, I'll keep the room free."

"I could give Christian that room, and you and I could share your room. I want him to feel like he has his own space. It's going to be tough on him. But I think this is the right move."

Share your room? Where will I have sex with girls? The last time I shared a room with my brother I was five and he was thirteen.

"Let's just see how it works out," I said, my eyes ablaze with worry. "I'm sure Christian will want to sleep with you for a while. It'll be new and scary for the little guy. And it's a big room. It's the master. There's room for two beds."

But if my brother needed a place to stay I would share a room with him, or sleep on the couch, on the floor, wherever.

"It's just not working out. I thought getting out of the Army would save our marriage. No more moving around, no more nights and weeks and months alone. Home every night with the wife and kids. I just don't know if that is what she wants. Sometimes I think she wants me gone. And sometimes I want to disappear."

We drove back to his house in total silence. I'd never been married but it didn't seem to me as if splitting up and taking your kids to near-opposite ends of the country could do any good for a couple and their family. But I couldn't say that to my brother.

We entered the house and the kids came running and Jeff and Melody kissed and embraced and I wondered what kind of nutty drama these people were living.

LATER I HAD my date with Iris, a skinny little Georgia punk goth with dyed black hair and combat boots and a foul mouth. She drove me around the rolling West Georgia hills to nearby cemeteries, many of which held dead Swoffords, and we listened to the Velvet Underground and some bands I'd never heard of. She smoked clove cigarettes and we kissed in church parking lots, at the edges of graveyards.

*   *   *

A FEW WEEKS later, back in California, I answered my home phone one afternoon. It was Jeff. He sounded small and far away.

He said, "Brother, I've got cancer. It's bad. And I'm dying."

OVER THE NEXT several months I visited Jeff whenever I could. His prognosis was never great, but he always put a positive spin on his illness: he was going to beat the thing, he was young and otherwise healthy and there was no reason he wouldn't survive— no reason other than that he had stage four non-Hodgkin's lymphoma and that the cancer had appeared on his spine, in his left lung, in his stomach.

The reason his back hurt so much when we were lifting weights that day was that the tumor on his spine was about the size of a grapefruit—a grapefruit on his spine, blueberries on his lymph nodes, peach on his lung, plum in his stomach.

Why when describing tumors do we invariably use fruit comparisons? Is this to soften the blow of the horrible news? Throw fruit, not cinder blocks.

So with my brother it started with a grapefruit. The word was on everyone's tongue, as if to say *grapefruit* was to not say *cancer.* You say grapefruit, I say live.

WHILE MY BROTHER died I lived in Sacramento, putting the finishing touches on my five-and-a-half-year bachelor's degree. I worked three or four nights a week at a unionized grocery warehouse, the swing shift, five p.m. to one-thirty a.m.

If it looked like overtime, we'd send a guy to the Texaco truck stop down in the shadows of the Highway 80 overpass to buy five or six cases of beer before the two a.m. cutoff.

I drank beer behind the truck stop two or three nights a week for five years. The beds of our pickup trucks and the hoods of our cars were our local bar, and we were the bartenders—tellers of bad jokes, keepers of dark secrets. Many of the older guys had fought in Vietnam. Most of the talk was about the shit work we did and the shit union that took so much of our pay and the shit bosses who constantly broke up our poker games because they regularly ran an hour or longer past lunch. Shop talk.

Most of the older men had been divorced once or twice. There was Dave who made ninety grand a year with overtime and still somehow managed to live from his car. There was Evan, who broke his ankle in a snake hole his first night in Vietnam and spent six months recuperating and screwing Navy nurses on Okinawa, clearly one of the luckiest men on the planet. For decades he'd played blues guitar downtown at the Torch Club. He told stories of playing with the legendary Johnny Hartman back in the day.

There was the other Dave, my age, smart as hell, but he loved the work of a forklift jockey. He'd start a semester at some college or another every year and drop out two or three weeks in.

"Just in time to get a refund. What a bunch of dummies," he said one day, after dropping out.

"The kids at college?" I asked, feeling implicated and hurt.

"No, man," he said, with a grand gesture toward the warehouse floor. "Douche bags like me who are gonna drive a forklift for the next forty years and break their backs three times humping hundred-pound bags of dog food."

But Dave would leave. His parents owned a massive dairy farm south of Sacramento, and the Valley construction crawl would soon take over the farm, to the likely tune of tens of millions of dollars. He knew that. Everyone knew that.

There was my best friend, Douglas Ahim, a former Ugandan child soldier who somehow in hell ended up in Sacramento after running with Jamaican gangs in London throughout his early twenties. I was one of only about three guys in the warehouse who could understand his Swahili/British English/Jamaican English/American English mash-up.

Supervisors were constantly yelling for me: "Swofford, what the hell did Ahim just say?"

I learned years later that his incomprehensible accent was a ploy when he said to me, "If they don't know what you're saying, they can't bust you."

Somehow he got a job as a plant mechanic and spent the next few years sleeping on the roof of the warehouse while making thirty dollars an hour, laughing at the rest of us as we sweated and cursed and loaded hundred-pound bags of dog food onto pallets.

They were all good men, solid working-class guys, but they called me college boy or college fuck, good-naturedly of course, but some didn't like me because they knew I'd get out.

But there were nights behind the Texaco, while my brother died, and I drank beer until five a.m. with this motley band of laborers, when I felt closer to them than I had to other men, closer than I'd felt to my marine comrades, closer than I felt to my father or brother or the boys I'd grown up with: they all knew my brother was dying in Georgia, but here in West Sacramento, behind the Texaco, no one mentioned it, and this not mentioning it showed they cared.

We sat in the shadow of one of the greatest highways in the Western world. I could jump in my truck, gas up, head straight east, and five days later I'd arrive in Manhattan.

While we drank and talked shit to one another dozens of big rigs idled behind us, truckers pissed next to their trucks, truck stop prostitutes worked their turf, dogfights and human fights broke out, drug deals went down, and we smelled the stench of commerce; the brilliant shine of vice assaulted us in the burning fluorescent lights of the truck stop; on the other side of a massive dirt berm rolled the Yolo Causeway, nectar feeder to the Sacramento Valley, feeder of the world.

And none of the men I drank beers with talked about my dying brother. This is the brute civility and humility of the working-class man, the man from Springsteen songs and Carver short stories. For many months this brute emotion held me up when otherwise I might simply have crashed to the pavement under the weight of my grief and the weight of the deadly flesh rotting in my brother's body.

A BIZARRE BEHAVIOR I acquired during the year Jeff was sick: The first time this happened, I had ordered through the intercom at a fast-food drive-through lane. Tacos. But as soon as I'd ordered I knew I did not want to eat those tacos. Tacos were all wrong. There was no way that tacos would satisfy me. And if I ate tacos my brother would die. But I'd already pulled forward, and someone else was behind me, so I couldn't back out. At the window I paid for the tacos, but before they had a chance to hand me the food I sped out of there. I drove around for a few hours trying to find the right restaurant. I sat in my car in dozens of restaurant parking lots: Italian, Mongolian BBQ, Chinese, French, New American, steak houses, burger joints, chain family-styles, fast food.

At the Mongolian BBQ restaurant I sat down, and then I

realized that if I filled that bowl with meat and noodles and had the guy behind the grill cook it, my brother would die. I sat at the table and drank iced tea for a while, glass after glass of iced tea. I hated iced tea. The nice waitress asked me every few minutes if I was OK and didn't I want to fill my bowl, didn't I know how it worked at the Mongolian BBQ, that you filled your bowl with vegetables and noodles and meat, and selected any number of tasty sauces, and then gave it to the man behind the massive grill; it was a grill, not really a BBQ, but the man behind the grill sautéed your bowl of food at high heat and then you ate it at your table, and you could return as many times as you pleased, up to three trips, before incurring a three-dollar surcharge for more visits? Did I understand?

I performed this extreme act of indecision a few times a week for many months until my brother died.

One night I did this with my girlfriend. We sat down and ordered food that I refused to eat at two or three different restaurants. Finally she said, "Why don't we drink some whiskey?"

JEFF CONTINUED ROUNDS of rigorous treatment throughout the spring and early summer. He'd lost his hair months before and had dropped about thirty pounds, but the athletic vitality that had always defined him remained noticeable in his graceful movements and his carriage.

I'd arrived for the July 4 holiday weekend and was told there would be hiking and a picnic during the day, followed by fireworks at night. A friend of Jeff's had made a big run to an Alabama fireworks mecca and once dusk settled we were going to light up the neighborhood.

Jeff had been in some pain in the morning and we had made

a slower start than intended. I could tell he didn't like Melody's driving. As we pulled out from their subdivision he sharply criticized her for not using her turn signal. My sister Kim and I, in the very rear seats, rolled our eyes at each other. There were times when Jeff reminded us of our father, and that scared us: Kim because of the memories of the stern authoritarianism of Dad, and me because of the fear that the father/son cycle was unbreakable and that regardless of will at some point every man becomes his father.

But I also considered that it might just be that the man was dying and that not using a turn signal seemed like a flagrant dismissal of the safety mechanisms he required for every aspect of his life, as though while he censured his wife he meant to say, *Honey, I might beat this goddamn thing, so please do not kill us in this car.*

Sweetwater Park teemed with families in full Fourth of July regalia: flag-printed shorts and caps and socks and shoes and blankets and coolers, shirts and backpacks and blankets. I couldn't scan farther than three feet without being assaulted by some form of Old Glory.

Jeff said, "Jesus, we don't even have a flag to wave. We must look like communists. Why didn't we think of this?"

I couldn't tell if he was joking or not. I assumed no. Jeff still defined himself by Country and God. I'd mostly given that up after the Gulf War. And then I realized that it must have just dawned on him that this might be his last Fourth of July with his family, and why not go all out and show your pride in your country.

Kelley and Christian wanted to play, so Melody and my sister took them to the swing sets and the jungle gym. Jeff and I decided to go for a walk on one of the trails. He wanted to do a three-mile loop.

I said, pointing at the map, "Maybe we should start with one of these little milers, just to see how you're feeling."

"I'm not an invalid yet, little brother. I can handle this. Last year this time I was jumping out of airplanes!"

I wanted to say: *Last year this time you didn't have a constellation of tumors attacking your body.*

We stepped off at a brisk pace. Since the night in January when Jeff had told me he and Melody were splitting up, we had not talked about their marriage. My mother had told me that they had renewed their vows at a ceremony at a new church they'd joined, but Jeff had said nothing about this to me. It was as though our conversation about the demise of their marriage and his probable move to Sacramento had never occurred.

I said, "So what's going on with you and Melody?"

"Things are great. We renewed our vows. The kids are getting along. We're going to beat this cancer, and we're going to remain a family."

"It would be tough to be sick and alone. I can't imagine that. I wonder what my girlfriend would do if I got sick."

"Every man always wonders that," he said. "What will this woman do if I lose my legs, get cancer, get my dick blown off at war? I always knew Melody would stand by me no matter what. All that trouble back there, it was a testing period. And then I got sick. Another aspect of the test. If we make it now, nothing will stop us. We've been together twelve years. That's huge."

"Do you think you'll be together forever?"

"I want to grow old with her."

We walked for a while in silence. The blur of red, white, and blue mingled with the oaks and the warmth of the sun. Jeff was holding up, a bit of perspiration gathering on his forehead. I hadn't noticed, but somewhere along the way he'd acquired a walking stick. I wanted him to say, *I'll grow old with you, too, little brother. Someday we'll be frail men walking in the woods with sticks, our children behind us, thick as thieves.*

Jeff said, "Don't rush into marriage, Tone. I did. It's been tough."

"I'm twenty-seven next month," I said. "I'm not rushing anything. You were twenty-two when you got married? I've already got five years of bachelorhood on you."

This struck a nerve with my brother.

"I guess." He paused. "That means you've probably slept with more women than I have. Than I ever will. Damn. That seems strange. You were such a little thin-lipped dork."

At this he jabbed me in the ribs, and we play-grappled there in the middle of the trail, other walkers looking at us as though we were two crazies come out from the woods.

I said, "What did Dad tell you when you turned sixteen?"

"To never drive drunk. And he gave me a box of condoms and said that Swofford men were blessed and cursed with a high-powered libido. And then he went back to tuning his Jaguar. What did he tell you?"

"The same thing. How old were you when you lost your virginity?"

"Seventeen. In the backseat of my Phoenician Yellow Mustang. No condom. Fifteen seconds, max. You?"

"Seventeen. Cab of my pickup, a Datsun. I used a condom.

I think I might have gone for thirty. I dropped the girl off and I rushed home and jumped in the shower and washed my dick with Ajax and Lysol. I got some crazy rash, obviously from the chemicals. I was sure I'd caught AIDS."

"You were one dumb kid."

We laughed.

I said, "Why did you get a tricked-out Mustang for your sixteenth birthday and I got a jalopy pickup truck?"

"I guess Dad liked me more."

"I guess so."

More silence as we walked.

Since Jeff had been diagnosed in February, our father had not visited him. I didn't know what kind of pain, if any, this caused my brother. I considered my father's willful absence completely unconscionable. But I couldn't say so to my brother, for fear that that might cause him further anguish. He had cancer to worry about so why add a dose of absentee father to the wicked emotional cocktail he ingested each day?

"I loved that Mustang," I said. "You picked me up at school in it one day. I felt so cool."

"There is no other smell like the interior of a '66 Mustang. It's a drug."

We finished the hike and returned to the van. Jeff had been correct—he'd had no problem with the three miles. But by the time we made it home, after feeding the kids and gassing the car, he felt exhausted and needed a nap.

The night was a festival of burgers and hot dogs and brats, firecrackers and bottle rockets and shrieking children. I flew home the next day. I wouldn't see Jeff again until November.

*　　*　　*

AS THE DREAD gray winter chill knocked leaves from their trees and the industrial pall of Nashville thickened, Johnny Cash lay in Baptist Hospital due to heart trouble. Nearby, at the Veterans Hospital attached to Vanderbilt University, Jeff lay dying. He'd recently suffered a number of grand mal seizures that led to the discovery of an apricot-size tumor on his brain.

I thought of the apricot tree in the backyard of the California house where we'd lived as children, and I thought of the sun glowing behind its branches heavy with soft golden fruit, and I thought of my brother running through sprinklers with neighborhood girls, but nothing lifted my gloom.

I'd flown in to be with Jeff and Melody and my sister Kim while Jeff's doctors decided what to do. Eventually they chose to operate.

The night before his surgery I went out to see some jazz at a club downtown: Joshua Redman performing with his band, including the legendary drummer Brian Blade. (Because of his talent he seemed to me decades my senior, but years later I'd discover he's just three weeks older than I am.)

I took a seat alone at the bar, drank a bottle of wine, and enjoyed my first live jazz show. I don't remember a lot about Redman's sax playing because I was so mesmerized by the drumming of Blade. He sounded to me like a maniac, a man totally in love with yet divorced from the sound and rhythms he made. Blade controlled the band and he controlled everyone else in the room too—the bartender took his cues from the drummer, as did the waitresses and every member of the audience. We didn't drink until Blade said drink, we didn't eat until Blade said eat, we didn't shift in our seats until Blade told us to shift in our seats, and we didn't clap like madmen in love with a daring religion until he told us to. It's still one of the best live music shows I've ever seen. After the show I went to the bathroom and found Blade standing at the urinal next to mine. It felt strange to compliment a musician while pissing, but why not?

I said, "Great show, Mr. Blade."

He said, "Thanks." And he nodded and flushed and left.

I made my way out of the club and into the musical chaos of downtown Nashville. In one bar I listened to a teenage girl do religious songs, way off-key and out of pitch. I could see she had the hunger, but hunger is never enough. I heard bad rockabilly and bad country and more bad country.

Outside one bar I asked if there was a Waffle House nearby, and someone pointed me up the road. I made my way up a dimly lit lane, and from the shadows a man called me over.

He said, "Hey, Rockefeller, can't you help a broke feller?"

I was drunk or dumb enough to not be afraid.

I looked at him. I said nothing. I thought about going for my wallet before he did.

"Come on, brother," he said. "I got two girls in my car. Take your pick or take them both."

He put his hand on my arm and squeezed. His fingers were scrawny and scratchy and cold. This guy was as hungry for something as the girl onstage singing Bible songs.

"How about some crack? You smoke cocaine?"

"I don't smoke anything. I'm going to the Waffle House. I'll buy you and your girls some breakfast." Once I spoke, it sounded like an absurd and naïve proposition.

He looked at me, suspicious. He seemed as if he was used to white men lying to him and to paying the price for the white man's lies.

"Seriously, man. I don't want crack or your girls but I'll buy you breakfast."

After he sussed me further he agreed to the meal and said he'd meet me up the hill in five minutes.

The Waffle House is a Southern staple. The food is generally awful and always bad for you. I can't imagine it's possible to escape a Waffle House without ingesting 1,500 calories and a million grams of trans fats. If a food is vaguely Southern and at least partially deep-fried you'll find it on the menu. They might as well serve a shot of deep-fryer oil with your meal the way Russians do vodka. All of this said, I've never not been satisfied after leaving a Waffle House at three or four in the morning.

I settled into a booth and told the waitress that I had a few friends on their way. The restaurant brimmed with the youthful well-heeled of Nashville. I imagined a few lawyers in the bunch, some IT guys, and they were with their girlfriends, professionals as well, lawyers and human resource VPs, and they all put off the slight odor of Greek brotherhood and sisterhood from their college days at Duke or Vanderbilt or Southern Miss.

I'd been out of the Marine Corps for almost five years. The next semester I'd transfer to a respectable university after a four-and-a-half-year slog through community college. These handsome folks, a few of them younger than I, reminded me of the complete and utter failure my life had been. I was twenty-seven, lived with a roommate in a four-hundred-dollar-a-month apartment in downtown Sacramento, and worked the swing shift at a grocery warehouse.

The crack dealer/pimp barged into the Waffle House with his ladies. The harsh fluorescent light did none of the trio any favors. Their clothes were dirty and I could smell them from where I sat.

The odors were of the body: sweat, urine, and vaguely, shit. The ladies and gentlemen of the white Southern upwardly mobile were shocked and appalled.

The waitress stepped forward to stop my new friends from advancing farther but I called out, "They're with me."

The waitress, an African American woman in her late thirties who probably held two other jobs and supported a large extended family, was too exhausted to argue with me, but the look on her face was one of complete puzzlement, as if to ponder, *What in the hell is this stupid white boy doing with this crackhead and his hos?*

I don't remember their names but I remember their vacant eyes and the desperation of their breathing and the pure insanity of their minds. I didn't know what crack did to a person's psyche. Did they know, I wondered, how completely gone they looked, how much like ghosts?

The Southern ladies and gents whispered just below audible levels but I knew they were joking about me and my companions. I stared at a blond girl, the VP of something, and mouthed obscenities. She turned away and mumbled at her date.

The dealer said to me, "Don't mind. Ain' nothing new."

One of his girls—she wore tight jeans and a blue-and-gold plaid shirt tied up like a bikini, braless—threw her menu down and said, "I don't know what I want but I want it smothered and covered!" That meant with cheese food and onions. She let out a cackle, and her friend, in a dirty black Snoop T-shirt, snorted loudly.

Only then did I realize our somewhat awkward seating arrangement: it was a small booth, and the three of them sat mashed together on one side with me on the other. I wondered if they were afraid of me or simply wanted to keep their distance and if at some level I wasn't, because of my whiteness, just like those fucking crackers in all the other booths. I offered to scoot over and have one of the women sit next to me but the dealer, sitting between them, leaned back and put his arms around them both and said, "My girls stick close."

At the time I didn't realize, or didn't want to realize, that I wasn't simply buying breakfast for a trio of down-and-out drug addicts: this man was a pimp and his girls were strung out on drugs; in fact he'd probably strung them out himself, and they had sex with men in order to get more drugs, the drugs that allowed them to blow their minds away and not think about the fact that they were having sex with men for drugs.

SACRAMENTO IS THE capital of West Coast homelessness due to its climate and the numerous public and private relief agencies, and the downtown air is always aflutter with the sound of shopping carts flailing through alleys. Being generous to homeless people seemed like part of the culture. I shared food on my porch with homeless guys, and more than once I gave my couch for the night to a homeless guy we knew as Mr. Incense because he sold incense, and another guy named James Brown because he did spot-on renditions of James Brown songs for all the young, drunk hip kids stumbling from the three bars worth drinking at.

Some nights James Brown made hundreds as kids flush with student loan money threw tens and twenties at his feet while he thrashed through a rendition of "Papa's Got a Brand New Bag." Before Brian Blade he might have been the only musical genius I'd seen in person.

BUT MAYBE I was just a fucked-up cracker and I thought it was cool and enlightened of me to buy a crew of drug-addled and sex-selling African Americans waffles and fried food at three in the morning in this yuppie town. Does it even matter? We all ate, and we ate well, and we laughed at the yuppies in their blue oxford shirts and khakis and penny loafers. Maybe that's all that mattered: as my brother lay dying a few miles away, his stomach empty for pre-op, his lips chapped and dried and yearning for an ice chip while he waited to be kicked behind the curtain of consciousness by a friendly anesthesiologist, I sat around a trashy, fluorescent-lit, and orange-laminated restaurant and ate like an animal with a few other people, in the middle of the night in Nashville in Tennessee.

We ate waffles and eggs and biscuits and bacon and sausage and fried chicken fingers and fried catfish and French fries and hash browns and fried whatever and most of it arrived smothered and covered with gravy, and we were happy, or I was, and I assumed they were, too, because they laughed with me and we high-fived and we laughed some more at the yuppies.

And then the show closed, a glaze came down over their eyeballs, the night darkened, and they needed to get high now and they needed money now and they needed to exit.

The man said to me, "Sure you don' want a girl?"

Both of the girls stared through me. Did they picture me in the backseat of the Olds, as they'd seen so many other men, sweaty dirty men on top of and inside them, whimpering because they couldn't get it up? Or just stupid, stupid men sleeping with prostitutes in the backseat of a broken-down car, ruining further these already broken-down lives?

"Nah, man," I said.

To pull the girls from their daze he squeezed them on the shoulders. They all three dragged themselves from the booth. It seemed as though they weighed a thousand pounds each, such was their effort to move their bodies.

The girls walked on ahead and out of the restaurant without saying goodbye. Some of the yuppies stared but most didn't care anymore. They were drunk and smothered and covered and that's exactly why they'd come downtown tonight.

The man looked at me and said, "Can you help me out?"

I pulled sixty dollars from my wallet and put it in his dry, scratchy palm.

He said, "Thanks. And for breakfast. I ain't eat that much in a long time."

He shuffled out. I sat for a while in the booth, looking at the detritus of our feast, looking at the glare and shame of the restaurant, the beckon to eat cheaply and to eat a lot and to not care about what goes in your body. I thought about the crackhead and his prostitutes and what they'd soon be putting in their bodies, what they'd been putting in their bodies for years.

I looked at my watch. It was four in the morning. In an hour my brother would be awakened by a nurse and wheeled from his room toward the operating room. He might die in there: they were opening his skull and extracting a ruined piece of brain.

I wandered around the city and attempted to grab a cab but there were none. It wasn't so far to my hotel and the hospital, so I walked. Along the way a man approached me from a side street. It took me a moment to recognize the same man I'd just fed.

His eyes as glassy and pocked as the full moon, he said to me, "Hey, Rockefeller, can't you help a broke feller?"

MY BROTHER FELL in love with Melody in the way that all Swofford men fall in love with beautiful women: madly and passionately, screaming down the street at three thousand miles an hour with their jockstraps on fire.

They met at a talent night on Fort Ord Army Base in Monterey, California. She'd arrived with a date and she left with my brother. Jeff sang a song—let's say it was "More Than a Feeling" by Boston. Because the event occurred on base no booze was served, but the GIs knew how to get around this, filling their soda cups from the mess with whiskey.

He had been with only two women in his life. He was a twenty-one-year-old enlisted dental hygienist. He'd dropped out of college a year before, after losing his football scholarship. His hair was as red as the core of the Earth and he'd ripped his physique down to 3 percent body fat. The freckles all over his white skin looked like small suns.

Melody cut a vaguely Mediterranean figure through the piney hills around Monterey. She, too, spent many hours a week in the gym and had the dark tan skin of a bodybuilder, though it came naturally. Later the two of them would laugh, in bed, when comparing their skins.

But this first night they went off base to a bar in town and had a few beers. The bar fancied itself a roadhouse or honky-tonk of sorts, a stopping place for wayward urban cowboys posing as GIs.

Jeff ordered cheap beers and cheap shots and they sat in a booth while all around them beer signs and country music and drunken GIs rioted.

"So where are you from?" Jeff asked.

"I was born on Long Island, where my parents ran an antiques shop. During the gas crisis they went bust. And we moved to Lanesboro and opened up another shop. We pulled into town, a caravan of crazy. Two vans, six children, seven dogs, fourteen cats, and two monkeys. That little town had never seen anything like it."

"Monkeys," Jeff said. "Where is Lanesboro?"

"Oh, right." She laughed and ran her hands through her hair. "It's in Minnesota. Bed-and-breakfast capital of Minnesota, they call it. I'm not sure why."

"Lots of bed-and-breakfasts?" Jeff asked with a smirk.

"No more than any other town. Where are you from?"

"All over. Military brat. Washington State. Seville, Spain. Tokyo. Vacaville. Sacramento. I guess Sacramento is kind of a home. My family lives there. I dropped out of college after two years."

"Why did you do that?"

"Boredom, I guess. I lived in a football house off campus. I got a few tryouts with pro teams. I went hiking in Nepal. Did journalistic work in South America. There was talk of me doing some speechwriting for Reagan."

"But you hadn't even graduated college."

"Neither did Andrew Jackson."

"Oh, geez," she said, and he heard the Midwesterner in her and he liked it. "What kind of lies will you tell me on our next date?"

"I'll pick you up at your barracks tomorrow at six. Clint Eastwood is loaning me his Ferrari."

AT JEFF'S FUNERAL the elephant in the room was his lies. He had never been a drunk, so no one could talk about his drinking. A few times during his chemo he smoked pot to keep the nausea at bay, but I doubt he took drugs at any other time in his life. He wasn't a womanizer. He didn't beat his wife or children.

But he lied. He didn't tell small lies, he told monster lies, the kind of lies that the listener was incapable of refuting. The listener might be able to say, "Ah, man, you're full of it." Jeff would laugh right along, and blow some more heat into the lie.

Thus, when he talked about having a walk-on tryout with the San Francisco 49ers football team, the first lie was a small one, a jest over a few beers one Sunday football afternoon, drinking with the guys from the church. Throw it out and see if anyone bites.

"I once caught a few passes from Joe Montana," Jeff says.

"Yeah, right. Me, too," his listener replies.

"It was 1984. I was trying to figure out what to do with myself. I screwed up academically and lost my scholarship at Sacramento State. But I knew I was a receiver. I was a born receiver."

And here Jeff would force his hands into the listener's face: he did have big hands, big strong football-catching hands. The listener would compare them to his own small hands and think, *Well, shit yeah, this guy could catch some footballs with those hands.*

And Jeff says, "The Niners' summer camp was up in Rocklin, you know, just twenty miles up the road from downtown Sacto. So one day I'm on my couch, trying to figure out my future, and I think, 'Why don't I try out for the Niners? What's to stop me from walking on and catching some passes and showing them I've got juice? I run a 4.2 forty.'"

And the listener whistles and says, "That's fast for a white boy."

The fact is very few people on the face of the Earth can run a 4.2 forty-yard dash. This must dawn on the listener. Jeff moves toward the listener. He thinks he's losing him.

Jeff's muscular legs are as hard as an oak. He stands. He flexes his legs, his quads and hamstrings taut, and he takes the listener's hand and puts it on his leg and says, "Squeeze. All of that is muscle. That is how I run a 4.2 forty. Yes, I am fast for a white boy."

And the listener nods.

Jeff says, "So I'm in Rocklin, and I just walk up to the fence. I've got my gear on. Little kids press their faces to the wire, fathers are reliving their glory days, there is Jerry Rice, there is Montana, there are footballs flying everywhere, whistles blowing, grown men yelling, other grown men crying, doubled over in pain. I see a guy in coach shorts, a whistle around his neck. I say, 'Hey, Coach. I'm a receiver. Give me a chance.'"

The listener says, "Just like that, you tell a coach to give you a chance? You're just a chump who walks up from the parking lot."

"But the coach," Jeff says, "the coach is trained to spot desire and talent. And he sees both in me, he sees fire."

And at Jeff's funeral, in the church foyer before the service begins, the listener walks up to me, the dead man's brother; the listener is now the dead man's mouthpiece, the carrier of the dead man's lie.

The listener says to me, "Man, your brother lived a crazy life. A full life. I just been in this little Georgia town my whole life. I admit I used to live a little through his stories. Can you imagine catching a touchdown pass from Joe Montana? I know it was just an exhibition game. But still. It was against the Raiders. Your brother caught a winning touchdown pass from Joe Montana against the hated Raiders. How many men can say that?"

"Not many," I say. "Not with a straight face, at least. Yeah, I guess I'd forgotten about that."

"How the heck could you forget that? I loved hearing him tell that story. A seventy-yard touchdown bomb from Joe Montana, fighting Mike Haynes off his back. Life don't get better."

Lies don't get better either. I look through the foyer to the front of the church, through the old ladies shuffling sideways across the aisles, through my uncles and aunts and cousins finding their seats, to Jeff's closed coffin.

The man dies. His deeds remain. And so, too, his lies.

My younger sister Kim corners me, mortified. "Oh, Jesus Christ," she says. "Some guy just told me about Jeff working with the CIA in Berlin. What the hell else will we hear?"

We will hear about the time he sang with the Mormon Tabernacle Choir.

We will hear about the time in Tokyo as a teenager when he practiced kung fu with Bruce Lee even though Bruce Lee died a year before we moved to Tokyo.

We will hear about the time Clint Eastwood loaned him a Ferrari for a date with a married woman. We will hear that the married woman's husband showed up at the hotel room carrying a shotgun and demanded that his wife leave the room; and somehow Clint Eastwood appeared, looking for his Ferrari, it would seem, and Clint Eastwood defused the situation, sent the married man home without his wife.

We will hear about the time he danced in Michael Jackson's "P.Y.T. (Pretty Young Thing)" video.

Jeff's son is at my side. He's a cute little five-year-old boy and he looks just like my brother. He has no idea that all these people are here to say goodbye to his father forever. He has no idea what forever means. He knows that for some reason his father is in the metal box at the front of this room. He knows that the tie around his neck is constricting and that the suit pants are scratchy and that he had to take a bath early this morning. He knows that his mother and his grandmothers and his aunts and uncles and all the adults in his life are crying.

Because my father has refused to attend Jeff's funeral I am the only adult Swofford male in our line. I lead the death procession, little Christian's hand in mine. We sit in the first pew, far right. Christian sits on my lap. He hugs my neck, and he cries, and he asks me, "Why is Daddy in the box?"

I can't answer him. I don't know how to say, "Daddy is dead." The three words, they are too cruel for his ears.

I kiss the boy on the cheek, and I smooth his pretty red hair.

The preacher talks about the things that Christian preachers talk about: salvation, the spirit; the afterlife, God's Army: this is garbage to me, smoke and mirrors.

A man is dead. The man is my older brother. His five-year-old son sits crying in my lap. That is all. That is the everything and the nothing of this day.

There was a military honor guard. They fired rifle blanks and I flinched at each report; they folded a flag and handed it to Melody. The corpse-laden hearse drove off to the funeral home, where later a worker whose name I'll never know would incinerate my brother's body.

The February Atlanta day was crisp but not bitterly cold. Back at the house, in the yard, I threw a football with Christian. We did not speak of his father. We threw the football. We played catch with a baseball. We shot hoops in the driveway. I wondered if Jeff also had some pro basketball and baseball lies that he bandied about. I hadn't heard them, but I wouldn't put it past him.

In the house my mother and sisters and Melody and a few of my aunts and uncles told stories about Jeff. Some of these stories would probably qualify as lies, or aberrations, but can you really lie about a dead man? The dead man is not present: he can neither confirm nor deny the reports. Death is the ultimate Fifth Amendment.

I remember that we drank some wine that day. No one called my father and he didn't call us.

I wanted to call and shame him for not being there, but I did not possess the courage. I knew that while nearly a hundred members of his nuclear and extended family buried his son in Douglasville, Georgia, my father sat in a shitty dive bar in Fairfield, California, getting drunk with other sad men. I knew the bar. I knew the pungent smell of the place, the combination of booze and vomit and industrial-strength cleaning supplies. I know what it is like to waste months or years of one's life drinking in one of these bars. Mine is on West Nineteenth Street in Manhattan.

I called my girlfriend in Sacramento. I felt bad for not having invited her to the funeral. I'd boxed her out. We both cried on the phone. She said she loved me, and she did, but I was unable to believe her. Within months we'd break up.

Later that night when enough wine had been consumed that we were all a little drunk, Melody asked me to follow her into the garage.

"I want you to have Jeff's pistol," she said as she pulled the plastic case from behind a toolbox.

She opened the case. It was a beautiful Czech handgun, a CZUB semiautomatic .45 caliber.

She said, "I want you to hold on to this until Christian is old enough to own it. And then I want you to teach him how to shoot."

"I don't want a gun around," I said. "When I get back to

California, I'll figure out a way to have it shipped to me. And I'll store it in a safe-deposit box. I don't—"

I stopped. The nearer truth was: I didn't trust myself with a gun in the house. I might blow my brains out.

"OK, fine. There's something else."

She fumbled through the toolbox and retrieved an envelope and handed it to me.

"Jeff would want you to have this," she said. "It's a thousand dollars."

"Why would Jeff want me to have this? I don't need it. I have a job. What were you saving it for? And why was it stuffed in a toolbox?"

"It was an emergency fund. That's all. Or vacation. I don't know. Just take it. Buy yourself something nice."

I felt like I was being bought off, but I didn't know what for.

I shoved the envelope in my suit pocket and returned with Melody to the dining room table, where my now-drunk mother cried uncontrollably, her head buried in her hands. I sat down next to her and rubbed her back.

Somewhere in the house Christian screamed for his mother. We found him curled up in Jeff's hospice bed, the green flannel Jeff wore when he died wrapped around his body.

This was the same room where Jeff had, a few nights before, asked me to take Jesus into my heart and life. It would have been easy for me to tell Jeff that I'd do this for him. He was in and out of a morphine cloud. I'd been reading to him the Christian inspirational verses he'd requested.

"Brother," he said, "I want you to live a good life. I want you to have a family. You need God for a family. For cohesion."

I said, "You know I'm an atheist. I have been since I went to war. I respect your beliefs. I just don't believe them."

"Pray with me," he said.

"I can't, Jeff. It wouldn't be right. It would make a joke of us both. I love you. I love your family. I love your children. I will do anything for your family. What do you need from me?"

"Let's pray for you."

"No prayers, Brother. Let's talk. What will your family need?"

"Mel has it covered. She knows. You're just a kid. Make your own family. Someday you'll find God."

I wanted, more than anything, to tell my brother that he was right, and that one day I would find God, but none of that would have been true.

I did say, "I will have a family someday. And I will be a good husband and father. And I will tell my children about you and how much I loved you. I can promise you that."

I read some more from the verses, poorly written inspirational Christian drivel. Jeff stopped me. He needed to piss.

He couldn't walk on his own. He asked me to carry him to the bathroom across the hall. I cradled his body and I carried him down the hall. His skeleton pressed against my body. Where once there had been so much muscle there was now only bone and skin. His chin rested on my shoulder and I felt his faint breath against my ear.

He wore the green flannel and gray sweats. I steadied him in front of the bowl and helped him shimmy the elastic-waistband sweats down his bony hips.

"I am happy to piss on my own," he said. "I need to keep pissing on my own. When I can no longer piss standing up I want this to end."

I looked at my brother's dick. It was shaped like mine, a natural bend toward the right. It was about the same size. He had no pubic hair. His piss was dark yellow with a faint trace of blood: the water in the toilet bowl looked as though a teaspoon of saffron had been dropped in.

"I haven't fucked in so long," he said. "I don't even know what sex is. Or what it means. I wish I could fuck my wife once more. No. I wish I could live and keep fucking her for the rest of my life."

I helped him back to bed. My mother and Melody came into his room. They administered another morphine patch and Jeff floated away.

I called Iris and met her at the Waffle House by the interstate. We ate the usual greasy mess of food. I didn't want to eat, though. I wanted to fuck. I wanted to fuck for my brother.

We jumped in her car and drove around for a while, our usual trip, the Velvet Underground our musical guides, from old church to old church, from cemetery to cemetery. It was late now, past midnight. I asked her to drive to my brother's house. We'd had sex here before, in the spare room, on the ground floor where Jeff now slept in his hospice bed. We entered the dark and quiet house through the downstairs patio.

I held Iris's hand and I walked her into Jeff's room. A reading light at the side of his bed lit his wan face. She stared at him for a moment and then she followed me down to the floor.

I heard my brother's soft breathing.

Iris giggled. "What are you doing?"

I took her shirt off. And her bra.

"Jesus," she said.

Yes, Jesus, I thought. I kissed her and took her breasts in my mouth.

"Jesus," she said.

She slid down my body and took me out of my pants. I looked at my brother. I thought his eyes were open but I couldn't tell. I thought I saw a smile, but I couldn't tell. I wanted him to watch.

I pulled her on top of me. I had never had sex in front of someone else before and here I was inside a woman in front of my dying brother. I was usually a fairly attentive lover but this time I was not. I was hard and I was deep inside Iris and I pulled her hips roughly against mine and all I thought of was my dying brother: his gap-toothed smile as a carrot-topped little boy; his high school football number, twenty-two; I thought of his Phoenician Yellow '66 Mustang; about playing catch with him in the yard, the way he taught me to use the laces on the football; I thought of his once-powerful body and I thought of women riding him, I thought of my brother fucking Iris; I closed my eyes and I saw him under the sexy young Iris and I saw myself dying in his hospice bed.

THE NEXT DAY occurred the party Jeff had summoned me for. And for the first time since Jeff had become ill, my father traveled from California to visit his dying son. I know that Jeff and Dad spent some time alone. I don't know what was said.

I do know that while a number of my aunts and uncles and cousins hung out in Jeff's living room and played guitars and sang songs, just as Jeff had wanted for his Dying Party, my father had cajoled me into joining him in a search for a bar that served his brand of scotch. I knew nothing about scotch at this point. Later I would know that other than a sexy ad campaign, this particular scotch had little going for it. But it was my dad's drink and in these dry and half-dry and downright parched counties of the

South, a man sometimes had to work hard to find a bar with his particular brand of scotch.

"Goddamn," my father said as we left yet another sports bar, out of luck. "I know when I was back here in '92 those guys had my Chivas. You can get a pot of black-eyed peas on every corner but they're damn near to kill you looking for your scotch. I got another idea."

I wanted to say, *I have an idea. Why don't we go back to Jeff's house and hang out with him and the rest of the family, since he's going to die in a matter of days, and the reason we are here is to spend time with him before he dies, not in shitty roadside bars all over Douglas County looking for your scotch?*

To my great shame I did not say this. I spent the afternoon and into the evening driving around the hills and towns of West Georgia while my father looked for a bar that poured his scotch. We'd pop into a place and have a beer, or a lesser scotch, and then head back out on the road. I suppose that if I worked hard I could turn this search of my father's into something symbolic, epic even. But it was neither symbolic nor epic. The search was sad and pathetic, my father's sick and deranged attempt to stay away from his dying son and his family. But wait, I could make this day about me and my father, my father's choice to bond with me, the living and thriving son: the father choosing to hunker down in the cave with the young, healthy son while out in the wilderness animals devoured the older son.

No, that doesn't work either. The only thing that works is this: my father was a coward. And so was I.

By the time we returned to Jeff's house the party had ended and the place was quiet and smelled of the dying: that humid, earthy smell of failing flesh. I went downstairs to apologize to

Jeff for missing the party, but he was already so high on morphine he had no idea I was even there.

A FEW DAYS after Jeff's funeral Melody called and asked me if I could convince my mother to watch the kids for the night while the two of us went out for dinner. I was leaving the next day and she wanted to talk before I left.

I dropped my mom off at the house for her babysitting duties. An animated movie of the Disney variety played on the TV. Melody always kept an extremely clean and tidy house, and the death of her husband had not changed this.

We drove to a strip mall nearby and went to a chain restaurant. Melody ordered a massive drink, a quart of blue liquor, the glass festooned with fruit and umbrellas. Bad pop music blared from scratchy speakers. The server looked at us intently while reading the specials, though there was nothing special about the specials. I'm certain that I ordered enchiladas. I drank one beer. Melody ordered another blue drink, and a playful and mischievous drunkenness descended upon her. I saw why my brother had fallen in love with her.

She told me stories about the years they lived in Munich. She talked about how sexy they had both been. They were gym rats, and everyone on base envied their bodies. Even after children, she said, they still had a sex life.

"Even when we fought," she said, "even then, we made sure to keep up a sex life. It's important."

I didn't want to hear my brother's widow talk about their sex life. I changed the subject to the children, or the weather. But she kept coming back to sex.

"God, he was a great lover. If it's there, you think it will always be there. And then he got sick. And it was gone. Like that, in a day, gone. At first we tried some things. Alternate things. At one meeting for cancer spouses they even had a pamphlet for it. Cancer sex. Can you believe it?"

She slapped the table hard enough to tilt and spill her drink a bit, the blue liquor cresting the levee of the glass.

"But that didn't work. I won't lie. I thought about other men. But I never did anything. A few men from the church made advances, but I pushed them away."

This got my attention: some dirtbag hit on my dying brother's wife? Where was he? I'd kill the bastard.

"Once." She paused. "I shouldn't say this. But once I thought of you. It seemed—it seemed normal. My dying husband's little brother. Isn't that how they used to do things?"

I didn't know if I had heard her correctly. Had she just said that she had thought of sex with me and that it had seemed normal? That was not normal. My brother's ashes weren't even in the ground. None of this was normal.

The waiter approached and she motioned for another round of drinks.

"Melody," I said. "You've had two huge drinks. That's probably enough. Let's get the check."

"I don't want the check. I want another drink! My husband is dead and I want another drink!"

Some heads turned and looked our way.

"OK," I said. "Have another. I just. I don't know what to say. I really don't."

"You're such a child," she said. "You will always be the baby. Your brother is dead but you are still the baby boy. As long as your father is alive you are the baby boy."

She told me that for many years she had thought the demons visited upon my brother by my father would never dissipate, but that they finally had when Christian was born.

"One child," she said, "was not enough for your brother to get out from under the sway of your father. But Christian did it. Christian was the magic bullet. Suddenly your father no longer haunted him. They became friends. I couldn't believe it."

She pulled a box from her purse.

"Here, it's Jeff's watch. It's a cheap thing. But take it. Keep it. And I still want you to take the pistol. Give it to Christian when he's eighteen. Will you do that?"

"I'll do whatever you ask." I'd do anything to get out of the booth, out of the restaurant, out of this time zone.

"Tell me about when you had sex with that girl in Jeff's room."

Melody had once chased Iris out of the house. It was the first night we'd slept together, the first time I'd come out to visit Jeff after his diagnosis. We'd parked her jalopy in the driveway and it leaked oil all over Jeff's pristine concrete. He'd been pissed. Melody had kicked at the locked bedroom door and told me to get the girl out of the house. We'd sneaked out the back and later in the day I'd spent hours washing the oil stain from the driveway.

"I saw you come home late with her that night last week. I saw you sneak around the back."

"Yes. I snuck her in. I had sex with her on the floor of Jeff's room."

She slapped the table again, harder. "I told your mother. I'll tell everyone in the family. They'll think you're sick."

"Maybe I am."

I'd been caught. But I didn't believe that she had told my mother or that she would tell anyone else. It wasn't her style. Melody liked owning secrets.

"Did he watch?" she asked.

"I don't want to talk about this. That was between Jeff and me. Maybe it was wrong. I don't know."

"Yes. It was wrong."

She finished her drink and I paid the bill.

I drove toward their subdivision.

"Let's get another drink somewhere," she said.

"I need to grab my mother and get back to Granny's and sleep. I have an early flight and I have to work at the warehouse tomorrow night. I'm already two over my grief days."

"How much do they pay you for a grief day?"

"It's normal pay," I said.

I realized she was toying with me.

"Use your grief pay to buy me another drink. I need a grief drink. I need to feel normal!" she screamed.

I continued toward their subdivision. As I pulled into the settlement Melody put her hand on my thigh and said, "Take me into the woods. Like your brother would have."

I slowed the car down. I felt a hollow sickness in my stomach, the vomitous stirring of my insides. I started to sweat and my field of vision sank down to a tunnel, straight ahead.

She said, "You can't. You're not a man like your brother. You are still a boy. But you want to. I saw the way you used to look at me when I first married Jeff. I caught you once, playing in our laundry at your parents' house, looking at my underwear."

This could very well have been true but I didn't remember it.

I said, "I was fourteen years old. I looked at any pretty woman that way. It's called puberty."

"Your brother would laugh at you, just laugh. He said you'd never get laid, what a sad case. Your mommy still cut your hair. You were such a dorky kid. We had a bet. He thought you'd be a virgin until you turned thirty. You're a boy. Still a baby boy."

I pulled into the driveway and turned off the car.

I said, "Mel, I'm going to go upstairs and sit with my mom and your children. I'm going to sit there for as long as you need. You stay here in the car. You think about Jeff. You think about your children. Think about yourself. We'll be up there playing games and laughing. You just sit here, and think about what you need from life. And I'll be upstairs with my mother and the kids. And when you want to join us, come on up."

Half an hour later she walked in the door.

Christian asked, "Mommy, where were you?"

"I just went for a walk, honey. I needed a walk. Did you have fun with Grandma and Uncle Tony?"

ON MY WAY to the airport I swung by the cemetery. There were already two Swofford men buried here, my grandfather and my uncle. I didn't know when they were going to inter Jeff. The Swofford plot was at the top of the hill, at the deep right curve of the horseshoe drive. I knew its position well. When I was a boy, every time we visited Georgia my father took us to look at his brother's headstone. I could find my way there in the dark.

As I banked toward the plots I saw two cemetery workers in the Swofford grounds. One man leaned against a shovel and another man sat atop a small backhoe, working the blade into the earth, working out the dirt, making way for my brother's ashes.

*   *   *

YEARS LATER, WHEN I begin to try to write about my brother I sort through boxes of notes, years of notes and photographs. I find an official Army portrait of my brother when he must have been going for a promotion. He's thirty or so and handsome in his rugged tough-guy-soldier way.

I find my DD-214, the military discharge, and also the DD-214s of my brother and father. And I find a note in my mother's perfect cursive script. The word *Jeff.* The words *Nurses Station.* And a phone number. I call the number. It is the VA hospital in Nashville. They instruct the caller to call the VA's 888 suicide hotline number if it is an emergency.

Well, is it?

5

Letter from My Father

On October 10, 2006, my father mailed to me a nine-page hand-written letter postmarked Sacramento, CA. The missives are dated July 06; August 06; August 10-06; Sun, August 13, 2006 (a day after my thirty-sixth birthday); Oct 4, 2006; Oct 8, 2006. All the entries but the last are written on one side of college-lined white paper with one-inch margins and three-ring holes. The last entry is written on the back of the eighth page: at two and a half lines it is the shortest of the lot, a haiku of the epistolary fistfight:

> *I have sat on this for much too long. The more I sit the longer it grows. It is well past time to shred or mail. So mail here it comes.*
> *With Love,*
> *Your Father*

With sickening clarity I remember removing this letter from my mailbox. It must have been the thirteenth or fourteenth of October. I'd had dinner at the apartment of my best friend, more a brother than a friend. Let's say we'd eaten delivery of some pan-Asian sort, the kind readily available in Midtown. Once their two kids had gone to bed after fighting the sleep demons for a while, Oren and Yael and I would have stayed up for an hour or so talking and drinking more wine, listening to music, getting drunk but not wasted, just drunk enough for a weekend night when the next day everyone had work to do.

Yael would have retired first, probably to sleep for a while with one of the restless children.

I would have sought Oren's counsel on the matter of my deteriorating relationship with Ava. We'd recently taken a number of breaks, meaning we'd cheated extensively on each other. From early on Oren had told me to leave her and he would have done the same thing again tonight. "Nothing good can come of this" is a typical Oren comment about my relationship with Ava. "Don't you want a family and real love?" Yes, I wanted a family and real love; yes, I needed to leave Ava in order to have a family and real love.

I walked home that night, twenty-seven blocks south and nine avenues west, a short city walk. At a bar or two along the way I beat the temptations of drink and women and kept on toward home. I called Ava and she didn't pick up. I guessed she was in a dank bar in the East Village, snorting cocaine in the bathroom with a man she'd just met. I knew the bar and the bathroom, but not the man.

I entered my building and checked my mail for the first time that week. I sifted through the various generic mailers and the other waste, tossed it in the recycling bin, and found among the remaining envelopes a thickish cream-colored one adorned with my father's recognizable steep script.

I thought, *This is the letter you've been waiting for.*

My father wrote a curse letter to my brother when Jeff was twenty-three. When Jeff died twelve years later my younger sister found it among his effects, in a binder, in protective wrapping. She and I read the letter together and wept.

We wept for our brother, our father, the death of our family, and the calamity in script we were experiencing, the father killing his son, the father backing his son against the stone firing wall.

In his memoirs Elias Canetti writes that the most awful thing a father can do is curse his son. Cursing a son is an invitation to the destruction of the family. Canetti's grandfather cursed his father and shortly after his father, a young and prosperous businessman, fell dead at the table.

SO WHEN I held the envelope in my hand, kind of drunk, rather heartbroken over a beautiful and fucked-up woman, thirty-six and alone in New York City, I knew these pages contained a curse from my father. I put the letter, unopened, in my top desk drawer.

AND ONE NIGHT a few weeks later I opened it.

Dear Tony,

July 06 [2006]

I write this because your schedule makes it impossible to have a sit down conversation or a meaningful telephone conversation. There are a couple of reasons why I am reluctant to do this. First it is the type of thing I think should be discussed in person rather than one-way communication. Secondly if you decide to save it—years from now someone may find and read it—assume it is something; it is not. Just as you assumed my letter to Jeff was my reply to his attorney letter. I have never seen that letter. I gave you a pass on that. The divorce was between your mom and me. I tried to keep you kids out of it. Some way you and Jeff got involved but not by my doing. Had you wanted to know—? Why the letter—? Why not ask?

My father is correct that at this point in my life my schedule made it tough for me to have a sit-down conversation. I lived in New York and he lived in California and I traveled often. And I was loath to have an important conversation about our relationship and my childhood over the phone. A friend of mine had recently been in therapy with her father in California, and I had for many months considered offering this option to my father: I'd fly out to California twice a month and we could sit with a psychotherapist to try to figure it out. But I spent enough time with my own therapist talking about my father that to add two more sessions a month might well have killed me. And my father is not exactly the therapy type.

The "attorney letter" he speaks of is a letter that my brother wrote to my mother's attorney that was put forth for the record in their divorce, wherein my brother outlined the various ways in which my father was verbally and occasionally physically abusive to his children, mostly my older brother and sister. I can't imagine that my father never saw this letter, and in fact in the letter he wrote to Jeff he referenced it. In return for this letter my father sent my older brother a scathing letter attacking his character and his manhood and challenging him to a physical fight.

The Cub/Boy scout thing was the first week or the first and second week. To that time you had only had overnight

and weekend visits with buddies, a week would be your
longest time away from home. This being your first summer
camp I was sure you would be ready to leave after the first
week. I explained it would be better to plan for two weeks the
following year, which did not make it into your book. But you
the big tough guy insisted on two weeks. I would have been
an asshole to keep you from going two weeks. Turns out I was
an asshole after all, trying to teach my young son that mature
people keep their word or if not take responsibility for the
convenience it cost others.

This camp episode is addressed in my first book. I wanked out of Boy Scout camp a week early and my father insisted I repay him for the second week that I missed. I hated camp. I couldn't tie knots, I was horrible at fishing, I had no friends, and I couldn't, for the life of me, get my hands around that greased-down watermelon as it floated atop the pristine High Sierra lake.

I missed my mother. Of course I came home early. So he was right. And maybe, years later, I was being a little punk to complain in writing about having had to repay him. But should twelve-year-olds be taught about maturity? Shouldn't they just be welcomed home and given another chance the next year, no questions asked? Perhaps a father should offer a model of maturity rather than a lecture on maturity? If life is all lessons, when the hell is a kid supposed to have fun?

But you the big tough guy. My father wastes no time getting straight to the gut shots and questions of manhood, even mocking the twelve-year-old me.

So, he seems to be saying, *you thought you were so tough when you were twelve, and how about now? I've got this pen in my hand, writer boy, and I'm going to kick your ass with it.*

In fact I hadn't thought I was tough: I had thought I was a weak, cowardly little boy and my father was more than happy to support me in this conclusion.

He doesn't even suggest that a reason he may have wanted me to go for just one week was that he would have missed me. But maybe he wouldn't have missed me at all.

My friend Oren is a wreck when his kids are at camp. He can't sleep. He calls it abnormal. He says, "You have children so they sleep under your roof, not to send them away to camp." If my father had similar feelings, he might have just told me.

There are other things you wrote that did not happen and others much different than the way you remember. Friends and family have inquired and said I must have been a real bastard. Which put me in the awkward position of explaining various parts of your book. Some of which I failed to recall, requiring a return read of the subject, which at times made me think you intentionally portrayed me as a "real bastard." You get a pass on that.

Truthfully the man *was* a real bastard. I spent most of my childhood in fear of my father. Rarely did I do the right thing. Rarely was he pleased. I understand that he might have different memories of events, but it is not my fault his son became a writer.

No one else will write about my father so I am his writer. And in the act of writing I hope to become again his loving son.

Everyone must understand: when someone writes a memoir people get scorched.

A couple of friends asked for autographed copies of JAR- HEAD. *Since I had to buy my own, I knew you would not furnish them one. It would have been an embarrassment to me having to tell them that my bestselling author son is such a cheap ass. I had to buy my own—so you'll have to buy yours. I purchased copies for them which you so graciously auto- graphed. Kim offered to buy me the book on CD but I told her you had half-assed said you would send me one. Maybe it will happen some time when I am still on the green side of the turf. She did buy me the music from the movie. I just purchased the movie for myself so cancel that request. Your continued fail- ure to send Art* [an old Air Force buddy of my father's] *a book and his continued asking embarrassed your mother so much that she sent him one. But she would never admit to this as being irresponsible on your part. Life is better if some things are never said. Just as my thoughts here may be, as I believe some should not be in your book, I took as first-timer's gloating. After the movie release the maliciousness continued. What is causing the unexplained behavior? Maybe you await a certain reaction. If so this may be it.*

I sent my father one copy of the galley and three of the hard- cover of *Jarhead*. For some reason he doesn't recall receiving them. And I explained to him that my publisher gave me only forty copies of my book and that there were a number of people I needed to send books to—former teachers, old friends, friends of the family. I also explained to him that if I went out and bought a book for everyone who asked me for one I'd be making about negative twenty dollars per hardcover, which seems like a foolish way to make a living—writing already being a foolish enough plan for making money. I know that my father wanted me to provide books to all of his bar and military cronies and some of the men who worked for him; I simply didn't think it was my responsibility.

And here is where I get angry for the first time, when he calls me a cheap-ass. He doesn't know the money I've provided to my niece for rent and some help with college tuition. He doesn't know the number of times I've bailed my older sister out of debt. He doesn't know that I'm paying my younger sister's university tuition and textbook costs. He doesn't know that I'm paying for a medical procedure my aunt in Pakistan must undergo. He doesn't know I paid my brother's widow's mortgage for six months. He doesn't know any of this because I would never tell him. I am not a cheap-ass. I just thought that if my father was so proud of his son he wouldn't mind going down to the bookstore and buying a few copies of the book for his buddies. Or, rather, tell them, "Go buy copies yourself, how do you think the little shit makes money?"

The purpose of this is an attempt to discover why you keep adding distance between us—do I contribute? A reply is not expected but perhaps I will find the answer, as I continue.

This is the first place in the letter where my father posits that he might be responsible for some of the distance between us. In typical John Howard fashion he asks the question and then tells me that I need not reply. By writing on, he'll figure the answer out himself. But does he even want to know if he contributes?

I would like to know more about your activities but I ask little, as you seem to feel it is an intrusion. I have asked you to do only a few things, but repeated requests have brought no results. I had hoped they could at least have been put in the form of a present—trip present—Christmas present—return from Europe present—Father's day present—Birthday present. Fake hope. Several months ago I repeated my request. You said that your novel was completed and you were going to spend the next couple weeks catching up on things. I had been unable to shame you into granting my requests but hoped that would be included in "catching up." Now after many months I see they are of no importance and I not much more.

I know a bit about shame. My father built a roof of shame for his family to live under. You do not shame your father with your poor manners. You do not shame your father with stupidity in public. You do not shame your father by asking foolish questions. You do not shame your father by talking to adults, by speaking unless you have been spoken to. This shame turned me into a treacherous little kid: I was sneaky, I was a liar, I trained my hearing so whenever I heard my name, anywhere in the house, I'd pick up on the fluctuations and intonations of the voices so that even if I couldn't hear all the words, I knew the intentions of the conversation: Tony will be grounded for not doing his chores. Tony will not go to Scott Seltzer's house for a sleepover. Tony's allowance will be reduced for eight weeks.

The thing my father didn't understand about shame was that once the son is in his early twenties the father can't shame him. In fact, the attempts of the father to shame the son look, to the son, like little more than feeble attempts to regain a control lost many years ago. So my father's attempts at shaming me backfired.

And I wondered why, suddenly, when I'd had some success, he chose to become so involved in my life. He'd never been involved in my life when I was a boy, an adolescent, a teenager, or a young man. The other Little League parents thought that my mother was a single mother because over my six years of playing ball my father never came to watch one game or pick me up from a single practice.

Once when I was in college he gave me two hundred dollars for books. When I loaded my rental truck to move for grad school he showed up and bought my buddies pizza and later took us out to a strip club. When at grad school in Iowa I eloped, he sent me and my bride a card and fifty bucks and he failed to show up for the marriage party at my mother's house, an hour's drive away from his. He didn't even bother to call.

You make trips to the area but no time to stop, not even time for a fuck-you phone call.

He's correct: there were times I traveled to Sacramento or the Bay Area and didn't spend time with him. There were other times when I went out of my way to make sure I saw my father and that we shared a meal or a few drinks.

And there is this, which he fails to recall or mention: during the spring of 2006 he'd been feeling rather fatigued each afternoon, and this, coupled with some low-level anxiety, had led the doctors to assume that there might be something amiss with his heart. All his other tests came back normal—his blood work was fine, they didn't find a bleed on his brain, there were no signs of a stroke, so they decided to go into his heart, take a look around, and most likely they'd insert a stent.

We talked on the phone about the procedure and I could tell that my father was quite nervous. I told him I'd come out. It was a Sunday afternoon, and his procedure was Tuesday. I booked an early flight out of JFK for Tuesday, which would put me in the Bay Area right around the time they'd be rolling him out of surgery.

I felt like a good son, like I was doing the right thing by my father and my family. After my brother's death we'd all been rather hospital-averse, so I thought being there with my younger sister, for my father, was the only right thing to do.

I took a flight at a hideously early hour and landed in San Francisco at around ten a.m. As soon as we touched down I frantically called my sister for some news, any news. I called my mother in Sacramento and my sister in Montana; no one picked up. I started to panic.

I picked up my rental and sped toward Fairfield and the big Air Force base where my father was being treated, the same base where I'd been born. My younger sister called and I picked up while ripping through the 880 exchange near Oakland.

"How is he?"

"Oh." She laughed. "He's fine. They took a look and his arteries looked great and that was it. They didn't do anything. We're on our way to Outback. Wanna meet us?"

I almost rear-ended a semi-truck.

"Sure. I mean. That's great. Amazing. Outback? Like, the steak house?"

110

"Yeah. In the mall near Dad's."

"I'm almost at Berkeley. I can probably be there in forty-five minutes."

"See you then."

I dropped the phone onto the passenger seat. My father's heart was fine. No stent. No worries, mate. Now, on to Outback. I'd flown all the way across the US to eat subpar steak at a chain restaurant.

I dropped my speed. I liked driving through the Bay Area. In the hills and waterways many fond memories of my early twenties lurked—epic drinking nights, making love in an almond orchard, houseboat parties on the Delta, making love in the Oakland Hills, circumambulating Mount Tam and making love at midnight in Muir Woods.

I drove toward Vacaville and, without thinking much about it, more on impulse than from thought, I got off the freeway and tried to find the house from my childhood. I found it. A simple shingled ranch, oak tree in the front yard, bay windows, flower garden.

I sat for a few moments and drove on to the nearby Outback.

My father and sister were in a great mood, already settled into a booth. An enormous appetizer platter of fried food-like items landed just as I joined them.

"So what's the doc say?"

"The ticker is fine, Tone. He thinks I'm suffering anxiety. Gave me some pills. Gonna check in in three months and see what he sees. Let's eat some steak."

The irony seemed lost on my sister and father: a few hours after my father had left the hospital for potential heart trouble, here we sat at a steak house, ingesting heart bombs.

My father didn't thank me for flying out for his non-procedure. After the lunch I drove to Sacramento and spent a few days visiting friends and my mother before returning home.

June has come and long gone with no greetings from you.
No passes there.

When I was a youth June loomed large as school ended and ceded to shirtless bicycle days and sunburns and poolside daydreams of girls I'd never kiss—and three family celebrations took place that month: my father's birthday, my parents' anniversary, and Father's Day.

June-time Sacramento sun warmed the pool and in it on those festive days we kids would splash and play, bark like dogs, while my father grilled burgers and brats and my mother made potato salad in the kitchen, occasionally yelling for assistance from my sister or me—we need more soda in the cooler! More napkins on the table! Gambler (our beloved Boston terrier) is chasing the neighbor's cat!

One particular Father's Day I remember well, if for no other reason than that the gift I gave my father resides with me now. I must have been eleven or twelve. A few days before the big day I rode my bike the mile or so to the nearest supermarket with a friend of mine and we perused the aisles for presents for our fathers. My friend didn't find anything that suited his father, but I thought I had.

I remember my mother helping me wrap the cumbersome object and tape it up, place a bow on top. I was excited because this was no run-of-the-mill Father's Day present, not socks, not a tie, not a new alarm clock or coffee cup or T-shirt. I gave my father a beer stein—which I now use to store spare change.

My younger sister and I had been swimming for hours and our hands were puckered like an old lady's. Picnic debris littered the table and the dogs ran circles around the pool, chasing the cat, chasing the rabbit, chasing their shadows as the sun dropped west. Country music drifted outdoors from my father's massive reel-to-reel setup in the family room. Johnny Paycheck. Johnny Cash. One of the Johnnys.

My father poured his Löwenbräu into the mug, and he drank from it, and I thought I was a pretty fine little son.

Our most recent face to face was a dinner at Arden Fair. [Arden Fair is a large mall in Sacramento, but actually the dinner was at a great Thai restaurant called Pardees in a swank little mall in Carmichael called Town and Country. My mother and younger sister were in attendance along with my friend Douglas and his wife Sachiyo.] *Which was well after your two weeks of "catching up." You were finishing your taxes and had gifts. You gave me "Sorry about that Dad." (No importance) I wasn't sure how to respond, so I didn't. What a snub! The likes of which no one deserves. Maybe payback for something in the past? No pass here.*

I recall giving my mother and sister textiles from a trip I'd taken to Vietnam. Before traveling there with Ava I asked my father if he wanted to join us, and he said no. I also asked him if he wanted pictures of any place, or any particular thing—a market in Saigon, a building, a street, a rice paddy, a particular stretch of jungle or river. And he said no to this as well. He told me he'd gotten out of Vietnam with his life and that that was the only thing he'd ever wanted out of the godforsaken country.

I asked him if I should look around Saigon for any half siblings and he smiled and said, "Why not?"

Giving my sister and mother gifts in front of him while offering him nothing was extremely rude. I feel horrible about it now. But I don't know what I would have brought him. Maybe one of those red T-shirts with Che splashed across the yellow Communist Party star? I plead guilty to the charge of showing up empty-handed.

He's correct: I may have been trying to get back at him for something, or for everything.

Last Christmas I sent you a check rather than a gift, which is what I normally do. I know it wasn't much compared to what you are now accustomed to, but you cashed it. I wonder why I didn't get a thank you, it would take very little of your precious time. Is thanks of no importance to you anymore? Or for such a small gift? Should a pass be given? Or should I chalk it up to an absent minded ~~professor~~ writer? Maybe even the thought behind the gift is of no importance to you? Should that excuse your ill-mannered conduct?

I distinctly remember calling my father when I received the check and thanking him for it. I told him I'd used it to buy a great bottle of wine that Ava and I would share around the holidays. This is the first sign that he's fixated on the sums of money he thinks I now make. The striking of the word *professor* indicates that he considers me a fool for walking away from a tenure-track teaching position to move to New York for a woman and to write full-time, as well his hierarchy of the two titles, professor and writer. A professor is, well, a professional. A writer is a bum.

114

Any man with a pen can say he's a writer. What man can say he's a professor and a writer? My father's maternal grandfather could; he taught music at Auburn and wrote church hymns. But I do not write church hymns.

Maybe this stems from the time you borrowed my GMC. You stated you only needed it for a short period of time, until you purchased one of your own. Several times in the past you used my red S-10; only once do I remember you replacing the fuel. Failing to get an estimated return date [on the GMC SUV] *other than "as soon as I have time to buy one of my own"—you offered to make monthly vehicle and insurance payments until it was returned. Since you were no longer a struggling student—it seemed reasonable to me. I have never had such a good deal and this arrangement would keep you from being rushed buying one of your own and cost you substantially less than renting one. You got distracted several times and kept it longer than most folks would consider reasonable and made no payments during that time. Maybe you felt for the first time you were in control of something in my life and were going to take full advantage. When you finally returned it, giving me a check which included reimbursement for one of your parking tickets; there was an air of arrogance as if you felt I should not accept your money. Which was confirmed later, when you accused me of gouging you—my own flesh and blood by taking money for the use of a vehicle. When it was time to renew the registration surprise—there were two more unpaid tickets plus late charges. Which had to be paid right there before DMV would validate the renewal. You had told me you were paying these tickets. What a lie!*

You never offered to pay for the oversight, which indicates you never intended to pay in the first place. I suppose you justified not keeping your word because I screwed you by having the audacity to expect and take payment from my own "flesh and blood" for the use of a vehicle. To this day I cannot understand why you would expect me to furnish the vehicle "fee gratis," then stiff me for your tickets. Especially since you were financially able.

In memory my father and motor vehicles are intertwined. Even the genesis of my parents' relationship involves combustion engines and speed: As a young airman in Moses Lake, Washington, my father ripped around town in a sleek 1957 Chevy. A high school senior with a bright red coiffure worked at the drive-in where my father and his military friends hung out on weekends. It was late in her senior year, she'd just turned eighteen, and she was supposed to start at Washington State in the fall.

My dad was a madly handsome Air Force kid of twenty, and he wanted to take her out. He spoke in a deep amber Southern drawl and words fell from his mouth like sex. But the redhead said no, and again no, and no again. This dark-haired handsome kid returned each weekend in his tricked-out hot rod and the redhead always said no and sometimes added *Go away*.

And then one night, near the end of her shift, a guy drove off with the tray and dishes my mother had delivered to his car. My father knew that the waitresses were charged for any loss of dishes and utensils, and he gave chase. As my father told it, the guy pulled over a mile down the road and handed over the tray, with all the dishes intact. My father returned the goods to my mother and finally she said yes. I now wonder if my father hadn't put one of his buddies up to the stunt, or if he had handed a stranger a few dollars to enlist him in the charade. What does it matter? The redhead said yes and the Swofford motor vehicle legacy began.

I use the word *vehicle* just like my father. Often when I employ it casually, say walking down the street with a friend and spying a Ferrari, I'll say, "That's a nice vehicle." And the friend will laugh at my use of the word.

"Why not just say *car*?"

Car seems so casual. *Vehicle* has a formality and manliness to it, the assumption that the person behind the vehicle knows the power and perils of said vehicle, knows how to fix it with his own tools if need be, understands the meaning of torque, the piss-your-pants sensation of blasting through the desert in a high-horsepower sports vehicle, taking hairpin turns up the mountain at fifty miles per hour, feeling death's breath on your neck as you dance at perilous heights and speeds along California 1.

On a bookshelf in my office is a simple wooden car my father and I made when I was three years old and we lived in Ohio. Making the car with my father is one of my first memories; the other is of a fierce lightning storm that took out the big oak tree in our front yard the same summer. I'm unsure which came first, the car or the lightning.

The car is made of simple scrap wood, two one-by-fours nailed together; one is one-third the length of the other and represents the roof of the vehicle. The wheels are made from one-and-a-half- and two-inch dowels, the two-inchers in the rear so that the car has an aggressive stance, as though it's always revving RPMs at the start line, ready for the go.

My father and I sat in the backyard and we used my red

wagon as a workspace. My father put my fist on the handle of the saw and covered my fist with his own, and together we sawed the one-by-four, two cuts against the soft pine grain. It would have been the first time I took a tool in my hand. I can feel now the reverberation of energy along the spine of the saw, up through the handle, into my tiny fist. From an early age my father taught me to respect tools, to respect their power and to know the consequences of abusing the power of the tool. Using the wrong tool was, for my father, tantamount to praying to the wrong god, or not praying at all.

My father cut the wheels from the dowels and he spray-painted the body pieces red and the wheels black.

While the paint dried he would have gone back to whatever father chore monopolized his time that day—building a fence, fixing a basement door, mowing the lawn. I involved myself in the intricacies of my mini swing set and the balance required to careen on my belly down the slide.

He called me back when the paint dried and I watched as he hammered the roof to the body with three nails. He handed me the car, my first and only homemade toy.

As a boy I logged hundreds, if not thousands, of hours playing with that car in my room or outside on the sidewalk or in the dirt, making car noises, running the vehicle through its paces—sprints, jumps, laps, smash-up derby. Six cheap simple pieces of painted wood made a boy so happy.

I occasionally take the car down from the shelf and place it in front of me on my desk. And as I roll it back and forth on my desk the feeling is the same—power, movement, escape.

I flip the car upside down. At some point, with a nail, I scratched axles, a drivetrain, and a transmission into the wooden undercarriage.

I doubt my father remembers this cheap toy. Sometimes I wonder why I have held on to it for so long. So many times I might have tossed it in the garbage like any other piece of the past, another junked vehicle.

THE CONTROVERSY OVER my extended use of my father's car might never die. We disagree on every element of the exchange. You've heard his story, here is mine:

In August 2003 I moved to Oakland, from Portland, in order to start a tenure-track teaching job at a Bay Area college. Back in Portland I never drove, the city being a bastion of public transportation, walking, and biking. I needed a vehicle for my commute from Oakland to Moraga. I told my father that I planned to do car shopping over a few weeks but that in the interim my friend Douglas had agreed to let me borrow one of his cars. My father told me that that was ridiculous, that he had four cars in his driveway and there was no reason for me not to drive one of them. He rarely drove the SUV and so offered it to me.

My father is very particular about his vehicles and his tools. They are always in perfect condition and any time a person tarnishes a vehicle or a tool he knows instantly. He knows if the mirror is a centimeter out of place, if the driver's seat or steering wheel has been shifted and not returned to its original position, if the head of the hammer has been chipped. I knew this about my father, and I knew that I should decline his offer, even lie—tell him that Douglas was on his way down from Sacramento as we spoke, delivering a car to me.

But I accepted his offer. The car wasn't really my style—it screamed soccer dad—but it would do the trick for a few weeks while I found my own car. He gave me the keys and we agreed that I'd return the car by the fifteenth of September, a little less than a month away. There was no discussion of money, car payments, or insurance.

My first day of teaching I rushed out of my apartment, running late as usual, and jumped in the SUV. I turned the key. Nothing, nothing but a cosmic joke. My first full-time teaching job, the first day of classes, which commenced in ninety minutes, and the car my father loaned me is a lemon. Speeding through the Oakland hills one can make it to campus in thirty-two minutes. I call a taxi driver I know, Singh, and luckily he's free. He's in Alameda but can be to me in ten minutes, he says. Singh is the only cab driver in the history of civilization, from donkey cart jockeys in the desert to Hummer limo cruisers in the city, to arrive in ten minutes when he says ten minutes.

After a few flights in and out of Oakland, Singh and I have built up a bit of a professional friendship. I know his kids' names; I know his wife wants to open a restaurant in Alameda; I know his brother is also a cabbie and that they grew up in Mumbai. He knows I'm a writer and that this is my first day of class at a new job.

He pulls up, the screech of his tires announcing his arrival to the neighborhood.

"Brother!" he yells at me. "Let's go. You gonna be late."

I'm sitting on my stoop. It's about eighty degrees outside and I'm wearing a wool suit and tie. Books and papers are splayed at my feet. I have the feeling that moving to Oakland and taking this job was a big mistake, and that my father's lemon car is only the first indication.

I jump in the back of Singh's cab.

He says, "Brother, your first class is at noon, right? Shit, we better move."

"Forty dollars on top if we make it in time."

"You da man," Singh screams, and he guns it down Fairbanks Avenue and into the Oakland hills.

I made it on time and my classes went well. A colleague gave me a ride home. I called my father and told him about the trial of my day and we shared a laugh about it and decided it meant nothing. He gave me his AAA card number so that I could get the vehicle towed and inspected.

I hung up and called Marin County, who lived now in Berkeley. She arrived a few minutes later and we ordered in and had sex a few times and I felt better. She asked me if I'd missed her body and I said yes, because I had. She asked me to do things to her she'd never asked for before, and I did. I hadn't slept with her in four years and I wondered what else she'd learned in the interim. In college we'd usually had sex in my truck, parked in front of her father's house in San Rafael, or in the bathroom in the house she shared with nine people in Davis. Everything about the sex felt new, though it also felt old and stultifying and I wondered again why I continually returned to old lovers. Comfort? Ease? Dread over the future?

The chill Oakland night sneaked into the room and we slept comfortably. In the morning I made eggs and bacon and we spent most of the morning in bed reading and fucking and talking about nothing of importance.

When she left I thought about my ex-wife, and I tried to remember why I'd left her. And then I remembered the dead car and I called AAA.

I'LL ADMIT THAT I am terrible at paying parking tickets and other fines. This is part laziness, part the scofflaw in me. Like my father,

I seek adversity. Adversity gives me a story, a narrative to write against. So I didn't pay a few parking tickets. But I swear I never told my dad I would pay his car payments and insurance.

Our setup seemed pretty good to me as well—my father, who owned a surfeit of cars, would allow me to borrow one of them until I bought my own. If he'd asked me to pay for the use of the vehicle I would have asked my friend Douglas for the use of one of his, which would have been free of charge. And it didn't seem far-fetched that a father would allow his only living son to borrow a car for a month, maybe six weeks at the outside, free of charge. Isn't that what fathers do for their children?

I'll admit that I took a bit longer than I originally intended to buy my own car. In the end I settled on a seven-year-old Mercedes 320, an old man's car if ever there was one: silver on silver, four doors, straight six with a bit of torque but nothing for the long run. I didn't want speeding tickets. I wanted transportation that wouldn't break down, with a low insurance premium.

Before I could get my father's car back to him, I had to run out of town for a weekend reading in the Midwest. I called my dad from Chicago O'Hare and told him that I was traveling again but that I'd have his car back to him Monday—I'd already enlisted a friend to help me in the handoff, and I'd be to his place by noon; he could check out my new ride and we'd run over to Suisun City for those great carnitas at Puerto Vallarta.

I heard the sigh, the Swofford Sigh, as I've come to call it. It's not always an indication of anger; sometimes it's mild irritation, or bemusement, but in this instance, listening from concourse whatever at O'Hare, I knew the Swofford Sigh meant anger.

"You promised me the vehicle back sooner than this, Tone."

"I'm sorry, Dad. I've had a hectic schedule, teaching, traveling every weekend. It took me longer to buy a car than I thought it would. I found one in Sacramento with help from Douglas and Cliff. They saved me from buying a clunker."

"You don't know how to shop for your own car?"

"It was more fun playing around with the salesmen with Cliff and Douglas. They know about buying cars."

"I know about cars. I could have found you a car in a weekend. What did you boys do? Play grab-ass, chase girls, drink beer when you were supposed to be looking for cars?"

"It took a few weeks. Isn't that normal?"

"Normal is sticking to your word. What did you buy?"

"A seven-year-old Mercedes. A sedan. An old man's car."

"Getting fancy, Tone."

"It's not fancy. It's German. It won't break down. It cost less than any one of your cars did brand-new."

"That might be. But listen. You're returning my vehicle so late I'm gonna have to charge you something."

"What? You wouldn't have even used it."

"But it belongs to me and you betrayed my trust. I'm gonna need the cost of the payment, and insurance, and wear and tear at industry standard, which is about twenty-two cents a mile, if I recall."

"Industry standard? What are you talking about?"

"That's what a company pays an employee for wear and tear on a private vehicle."

"My flight is boarding. I've got to go."

"See you Monday, Tone."

My flight wasn't scheduled to depart for two hours. I went to the Bennigan's and ordered a double vodka.

*   *   *

MY FATHER LEFT town for a few days and informed me that I should leave the vehicle in his driveway, locked, with the keys in the glove compartment. He told me that he'd put an invoice in the mail.

I FORGOT ABOUT the invoice. The semester had bogged me down, teaching full-time filled up my schedule. I was trying to get in shape, riding my mountain bike through the Oakland hills every day I could. The casual, regular sex with Marin County was a bonus that I hadn't counted on when I moved to Oakland, and the sex kept me sane. I had no time to waste on dating.

And everything I did—cook, write, eat, teach, read, screw—was an attempt to banish my ex-wife from the currents of my daily life.

Then one day the handwritten invoice arrived. All totaled, my father wanted about seven hundred dollars. I fumed. I couldn't believe the old bastard had actually gone through with it. My own father wanted to charge me for the use of his vehicle. I went for a bike ride. I shot some hoops alone in my driveway. I called a friend. He agreed my father was a jerk. I called another friend. He agreed my father was a jerk. I called another friend. He told me that my father and I were both jerks. I told him he was a jerk and that that was the last time I'd ever ask for his opinion.

A few days later my father called and told me he was going to be near Oakland, and that he hoped to swing by my place to pick up the check I owed him because he didn't know whether or not a guy like me even used the post office.

He stopped by late, around ten, when Marin County was already in my bed. She wanted to say hello to my father, but I asked her to stay in my room.

I let my father in and he glanced around my apartment.

"Nice place, Tone," he said.

"Thanks."

"Where do you write those masterpieces?"

"The large bedroom in back is my office. I sleep in the smaller room."

My father, an amorous man, always in tune to the presence of a woman, glanced at the couch and Marin County's purse and sweater, draped over an arm. He smiled.

"Girl in the back?"

"Marin County."

"Oh, sure. Pretty girl. You're never gonna give that one up, are you? She's too shy to say hi to your old man?"

"She's asleep."

"I gotta hit the road, Tone. You got that check?"

I handed it to him and he put on his glasses in order to read. "Looks about right," he said. "All righty, then. I'd say let's get a drink but I bet you got business to 'tend to. Catch you on down the road."

He clipped my shoulder with his open palm, an attempt to bring me in for a hug, but I stood as still as a flagpole.

"Give your old man a hug," he said with obvious glee.

He knew the matter of the check was burning me up inside, that I considered him a complete bastard for charging me to use his vehicle, and that I would say nothing about it because I was a coward and I never challenged my father.

We hugged and he departed.

I returned to bed and the only thing that might offer solace.

We have never discussed the voicemail you left shortly after events mentioned in the last paragraph. I felt we should have discussed it, but you said you were ok—which I took to mean you weren't interested in talking about it. The preposterous accusation that I stuck your face in dog shit; is untrue and makes me wonder what other atrocious memories of me you hold. I turned your head down toward the ground for you to see but never stuck your face in shit. How did this not make it into your book? It may seem real to you and you may go to your grave believing I did but it simply did not happen.

This episode has never appeared in any of my writing, but I can't let it go. I had tried to write the scene into my first book but it was more painful than any of the wartime scenes I wrote. I gave up. I'm not sure if my father believes it appeared in the book and I misrepresented the event or if he is asking me why I *didn't* put the scene in the book.

Either way, one Saturday in 1977, in Vacaville, California, I woke up at the usual kid hour and watched cartoons from the prone position, a few feet back from the television, my porcelain-white chin resting in my hands, bowl-cut ink-black hair hanging in my eyes, diaphanous curtains. Let's say Bugs Bunny, Donald Duck, Speedy Gonzales, Elmer Fudd. I wore pajamas, a super-hero of some sort emblazoned on the front. Aquaman.

The Saturdays of my boyhood were as regimented as the process for docking a nuclear sub: watch cartoons and do not disturb late-sleeping parents; eat the breakfast mother prepares; dress in yard clothes; perform yard duties; stand by for father's inspection; if inspection is passed, go play with friends until dinner; if inspection is failed, redo yard chores until perfection is achieved.

My sisters followed a similar routine, though they helped my mother with the indoor chores. My older brother had some leeway. He'd leave the house early and ride his bike with his buddies, shoot hoops down at the school, cause chaos in the neighborhood—later in the afternoon he'd help my father tune up and wash and wax the cars, or assist in major reconstruction works: mending a fence, patching the roof, planting or tending our mother's flower or vegetable garden.

As a child, I never understood why my parents refused to wake up with me and join in my world, but obviously they were catching up on sleep and romance.

When my cartoons finished, my mother emerged from the back of the house and made pancakes and eggs for my sisters and me. My older sister, Tami, helped my mother with the boxed batter, beating hard with a wooden spoon in order to remove the lumps. My younger sister, Kim, and I sat and talked about the things a seven- and four-year-old talk about—our bikes, her dolls, school, coloring books. We shared the Saturday newspaper comics.

The big breakfast—eggs, bacon, pancakes, orange juice— sated us all.

I went to my room and changed into my yard clothes—a worn pair of plaid Toughskins, a faded Tokyo Giants T-shirt that read TOKYO GUTS on the back, and a football jersey from my time as a linebacker with the Tachikawa Steelers, way back in '75.

I gathered the week's newspapers from their haphazard pile in the garage and placed them in a paper shopping bag and placed the bag in the backseat of my mother's car. Later, when she and my sisters shopped for groceries on base, they'd drop the papers off at a recycling bin.

At the time we owned two dogs, French poodles, a mother/ daughter super-duo of black curly hypoallergenicness. I loved the two dogs, Gini and Fifi, but they were not a boy's dogs.

G & F did not play catch like my friend's lab; G & F did not run the grassy amber hills behind our house with me and the neighborhood kids, the way another boy's German shepherd did; G & F had assumed a snooty French pose and for the most part looked at us as the French look at most Americans—as uncivilized brutes. They never rushed to the door upon our return; their tails knew not the excited wag of canine recognition for dear owner. Never once did either dog lick my face ecstatically, bestowing on me the slobbery dog kisses called love.

Someday boy-appropriate dogs would enter the family.

The worst dog chore in the family fell to me: every Saturday morning I skulked around the backyard, a double-thick paper shopping bag in one hand, a pooper-scooper in the other.

In a singular stroke of parenting genius my mother and father allowed me to choose my own pooper-scooper every few months—they were way ahead of the curve on the concept of "ownership." Whenever the wear and tear of G & F's intestinal tracts had put the damage to the tool of my trade my father took me down to Lumberjack, the lumber and hardware store of choice in Northern California, and allowed me my pick of the litter, so to speak.

Back in the mid-seventies pooper-scoopers were rather rudimentary compared with today's options—Four Paws, Yard Pup, Little Stinker. The tool I used looked like a fish spatula. Design and decoration variation occurred only at the handle: with my handle choice I expressed both my character and my aesthetic principles. I admit I favored flower prints.

On this October day the grass shone a brilliant green and among the blades a riot of dew softened my step. I was a sojourner, a Native American tracker in search of scat. My life depended on it. The backyard became my jungle, my Laos, my lost country. There—evidence of G & F: I bent and scooped. My father had taught me a system of poop appropriation that many years later in the Marines I would recognize as "policing." You walk a grid: you leave no swath of ground uncovered by the eyes. If it doesn't grow, it goes, the saying went: cigarette butts, bullet casings, ration packaging, and bandoliers. But here in southeast Vacaville I looked only for the evacuations of our stuck-up poodles, the ladies, as my mother called them. Here: bend and scoop. There: bend and scoop. Everywhere: bend and scoop.

I held my little nose. I breathed into the bend of my elbow. I dragged the increasingly heavy bag along the damp grass, toward the garage. My chore done! Another weekend in the trenches and I had survived. I heaped the bag into the open garbage container—the weight of nations no longer taxing my shoulders.

On Saturdays my father woke up late, or left the bedroom late. He's neither a reader of books nor much of a television watcher, so I'm not sure what he would have been doing in the bedroom a few hours past my mother other than sleeping or daydreaming. He was famous for his stash of candy, and he always had a bit of a belly, so he might have been feeding himself candies and relaxing in bed and dreading coexistence with his family. For most of his life work allowed him an escape. The man must leave for work.

But not on Saturdays—on Saturdays the father cannot escape the brood, and the wife, and the building we call a home. Some men escape with golf, or race cars, or the local bar, but my father never had a hobby that I know of.

I reread the comics at the kitchen table while around me my mother and sisters created a portrait of efficiency and cleanliness:

laundering, dusting, vacuuming, poofing pillows, shining furniture, making early preparations for dinner.

When my mother passed me she'd muss my hair and kiss my forehead and I was then and would always remain her baby boy.

My father exited the marital chamber and told me to get ready for the yard inspection. With a start I ran to the backyard and stood on the patio. Nerves rattled my knees; my heart raced: I generally missed a spot, but lately I'd been on a roll, say five or six weeks straight without a penalty. I wanted an undefeated fall season.

"What is this?" my father called from about twenty feet away.

"I don't know," I said. Knowing exactly what this was. My undefeated season had been crushed.

"Well, why don't you come take a look?"

"I don't know."

"I don't care if you don't know. Come here, Son."

I sidled up next to my father. Usually he lectured sternly about the finer points of policing the area, of paying attention to my surroundings, of the responsibility we each had in making the family ship run properly. I suppose this is what most fathers spend their time doing: making minor corrections in the navigation.

But this time my father grabbed me by the back of my neck and he forced my face down toward the pile of dog shit; I fell to my knees, my nose now inches away from the pile. So close I could smell and taste it, the wet meaty aroma of dog shit. My stomach heaved.

"What is that?"

I cried. I gagged. I failed to speak when spoken to.

"What is that, Son?"

"Dog. Poop," I said through tears.

He held my face an inch or two above the dog shit for a few more seconds. And then snatched me away as though he'd saved me from something.

"Now go get your scooper and clean that up."

I did as told while my father watched me from a chair on the patio. When I finished he called me over. He sat me in his lap.

He said, "I don't want to do that. I don't want to have to look after you all of the time. You're a big boy. You know what your job is. If you don't do your job right then no one else can do the right job. And then nothing works around here. If you don't do your job I can't mow the lawn, and then you can't hose down the patio and the driveway. You see?"

I sniffled. I nodded.

"I can't be mowing over the dog poop. That just causes more of a mess. We gotta be on top of this stuff, Tone. OK?"

I sniffled. I nodded. I went about my Saturday.

AFTER PAYING THE car invoice from my father I left him a phone message asking if he remembered that backyard event. I asked him if he remembered shoving his son's face in a pile of dog shit. It is true my face never touched the dog shit, but this seems to me a matter of semantics. I could have used the word *toward*, or *near*, but neither seems specific enough, or close enough to the experience of a seven-year-old boy.

I don't know what the car invoice and the dog shit event have in common. I remembered the dog shit event after ranting to a friend about the car invoice: we sat in a bar in Oakland,

King's Lounge, and we drank cheap drinks and looked at girls and I told him what a prick my father had been about the car, and in the middle of telling him the story I saw myself and my father in grainy sixteen-millimeter memory film, in that back-yard in Vacaville, a father and son already locked in emotional combat.

For the use of his vehicle my father received from me more than a check. I handed back to him this awful memory.

It appears that most fond childhood memories are shared with your mother. Imagine life without them. Mine are imagined, based on my grandmother's love, which I share at my mother's grave.

Here is my father's best writing yet. He acknowledges that my childhood was smoother and sweeter under my mother's watch and invokes the fear of every person who walks the Earth: life without Mother. What is life without Mother? Nothingness. He finalizes the paragraph with an image of himself at the foot of his mother's grave. *Whatever you might think of me*, he says, *don't forget this fact.*

My father's mother died a month after he was born.

I DECIDE I need to move the TV from the foot of my bed into the closet. I don't have cable and rarely watch DVDs and the TV is an eyesore.

My closet is full of five or six boxes of books and miscellaneous papers from the office in Brooklyn I moved out of a year ago.

In the boxes of books I discover a few gems I haven't seen

in a while: *The Oxford Companion to Italian Food*; the Leonard Michaels novel *Sylvia*; *The Letters of Sigmund Freud*; Gary Snyder's *Mountains and Rivers Without End*.

I find three pairs of earphones, scotch tape, rubber bands, tax documents, a Japanese foot massager, and a stapler. And a manila envelope with my aunt Janna's familiar script: *Forms to Keep*. I have no idea what this could be. I pull out the forms and the top form is a photocopy of the obituary page of the *Opelika Daily News* from Monday, July 21, 1941:

Mrs. Annie Swofford, Auburn Route 1, Dies at Opelika Infirmary

Mrs. Annie Laurie Swofford, age 20, of Auburn Route 1, died at the Opelika Infirmary Sunday, at 2:45 p.m., following four weeks illness and funeral service is to be held at 4:00 p.m. daylight saving time today, from the Baptist church in Auburn, internment in Auburn cemetery. Short Funeral Home is in charge of arrangements.

Deceased was born Annie Laurie Howard, on Auburn Route 1, residing there all her life. She was married August 29, 1937 to J. C. Swofford, who survives. Other survivors are: baby son, John Howard Swofford, mother Mrs. S. L. Howard, twin brother, Hodge Howard, now at Camp Blanding, Fla, David Howard, brother, of Auburn Route 1; sister Mrs. J. H. Crawford, Opelika, sister, Mrs. H. S. Strickland, Selma, ALA; brothers, Robert Howard, Auburn and Lafayette Howard, Perry, Fla.

Dr. J. R. Edwards is to conduct services and the following are to act as pallbearers: Earl Wood, Carson Cooper, Cecil Waller and Wilton Thorp.

Mrs. Swofford's father, Samuel Lafayette Howard died in October, 1940.

Baby son, John Howard Swofford

My father was just a month old when his mother died.

She came from a well-to-do family in Auburn, Alabama. Her father taught music at Auburn University. Her mother was a homemaker. My grandfather was a young guy trying to put together a chain of gas stations and sundries stores, but he never pulled it together. His young wife died, he took his son home to Georgia, a few months later he went to the war and his parents raised his son until he came home in 1945.

I have always heard, money changes people. I met people who were down to earth folks, with class and integrity and sound moral and ethical strength and did not wear their money on their sleeve. It took a while for me to see they had money and I could not imagine it changed them. I hoped that if I ever got money (too late for that now) I would have the fortitude to keep it from changing my character. Other money people show it right away, they act like their money makes them better than others and entitles them to royal treatment, usually believing they are not subject to normal social behavior. I would like to see how they are treated on their way back down, by the ones they treated with arrogant indifference as they passed on their way up.

You had as much choice in choosing me as father as I you son. Do memories justify rude and irresponsible behavior—? Did you blind me—or have you changed that much in the last few years? Maybe a combination, whatever my contribution—it is unintended.

Another brilliant rhetorical turn on his part—after reminding me of the tragic death of his mother and softening me, he goes back on the attack.

I remembered the last line of that first paragraph as "See you on your way down." Here my father is trying to be sly and anecdotal, trying to impart folksy Southern wisdom.

He believes money has changed me. Yes, for a few years I made very good money, banker money, but my father doesn't understand that the writer's life is feast or famine.

My father can't imagine that the rift in our relationship has anything to do with *our relationship*. He's looking for someone or something to blame, and money and I are to blame. *Money, money changes everything.* For my father, it's as simple as that. Also, he'd like the past erased.

And more than anything, perhaps, he is hurting inside: still smarting eight years after my brother's death, as is everyone else in the family. But he needs to lash out. A part of him, I'm certain, hates me for being alive while Jeff is dead. Just as if I'd died and Jeff had lived, he'd hate Jeff for the same reason. He had been waiting for a reason to hate me, and suddenly he had it: my first book, wherein he thinks I treated him unfairly, when in fact I treated him with kid gloves; what he deems my wild financial success; and the fact that I have failed to put a few things in the mail, which is a behavior common to me since I was a little boy: I'm a daydreamer; I don't always follow through on the directions I've been given. This angers him, too. He can no longer boss me around, he has no control over me, and he doesn't like that at all.

My father has cursed me: *See you on your way down*, he says.

> *This turned out to be rather lengthy. I am proud of you and your accomplishments, more than you will ever know. You have many more to come. Stop and smell the flowers once in a while. Don't forget your roots. I fear that money is bringing unfavorable change. Keep that from happening! As I said before I can't expect an acknowledgement and at this moment, am not sure this will be sent.*
>
> *Love, Dad*

My father, whatever else, has chutzpah. I believe he knows he will send the letter. But this is a great narrative and emotional punch: I get to the end of his six-page-long assault and I read that he might not have sent it. What would have happened if he hadn't? We'll never know.

Sometime in August he picks his pen up again:

> *August 06*
>
> *Granny told me you didn't call her to let her know that you were not interested in receiving the cross of military service. You simply did not send a copy of your DD-214. What a way to let her know——. Even though many would like to rewrite history it cannot be changed. Your Swofford roots go back through the Southern Confederacy. Your great-great-great-grandfather was a Confederate soldier. If he had been killed and not made it back to Dog River neither of us would*

be here. You can be proud or ashamed but you can't change it.
Your Warner roots [my mother's] *could go through a Union*
Soldier. How many people know where their great-great-
great-grandparents are buried?

Granny is Anice Swofford, my father's stepmother. She's a
sweet old lady, my sweet old granny, with a gleam in her blue eyes
and she likes the acronym GRITS: girls raised in the South. She
makes the best sausage biscuits in the world and she's a member
of United Daughters of the Confederacy.

The Cross of Military Service is a medal the UDC gives to
combat veterans who are direct descendants of Confederate soldiers, and as my father outlined above, I seem to be one of those.

It's my understanding that when Granny accumulates cita-
tions and awards for her family she gains esteem from her colleagues. And I don't begrudge Granny her hobby. But I couldn't
accept a medal from an organization that associates loosely with
neo-Confederate groups that would gladly wipe half my friends
off the face of the Earth.

Sure, I could've called Granny and told her that, but it seemed
easier to simply ignore her request for my military discharge
papers. She's a smart lady. She knows I'm a progressive. She'd get
the hint. No need to smack down Granny over the phone, was
my thinking.

Of our Southern ancestry my father writes, *You can be proud or*
ashamed but you can't change it. This is true. And I like the South,
and as a kid I loved visiting all the family down there, and still
do, but I can choose to not accept an award from an organization
that fights to keep the rebel flag flying.

Aug 10-06

Now that we have had this pissy phone call I will
probably be sending this and still no response is expected.
Helping Tami is not the issue. You will know this will not
be the last time she hits bottom and needs financial aid. I am
glad that you are willing and able to help. I no longer have
the resources, mainly because of being on a fixed income, which
is much less than when I was working. You having the money
to pay me back is not the issue. The issue was the question
you would not answer. There you were being evasive, not
answering the question, but asking others that had nothing to
do with a re-payment date. Why do you think I was pressing
for a re-payment date?

My father was visiting my older sister in Billings and she had gotten into some financial trouble. She needed some cash, not a large sum of money, as I recall, around a thousand dollars. I was cheating on Ava in Vancouver at the time and didn't have a checkbook on me so I asked my father if he wouldn't mind writing Tami a check and then as soon as I was back in New York, in a few weeks, I'd drop one to him in the mail.

For whatever reason this threw him into a rage. I remember well the argument. He wanted an exact date that I would put the check in the mail and I refused to give him an exact date because I hadn't bought my return ticket. I was sitting on the terrace of an apartment in Vancouver BC. Inside the apartment was a woman I had just made love to. I drank coffee and took in a view of the sea, and I let my father scream at me and I refused to respond.

I ended up wiring Tami the money. Cut out the middleman.

*Since you have made it "Big Time," I am no longer dazed
at your treatment of family. You should be embarrassed at
not calling Granny and ashamed about James's books.* [I was
delayed in returning signed copies of *Jarhead* to a cousin
of mine.] *Your mother will take exception, as usual. You seem
to gloat at being an arrogant, self-centered person exhibiting
the lowest level of responsibility. Why would your time be
more valuable than theirs?*

Love, Dad

Perhaps I should have called my grandmother and said,
"Thanks, Granny, but I'd rather not receive an award from your
neo-Confederate organization."

Sometimes silence speaks wonders, even to your sweet, sweet-
tea-drinking granny.

I should've returned those books to my cousin James sooner,
but I didn't. I'm unorganized. I lose stuff. I don't write things
down. I miss appointments. I piss people off. It has nothing to do
with any success, or any sums of money. It's just who I am. When
I was a dirt-poor college student subsisting on ramen and PBR I
behaved exactly the same.

None of this makes me arrogant or self-centered. But if your
father thinks you are arrogant and self-centered, you are.

Sun Aug 13, 2006

*It was good to hear your voice, know that you had a good
birthday. You may not open this for three or four months or
for that matter ever; since you said you have no reason to open
mail as you have no bills. How fortunate for you. If it were
a publisher or Hollywood type, would it sit that long? Now*

that I see most family matters are of little importance to you—
should I call James and tell him he will be lucky to ever get
his books back? Is it unreasonable that we expect responsible
behavior from you?

My father the pit bull: *It was good to hear your voice, know that*
you had a good birthday—now let me reiterate the myriad ways
in which you are a failed son and a failed person and rip your
throat out.

Guilty, guilty, guilty: I suck at paperwork. I don't open mail
for months. In my mother's study in Sacramento is a box of my
unopened mail from the Portland years, 2001 to 2003.

Are these *character* flaws? And who is *we*? Above, he writes
that he knows my mother will take exception to the notion that
I am flawed, so he can't be including her in his *we*. This is the
global We, the world knows I am a failure, that I let my family
down, that I don't follow through, I am a bad citizen and a worse
son and my father is here to teach me a lesson.

I've just turned *thirty-six* years old. Who the fuck does he
think he's talking to?

He addresses my financial situation in a rather snide way, but
shouldn't a father be pleased that his son is unencumbered by
debt?

I like the part about *publisher or Hollywood type*. Another fine
rhetorical flourish—I have somehow come to represent the world
of wealth and fame, the world that debases family in the name
of self.

I don't know my cousin James well; in fact, I've met him only
two or three times. He's a nice fellow, with a pretty wife and a
cute scrappy young son whose face is all freckles and smile and

teeth. And he seems like a pretty understanding dude who wasn't stressing over the fact that it took me a while to get the books back to him.

August 13 is the day after my birthday. My father and I have a habit of missing each other's birthdays—sometimes by weeks, or days, or even months, but for some reason my father nailed it in 2006.

He's been stalking me for months, he's on top of me, he knows my birthday, he'll nail the date this time, show me that he cares even though he knows—he knows he's about to light the fuse of his epistolary cannon. If during one of our phone conversations I'd said the right thing, apologized for my indecent and selfish behavior, he might have folded the letter away in a drawer, or burned it—he's giving me the chance to avoid this attack without telling me. *If you turn around and apologize I won't punch you in the back of your head.* He knows I won't say the right thing, he knows I'll be the self-centered prick he's come to consider me, and then he'll have to light the cannon and wait, and wait, and wait for the sound of the explosion. He wants fury and he will get fury.

> *Oct 4, 2006*
> *I enjoyed our conversation last night. Best visit we've had*
> *in a few years. Do you see us as having so little in common?*
> *You seemed in good spirits, more relaxed and upbeat than the*
> *last couple of years. I hope it is a sign that you are happier and*
> *more comfortable with life. But you're still reluctant to share*
> *life experience and that underlying bitterness remains.*

I don't recall this conversation at all. But in fact my father and I have very little in common. We share no hobbies or recreational pursuits. He doesn't read, he rarely sees movies, and he doesn't cook. I have no idea what my father does with his time other than sit around his house and think about what a shit son he had the great misfortune of bringing into this world.

When he mentions my mood, *relaxed and upbeat,* I recognize that he cannot conceive of me in the world without his view of me in the world. He doesn't understand that with friends and lovers I have been *relaxed and upbeat* for years, that in fact with my mother and sisters and the rest of my family I have been *relaxed and upbeat* for most of my life. My father thinks he still owns me.

Oct 8, 2006

> *I have sat on this much too long. The more I sit the longer it grows. It is well past time to shred or mail. So mail here it comes.*
>
> *With Love,*
> *Your Father*

I didn't call my father after reading the letter. I didn't respond with a letter of my own. I didn't know what to do, really. My father had shipped a letter bomb and it blew up in my face, the particles of sharp ink marred my face and hands, disrupted my spirit, unhinged me.

I called friends who had trouble with their fathers and they all confirmed for me that my father was a complete asshole, and that he hated me for some reasons I might never comprehend. Some went Oedipal, others went *Great Santini*; others took his side and said that when I became a father all of this would change (of course, they were fathers).

My therapist told me to write my father off, that we couldn't choose our birth parents but that we could find other parents in the world. I'd already turned a few teachers and older friends into father stand-ins. And my therapist's willingness to write my father off so casually caused me to take my father's side, something I did fairly often when discussing the man with other people who might not take such a generous view of his verbal and sometimes physical abuse, his womanizing, his combat-deranged mind.

In late December 2006 I found an opportunity for a peace offering to my father: my publisher had sent me forty hardcover copies of my forthcoming novel. My father had complained so bitterly about how few copies I'd given him of *Jarhead* that I decided I'd make amends here: I'd send him ten copies; he could hand them out to his work and bar cronies. This time around I'd be the good son, the dutiful son. I'd not make my father look like a chump in front of his buddies.

I was in upstate New York at my winter rental, in Germantown. I drove to the post office and boxed up ten books, having signed a few of them, and having dedicated one to my father: DEAR FATHER, THANK YOU FOR YOUR SUPPORT, YOUR LOVING SON.

I didn't know what support he'd given me, but it felt like the right thing to write, the kind of sentiment that would resonate. When it came time to address the box, I realized that I didn't have my dad's PO box information memorized. I knew his home address but he didn't like receiving mail there. For some reason he felt that the government had more access to his private life if he received mail at home. More than once I'd forgotten his injunction about using his home address and gotten an earful. So I decided to call for his address. It would be the first time we'd spoken since I'd received his letter. I thought it best to not even mention it.

"Hey, Tone," he shouted on his end of the line.

My father is one of those people who have decided that the louder you talk into a cell phone the better your reception.

"Hey, Dad," I said. "I've got some copies here of my new book and wanted to send some out to you. I'll send ten, so you can hand some off to your buddies. I need your PO box number."

"Ah, hell, Tone. You don't gotta do that. I already read that, um, that, what do you call it? The gallery? I got it from your mother."

"Galley. Yeah, I know, but you got upset with me last time over how many books I sent out, so this time around I thought I'd send you some stock."

"That's all right," he said. "I'm not really sure any of those guys would be interested. And I don't need to read it again."

I'd set myself up for this: the contrite son returns to the father for approval, possibly even for a joyous embrace, but receives instead a beating.

"OK then. Goodbye," I said.

I hung my phone up without hearing his response. I stood in the small Germantown post office, burning with rage. It was a familiar feeling, my father denying me: this time praise, acceptance—he didn't say that he liked or hated the book, simply that he'd read it and didn't need any more copies hanging around, littering up his place. I wanted to burn the box of books. I wanted to burn the post office down. I wanted to burn all of Germantown, all of Columbia County—to scorch the entire United States, east to west, and my father there in Fairfield, California, on Meadowlark Lane.

It was a week before Christmas and I was alone upstate.

I sat in my BMW M3, the engine idling mean. I was a cliché: an angry man in a sick-fast car—zero to sixty in 4.3 seconds. My shifts weren't expert enough for me to have hit a track time like that, but my shifts weren't bad, and no matter what I did, I *felt* fast driving that car, and the speedometer said so, too.

For sex, which might have calmed my rage at my father, I had a few options: both of them were in the city and neither of them was my girlfriend, she who was in Miami quite probably engaging in sex with someone other than me, her boyfriend.

I could drive to the city and be out at dinner with a beautiful one of those options by nine o'clock, or I could invite one of them up to the country, Amtrak to Rhinecliff—I'd done it before.

Or I could drive country roads like a madman and sleep alone.

I headed up 9G North, toward Hudson. I didn't speed along this stretch, but occasionally I downshifted and jacked the rpms toward the red line, feeling the torque, feeling the tires chew into the road. The desolate months had begun to settle on upstate New York: frozen ground, brittle tree branches signaling the death of another autumn, the occasional pine straining green through the gray muck of it all. Darkness fell early these nights. I had only an hour or so to drive wild without headlights.

I booked across the Rip Van Winkle Bridge and ambled through Catskill, driving like everyone else, the parents on their way to retrieve a child from some practice or another, or a rehearsal, or detention. But my car was faster than most on the road.

Out of Catskill I turned onto 9W South and began to rip through the gears. From the left an asphalt truck abruptly pulled out in front of me and I gunned it around the guy, not looking for oncoming traffic, nor caring. The speed limit was forty-five and I was going ninety. The week before I'd hit 120 on this road, and I wanted at least that much again. I wanted more. The governor on the car would stop me at 133. What value did the car have if I didn't run it out like that? None. Who wants to say *I once owned this incredibly fast German sports car, and one time I went eighty-five in it?* Only a fool.

The road ahead thinned to one lane, beneath a railroad overpass. I slowed down for the red. Between the stop line and the tight underpass lay about thirty yards of road. We went green. I gunned it, I ripped through the gears, and I shot through the short tunnel at forty-five, the traction holding deep on the slight right bend. In front of me was about two miles of mostly straight road, and I killed it, I chewed it up, the speedo climbed to ninety, and then 105, and then 120, and then 130, and then it hovered and ticked at 133; the world flew by, seasons changed, my heart hung at the edge of the world. I could die, I could kill myself with a flick of my wrist and it would look like a mistake, a daredevil young writer, war veteran, pushing all the limits at once and doing a header into a tree with his sixty-five-thousand-dollar car. But I took her down, slow, descending, 115, 105; let's hold on here at a hundred for a moment, it feels good, it feels fine, brakes now, eighty, sixty-five, fifty; there we are at forty-five, the speed limit, the boredom experienced by every other man and woman behind the wheel of a minivan.

The quiet. I hated the quiet.

I drove back across the river to Tivoli. I'd decided that in fact I wanted to have sex with someone this night, a stranger. I thought, Bard grad student! Perfect. Smart, possibly a bit crunchy and certainly young.

I ate at the bar at the Mexican joint in town. Bad chicken something, so-so margaritas, at least a few, possibly many. Nothing happened in the girl department there, a stringy blonde tried to chat with me but stringy blondes are not my style.

A fake English pub down the street drew my attention. I parked behind the bar. I started with whiskey. I remember the bartender being a friendly young guy. At some point he stopped charging me. I talked to a few locals, and a few male undergrads killing time before their flights home for winter break. Word on the street was all the girls were gone. Tivoli: Land of the Hand.

I can't tell you that I was wasted but neither can I tell you that I was sober. Certainly I'd had too much to operate my car completely safely. One of those families from the minivans? I might have taken them out: band instruments and soccer clothes tweaked in the jumble of metal and flesh. But I didn't.

I drove faster than I should have on the country road leading to my place. I pulled into the gravel driveway, safe, but decided I needed a late-night snack. Some popcorn, perhaps.

I headed the three or so miles back to town. At the Stewart's I bought chips and salsa and a pint of ice cream. I started for home. I had the sunroof open, the bitter cold air ripped through the car. I'd driven this road hundreds of times. I remembered the exhilaration of my late afternoon speed fest, and I kicked the speed up. Yes, a stupid move. The road, I knew this road, and about a mile before my house it made a kinky tight S, posted speed limit fifteen mph. I'd hit it at forty a few times without a problem, but also without a few margaritas and whiskeys coursing through my bloodstream. But this time I pushed fifty, and fifty was no good, the S in the road became an M and then a Z and then a Q.

The sound was deafening and people from three or four houses along the road emerged to witness the results of tonight's match. Man and BMW versus Three Trees and a Telephone Pole.

Man and BMW lost.

I'd concussed myself against the now-shattered driver's-side window. I smelled gasoline, and all I saw from the windshield was hood, the beautiful crumpled racing silver hood. I heard the noise of the onlookers, cheering me out of my car, the loser. The shattered window was still intact, but I broke it away with my upper arm and climbed from the car. Dizzy, I sat along the side of the road and waited for paramedics or police. The onlookers inquired about my condition and I told them that I was fine and that I could just walk the half mile home and have my car towed in the morning. It seemed like a good plan.

The paramedics arrived first. They checked me out and said I was free to go.

The cops were young and polite, early thirties. They asked me to blow into a Breathalyzer and I refused. The few lawyer friends I had said to always refuse, if you've had more than two drinks, refuse the Breathalyzer. In order to avoid paperwork the cops tried to convince me that blowing was a good idea.

"If you just blow, no matter what the reading, we'll drop you off at home. Otherwise, we gotta pull you in front of a judge tonight, and the judge will not be happy, I assure you. And you will spend the night in jail."

"I still refuse," I said.

"OK, sir, have it your way."

Somewhere along the Taconic State Parkway on the way to State Police Troop K headquarters, one of the cops said, "Hey, wait a minute. Swofford? Didn't you write that book *Jarhead*?"

I felt like a fool. "Yes," I said, "I did."

"I got a marine buddy. He hated that movie. I thought it was pretty good. My wife read the book. Nice to meet you."

At the station a bit of hell had broken loose. A local kid had gotten drunk and somehow made it into his neighbor's house, where he'd decided he'd eat some leftover pizza and watch a movie. The captain knew both families and was trying to decide how to proceed. Most people were of the mind to give the kid a break, bust him on some bullshit misdemeanor trespassing charge, but scare the shit out of him and teach him a lesson. I thought how I might like to get a bullshit misdemeanor charge and be taught a lesson. But it didn't seem as if that was going to work out tonight.

The station had just taken shipment of an electronic finger-printing device and my boys were having a bit of trouble operating the touch pad. While somebody got on the horn with IT, one cop said, "So how did you like the movie? I mean, that must have been weird, some pretty Hollywood kid playing you, your name and everything."

Over the years since my first book had been turned into a film I'd had this question thousands of times. But never from a cop while waiting to be fingerprinted. But I didn't flinch, and I gave my standard reply: "He's a good actor. I think he nailed it. But my abs are tighter."

The cop laughed, like he was supposed to, as thousands of other people had over the years.

And he was right. The judge did not appreciate being dragged from whatever she'd been dragged from in order to send me to jail for the night. The charge was driving under the influence, but they had no evidence, other than the observations of the police, who told the judge that I'd been polite and cooperative throughout our evening together.

The orange jumpsuit fit snugly and the deputy taking my mug shot said, "So you're the *Jarhead* guy? Nice to meet you. Who you gonna call, Mrs. Jarhead?"

I called Ava and asked her to post bail, which her father did the next morning around ten or so. The night in jail had been uneventful. No lunatics, no murderers, nothing exciting, just the same old jailhouse Bible and rubbery chow I used to be served in the Marines.

As the sheriff handed me my clothes and a check for the cash that had been in my wallet he said, "Goodbye, Jarhead. Hope to never see you again. Good luck."

I took a cab to the wrecking yard where my car had been towed. I pulled my warm winter jacket and the box of books from the trunk. The car was totaled, crumpled down to economy size from sport coupe. I noticed my chips and salsa in the backseat, so I grabbed those, too, and headed home.

MY BROTHER TOLD me this story about our father. It happened in 1974, when my brother was twelve and I was four.

My father's squadron had given him a going-away party before our family shipped off to Japan. He had a long drive home, from Sacramento to Vacaville, about fifty miles. He was drunk, and somewhere along the way the highway patrol red-lighted him, but my father didn't pull over. He was driving a fast Jaguar XK-E, and he didn't feel like stopping, so why stop?

My brother claimed to have been in the garage, working

on his bike, when my father ripped around the corner followed closely by three CHP cruisers. My father slid the XK-E perfectly into the driveway and made a dash for the front door, at his heels the three cops, but my father slammed the door in their faces.

In my brother's version, my mother talked to the police and told them that she would take care of her husband, and the police left.

Both of my parents deny the veracity of this story. I've queried my father about it numerous times and he always says, "Never happened."

This story might be one of the first lies my brother told me. But it might also be true.

Maybe most important was the fact that my older brother believed he had a father who took such extreme risks with his own life and the safety of his family. The police chase might have happened only in my brother's twelve-year-old head. The father he knew was a veteran of the Vietnam War and a pretty tense and keyed-up thirty-three-year-old man. My father loved and owned fast cars. My brother must have felt that he was a passenger in one of those cars, always moving at unsafe speeds.

6

Bethesda

Somewhere between Elizabeth and Princeton I looked at my speedometer and realized that I was going 120 miles per hour. In my mind I'd been back in the desert driving a Humvee. We were spraying fire everywhere, me driving with my left hand, my M16 in my right, the barrel out the window and me letting loose on burst. I didn't care who or what I hit.

Now I let the engine drop speed slowly. On the shoulder ahead of me a guy changed a tire on his beater truck. My first thought was VBED, vehicle-borne explosive device. Then I saw the wife and child holding hands at the rear of the vehicle. They waved. The man wore dirty ConEd overalls. In black and white it could have been a scene out of Dorothea Lange or in a novel it would have been Steinbeck.

People driving shitty cars in art and books: someone should write a dissertation.

My right hand gripped the gearshift as though it were the pistol grip on my rifle. No, as though it were the pistol grip on my life. But I had no ammunition here on the road to Bethesda, and the targets remained unclear. I poured water over my head and blasted the radio. I took the speedometer back up to ninety. I thought of the young kids missing limbs at Bethesda. What would I say?

I ARRIVED AT the Naval Hospital at three in the afternoon. The lobby was enormous and tile-floored, dotted with large planters housing massive, boring plants: the echoes from boot heels driven hard into the ground moved through the space in the timbre of death. Like most other military buildings it was well signed, but all the signage bore acronyms, so that if you didn't know what CFSSB stood for, even if you were looking for someone inside that particular labyrinth, you were totally lost.

As on any military installation people in uniform, mostly fit and youthful, hurried from one destination to another as though the world were on fire. And of course, it was. From the uniforms each wore you could tell very little other than rank. One colonel might be a bean counter in the motor pool, and another might be a Special Forces genius who'd been killing for America since the age of twenty-two, but you'd have trouble telling them apart. Only the eyes gave a clear portrait: the bean counter witnessed the world with bemused detachment, aware of how lucky he was to have worn the uniform for so long and to have missed combat; the genius killer watched the world with a weary gaze, constantly tuned to the threat wave, looking for danger real or imagined. Men and women in unfortunate naval khaki uniforms entered and exited the building, as well a few marines in short-sleeved dress blue uniforms. It was one of the easiest uniforms in the world to get laid in. It still made me proud.

AND UNFORTUNATELY FOR me hospital acronyms were some of both the most complicated and the least-known in the Marine Corps.

No marine planned ever to enter a hospital. I noticed across the lobby an office with maroon-and-gold signage, which lead me to the correct assumption that this was the liaison office for injured marines and their families.

A staff sergeant greeted me, "Can I help you, boss?"

He wore a shrapnel-enhanced smirk and in his eyes swam the deep constant pain of having killed and watched others die.

"I'm here to meet up with the DAV," I said.

"Swofford?"

"Yes." It had been years since I'd spoken to a marine staff sergeant in uniform. I hadn't done anything wrong, but still he made me nervous. This guy had been jacked up overseas, he was probably ten years younger than I, but he looked hard and he looked mean, and I knew he had lived some years. When I was a corporal in the Corps I looked up to staff sergeants as if they were gods.

"Fucking Jarhead," he said. He half smiled. But I wasn't sure if he wanted to shake my hand or punch me in the face.

I was wearing a suit. I must have looked like a real civilian piece of shit to him.

"Yo, PFC Colon, weren't you with 2/7?" the sergeant yelled over his shoulder.

"Hells yes," a young voice called. "Who wants to know?"

"Jarhead is here," he said.

In the Corps I had gotten used to being called fuckface and retard and shit-for-brains. But for many years now people had called me Tony or Anthony, or Swofford, or Swoff. I had not yet acclimated to being called by the title of my first book.

"You can call me Swofford," I said. We finally shook hands.

Colon came from behind the cubicle. He had the youthful

gleam and game on his face of a Dominican from New York, a kid who had probably seen as much crazy shit in the neighborhood as he ever had in the Corps, other than the IEDs and car bombs. He was in a wheelchair.

"Swofford," Colon said. "Fucking Jarhead. We all read that fucking book. Man, and the movie. That is some lucky shit. Me, not so lucky. Fucking sniper, spinal cord. Paraplegic. Can't even jack off. But fuck it, I coulda been killed dead."

"When did you get hit?" I asked.

"August oh-five. I think it was a Chechen. The fucker shot me like no Koran-drunk hajji ever could."

"That rash of sniper casualties. And then they stopped," I said.

"We either killed the fucker or he went back to Chechnya when his visa expired!" Colon laughed.

That was the thing that always blew my mind about injured marines. Here was Colon, a fiercely handsome young man of nineteen or twenty who would never get laid again—to fuck is the only thing any nineteen-year-old marine thinks about—and his attitude was so overwhelmingly positive and so filled with humor and delight at the madness of it all. I'd seen the same attitude while hanging around Camp Pendleton a few years earlier, and it was hard for me not to break down in front of this overwhelmingly positive outlook. Didn't he want to know why, didn't he want to rage against the world? Someday he would, when the Corps's goodwill ran out and it canceled his sweet desk job, or when he showed up at the VA one bright day with a broken wheelchair and they handed him a wrench to fix it himself. It would happen. But for now let Colon have his humor and his youth, I thought.

"Hey, Swofford," the staff sergeant said. "Have you heard of these Warrior dinners the big shots in DC throw every Friday night for outpatients? It's like, they got a band and some minor celebs. I saw Bob Dole a few weeks ago. And Chelsea Clinton one weekend. And TV types from New York, and they put on this big dinner for guys in long-term care, take about a hundred of them a week out for a night on the town, steak and shrimp and a shit-ton of beer. And their families can come. You want to attend tonight? We got an extra slot for a non-injured. No shit."

"I'd love to go, Staff Sergeant."

I'd heard of these dinners. A local restaurant had been putting them on since the first injured had begun to arrive in a slow stream, and now that they arrived from overseas in a river of carnage, the popularity of the dinners had soared.

"So you want to go see some injured marines?" the sergeant asked.

Colon said, "There is some fucked-up motherfuckers up there, Swofford. This ain't no hundred-day war. This ain't no friendly fire. This ain't no boo-hoo-I-didn't-get-to-shoot-back-at-the-bad-guys bullshit."

He popped wheelies in his chair and he looked right through me. I knew he was challenging me and my easy little war, and I'd let him have it because he was right. My war was not shit and his was. I wrote a fucking book out of my little war and from his big war he got his dick blown off. You do the motherfucking math.

"This is the real fucking deal, I mean, double amps, faces blown off, brains splattered to the Funky Cold Medina and back. You think I got it bad? I ain't got shit bad on some of those fucked-up motherfuckers. You want to see some fucked-up jarheads, go on and see the show."

I'd forgotten how much marines curse. *Motherfucker* was the equivalent of *oh really* or *no kidding*, or you could use the word to talk about the cosmos and life and death. Two guys could sit on watch for four hours in the middle of the night and the only word that would pass between them would be *motherfucker*, but that word meant: Here come some suspicious bastards; I don't think she's fucking around on me; I go home in three days; Do you think the *Rig Veda* is correct when it says, "Breath of the gods, embryo of the universe, this god wanders wherever he pleases"?

"What is the mood up there?" I asked.

Colon was popping wheelies and doing 360s in his wheelchair, and he said, "Most of the guys got a pretty good attitude. If a guy didn't lose his dick, you know, that's good. When a guy wakes up, you know this, Swofford, the first thing he does is reach down to see if he's still got a cock on him, and then he looks at the doctor or the nurse and says, 'Is it gonna work?' Or if he no longer has hands, he just looks, cranes his neck to see the bulge."

I did know this: that at one level the carnage breaks down to the dudes who lost their dicks and the dudes who didn't.

"Penis, big fucking erect penis, Mom," as Tom Cruise playing Ron Kovic said.

I'd need a year on the ward to figure out all the other layers of love and hatred and confusion and ecstasy.

"How long will most of the guys be here?" I asked.

"Of course, that's up to the docs. A month for some, six for others. And then some guys they'll send over to that fucking hell-hole Walter Reed and fit with a bionic arm or leg. A guy might not even want pussy after jacking off with a bionic hand for a few months. Bionic hand won't tell you to take out the garbage, bionic hand won't tell you it's got a headache."

Colon sad this loudly and it elicited howls from all corners of the office. I'm sure they'd heard it before. And I had no doubt it would remain funny for many years.

"And you see with me, Swofford, I got some new territory to explore with the ladies. 'Cause, like, I never went down before; we just don't do that that shit where I'm from. But if I want a woman now I got to rethink my strategy. You ever see that movie *Coming Home*? So the crippled Vietnam vet Jon Voight goes down on Jane Fonda like crazy. I think it's the best movie orgasm of the 1970s. Honestly, I don't think Hanoi Jane could've faked that."

The sergeant said, "Colon Googled 'cunnilingus in films' and got back about five thousand hits. He's renting all of those movies and learning technique."

Colon continued to pop wheelies. "What I'ma do is write this manual, right? It's gonna be called *The Finer Points of Going Down*. Maybe the Naval Academy will publish it for me and it will become a textbook."

More laughs from behind the cubicles.

I'd heard differing opinions about the quality of the health care the injured were receiving. Without any medical training and without talking to the troops, there wasn't a lot I'd learn, but I thought I could hang back and observe; to observe and deduct had been most of my job in the Corps, and it was now, too, so I'd do it here and see what I could come up with. Word was that Bethesda was running a cleaner operation than Walter Reed, but I didn't know if that was bullshit marine pride getting in the way of an honest appraisal of the treatment.

A NAVAL OFFICER from the Bethesda media team arrived to escort me to the injured marine floor. I made plans with the marines to meet up with them later at the dinner in DC.

As we walked onto the ward my first impulse was to bolt. I hadn't been to a hospital since my brother died. I knew the smells and the sounds, the antiseptics and the low whirl of machines that give and take life—I knew the collective heartbeat of a hospital floor holding so many lives in fine balance. I did not belong here. I would wreck the balance.

I wanted to be back in Manhattan in my clean little life, in my Chelsea apartment with clean white museum walls and art pieces hanging from those walls; I wanted to drink Burgundy wine from my cellar; I wanted to cook in my professional kitchen; I wanted to eat at my eight-thousand-dollar table while wearing my two-thousand-dollar cowboy boots; I wanted to take a woman other than my girlfriend out to a five-hundred-dollar dinner and take her home, and upstairs while staring at the Empire State Building I wanted to fuck her and forget that a place called Bethesda Naval Hospital existed exactly 230 miles away from that clean Manhattan life.

But that was not the plan of the day. The naval officer showed me into a room where a mother bent over her young marine son. He'd arrived two days before. They were not sure the kid would live. A week earlier he'd taken a sniper round to the forehead. The swelling was down. He blinked when his mother spoke to him. But he could blink for only a few hours a day. I remember that the family was from Ohio. Someone from the naval media team asked me to sign a copy of *Jarhead* for the kid. I wrote it out to Tommy or Timmy or whatever his name was, knowing he'd never read it. His mother took the book from me and smiled and said she'd read it to him.

I thought, *Jesus, please read the kid something with a little bit of hope, not my bleak book.*

What are you going to give a mother from Ohio to read over the deathbed of her nineteen-year-old son?

I walked out of the room with my minders. My brain hurt. I was short of breath and thirsty. The minders got called away for a moment and they asked me to stand by.

Ahead of me in the hall I saw a man in his fifties leaning against the wall just outside a patient room. He wore a red T-shirt emblazoned with MARINE DAD. The guy was big, he'd once been an ox of a football player, somewhere in the Middle West, I guessed. I approached him.

"Excuse me, sir, can I ask you a few questions?"

"Who are you, son?" I read former marine officer right away, Vietnam, '68 to '70. I saw it in his eyes.

"I'm a former marine and a writer. I wrote a book about the first Gulf War. I'm here to listen to some stories, find out about the quality of the treatment. Who are you here visiting?"

"My boy," he said, and he pointed at his sweatshirt and looked at me as though I were stupid.

He continued, "He's in surgery right now. Below the knee on one leg, above the knee on the other, once it all shakes out. Goddamn it, son, I was in 'Nam, I saw a lot of men die, but I've just spent three weeks up here, and I never saw men injured so heinously. The boys are ripped to shreds. Go room to room and you'll see. And look at all the mothers. I'm one of the only fathers up here because the fathers are back at home earning money or they've never been around. I'm lucky, after my time in the Corps I was an executive at a bank. I retired a year ago. I've got two pensions. I can afford to cool my heels here and look after my son. I can do this for the rest of my life. But look at the mothers. Some of them are married, but you know the story, many of these boys come from broken homes, poor homes, single mothers. These women, they thought they were going to refashion themselves after fifty, live new and dazzling adventures. But they're going to be feeding and bathing their sons for the rest of their lives."

He placed his hand on my shoulder and asked me to look after any marine I could. A woman approached. She was clutching copies of a newspaper article to her chest.

"This is the article they ran on Sam yesterday in the paper. It's so touching. They captured him. He couldn't speak but he blinked his eyes and they captured his soul."

The woman began to cry and the Marine Dad comforted her.

"May I give you one of these about my son?" she asked me.

"Yes, ma'am," I said. I glanced at the article, a front-page story with color photo from Wednesday's paper, this woman at her son's bedside, the son immobile, neck brace, oxygen mask, legs in traction, the boy barely visible beneath his bouquet of medical matériel.

"Who are you with?" she asked.

Just then my minders arrived and introduced me to the woman. She asked for a signed book and I gave her one. She told me that a week or so before Wolfowitz had been on the ward but she was much more excited to meet me.

The woman told me that the care her son received was top-notch and that the support staff had been wonderful. I glanced at the photo of her son on the cover of the newspaper.

"He's a sweet boy," she said.

The Marine Dad walked away.

The woman looked at me and said, "I'm happy for him his son has a small wound."

When losing most of both of your legs was a small wound I

would never be able to truly understand the depth of the despair these marines and their families were suffering. During my war I'd spent a short time at the entry point of this calamity, at the end where the bombs blew and rifles and RPGs shattered bodies, where Warthogs sometimes fired on friendly troops, and I had totally forgotten about this end, the sick end, the destroyed end of it, the utter ruin of families.

"May I hug you?" the woman asked.

"Yes, of course." I felt awkward but I couldn't say no, could I?

And she hugged me tight: she gripped me for life, for a memory of who her son had been: young, clean-shaven, strong. She would never again hug her son while he stood upright. She wept into my shoulder. The lioness had lost her family. The moon darkened. Ice caps melted. How could we go on?

She locked on to my eyes in a mildly wild and erotic way, her face full of tears. She was attractive in that high school librarian way, orderly and considered. Handsome, that's what she was, and sturdy, and she possessed the orderly smell of all good mothers. Her son would be fine. He would never walk and he might not talk, but he would have his mother and somehow they would both know this and be well.

This could not have been true but it is what I told myself then and it is the same lie that other Americans have been telling themselves for a decade, and we believe this because we have to.

Nurses and orderlies swam around us in a school of green and blue scrubs. From every room came the nauseating white sounds of resuscitation, prolongation, the beginnings of altered lives.

One of the minders grabbed me at the elbow and ushered me on to another room.

In the two visitor's chairs of the room sat an extremely old woman and a girl who could not have been older than ten. They wore colorful indigenous clothing that to my untrained eye shouted Bolivia. The old woman chewed at her leathery lower lip and the young girl beamed a smile that was as incongruous as their dress.

My minders introduced me to the marine. He was an infantry staff sergeant and had been blown up in a convoy. Both of his legs were in traction.

He said, "I'm gonna walk, man. I'm gonna walk again."

His face bore the burns from human shrapnel.

He said, "My guys got blown up. I lived, you know? I lived. I got blown up, and I woke up right here in this bed, how many days later I don't know. I was having this dream of the Philippines, like a little island and there were women and I was with my platoon and we were partying with the women. But I open my eyes and look at the end of the bed and there is sitting my grandmother and my niece, and I haven't seen anyone from Bolivia in fourteen years, since I left, and I think, 'Well, goddamn, I died in Baghdad and here I am in heaven with my grandma and my niece. Isn't that nice.' But then I think, 'Wait, they aren't dead, how can they be dead?' And they walk up to my side and say, 'You are alive.'"

The grandma eyed me suspiciously and the little girl continued her intense and beautiful smile.

"I love the Corps. Can you believe I got blown up in Baghdad and before I wake up here in the US they bring in my grandma and my niece?"

I had to admit that I was totally impressed.

"All I want to do is go back over and fight again. Fight for my dead brothers."

I could see he was slightly doped up and it looked as if he got shot up again through his IV because he faded away into a deep mind wander. Where did the drugs take his brain? Back to the desert or that Philippine island stalked by willing women, the West's Shangri-la, not unlike the Moslem's promised land overflowing with virgins for every martyr?

My minders showed me out of the hospital.

I HAD NEVER driven in DC and had only the slightest idea where I was going. I wanted to visit the Marine Corps War Memorial, which abutted Arlington, prior to heading somewhere near Capitol Hill for the dinner, which started at seven. I found the memorial. It was a replica of the famous flag-raising at Iwo Jima, the second one, of course. Everyone knew the story about the poor bastards who'd done it the first time, stupidly, without a photographer in tow. Never go to combat without a camera (or a blog).

Around the massive base of the memorial were stenciled the names of every campaign, large and small, that the Marine Corps had ever participated in. The crowd was one of those truly American collections of people: white, Latino, black, Asian, Middle Eastern, and recent Eastern European immigrants. Some of the men were Vietnam vets, others the sons and daughters of vets. A man being pushed in a wheelchair had to be from the Island Hopping Campaign; he wore a cap emblazoned with the badge of Guadalcanal and the 1st Marine Division, the division created specifically to jump the islands all the way north into the heart of mainland Japan.

I wanted to feel deeply patriotic. I smelled burned sand and scorched asphalt. That was all.

I walked toward the edge of Arlington. There were two

funerals under way, each held beneath a blue plastic tarp. One coffin had already been dropped, the family and friends staring into earth; at the other a priest hovered above the box in mid-prayer, offering absolution. I wondered who rested in the coffins, young men from the current wars or old men passed on from emphysema or colon cancer, mad in the head from Alzheimer's, or a peaceful sleepy end, just one last breath, a snore.

Arlington's austerity chilled me, a tapestry of green-and-white silence. The tapestry did not hide the fact that most of those men and women had died horrible deaths in combat.

TWO TOUR BUSES unloaded their passengers in front of the appointed restaurant, a few blocks from the Hart Senate Office Building. These were the men and women, soldiers, sailors, and marines, undergoing outpatient care, on their way to recovery. They used crutches and walkers and wheelchairs, and some of them walked on their own: he with a prosthetic leg, I could tell by the slight flag-like snap of the pants leg, or she missing an arm and choosing thus far to go without the prosthetic, the left shirt sleeve delicately folded and pinned to the front of the shirt, the single phantom hand in a gesture half of prayer and half of defiance.

And here now more mothers. Of the many legacies this war would produce the one not yet considered by most observers was this, which the Marine Dad had pointed out to me in the hospital corridor: mothers—a few as young as forty, women a man my age might date—looked at the horizon and saw themselves escorting their sons to VA hospitals for the next forty years. The greatest burden of a war always falls on the mothers. The men on both sides kill; the men have their mortal fun, they blow each other up and post the deeds on YouTube, and the mothers carry the casualties to the Rasa River, wash and dress the wounds, count casualties. The mothers bathed the wounded at Hiroshima. They have done so on the Seine, the Thames, the Missouri, the Danube, the Oostanaula. Name a river. It has received our wounded from the backs of mothers.

I heard someone calling my name. I watched the staff sergeant push Colon up the hill. Both men were wearing dress blues and Colon surreptitiously took a nip from a bottle of whiskey. It was a prelude to a horror film or a Dada fantasy, and I couldn't decide which.

Colon said, "We got big plans tonight, brother. After this proper sit-down meal we are going to show you how to get it on in DC. The girls are wild, man. There's like forty thousand college girls within the city limits. How can that be bad?"

"That sounds perfect, my friend."

"It's a circus. Didn't you come up here and party when you were in Jacksonville?"

"Not really. I had a girlfriend in California. I spent most of my time running up a long-distance phone bill with her."

"A girlfriend," Colon said. "I got one of those, but she's in the DR, left me for the motherfucking pizza delivery man, I shit you not."

I could see this conversation turning south in no time. We were under the awning in front of the restaurant and the other injured servicemen and -women walked between and around us. Infidelity was a hot-button issue in the military that no one wanted to touch. Other than beer and sports and hamburgers, it was the main thing enlisted men talked about. Infidelity, the fear of it—real and more often imagined—haunted the ranks; it ranked just behind the fear of dying.

I motioned to the two marines that we should head in. There was a serious queue at the elevator, we were expected in a ball-room on the second floor, and most of these men and women weren't exactly prepared to climb the stairs. The guys told me to take the stairs and that they'd meet me up there. I offered Colon a piggyback ride but he said he didn't trust my scrawny civil-ian legs.

The reception looked like a middling version of the New York parties I'd casually attended for a few years. The food spread was not as ambitious as at a Hollywood party and about on par with something for a party a poetry magazine might throw. In rank-ing New York parties in terms of sex appeal and food and booze I'd give hedge funds the number-one spot, then the art world, television, magazines, books, and in an ugly and distant last, the NGOs.

The bar here consisted of one guy behind a folding table, two kinds of bad wine, red or white, and a number of sixty-gallon coolers full of ice and beer and soda. But it didn't matter. The arriving troops were pumped. They weren't eating hospital food tonight, but rubbing elbows and wheelchair wheels and pros-thetic limbs with the affluent and influential.

I saw the secretary of the Army and an admiral whose face I recognized from some congressional hearing or another. I saw Bob Dole. I saw half a dozen congressmen and a few senators whose faces I knew from the papers but whose names I couldn't recall. Most if not all of these politicians were Republicans. Of course, this party didn't hold priority this evening for these kings of social DC. They were the power wave in this room, the surge, and in this city, as in every other city in the world, when you are the power and the money you can spend only so much time around the masses before an uncomfortable silence falls over the room.

The troops and their families will not be able to hold conversations with you about holidays in Europe, about that new sailboat, the new nanny, the summer home remodel.

This gathering is supposed to be a casual social hour but eventually the masses will want to talk about health care and prescription drugs and a living wage. And how many times can you ask the kid with a metal plate in his head, the kid with no legs, the bomb-blinded kid, where he grew up and where in Iraq or Afghanistan did this horrible unfortunate awful thing happen and how he was progressing and if he missed the men in his unit; how many times could you ask these questions without the guilt and horror blinding *you*?

I sensed that these princes of the ocean would debark from our listing cocktail lounge within twenty minutes and jump in a schooner and sail to a party where none of the tough questions had to be asked: calm seas, no visible injuries, good martinis, Beltway bottle blondes. And I was right. Twenty minutes later someone on a microphone asked us all to be seated and the power left through the back door having done their good deed for the week.

I sat at a table with Colon and the staff sergeant, two injured army personnel, two female volunteers for a nonprofit veterans advocacy group, and two members of a lobbying firm who seemed to be a couple. I gathered that the guy from the lobbying couple ran a celebrity gossip blog on the side. He had a digital recorder in front of him and he was talking about Britney Spears. I wanted to tell him that his marks had just escaped through the emergency exit, that the famous among us had left. As the salad arrived I began to talk to the woman at my right, his date.

She introduced herself in a Texas accent that sounded like summer and smelled of the color yellow and tasted of watermelon and pit BBQ.

"I'm Amy. I work for a lobbying firm. Health care, mostly. But in my spare time I shoot short docs."

"You kill vertically challenged physicians?"

She didn't like my joke.

"I direct and produce short documentary films, films with a social conscience. Films about America. What is your name?"

She stabbed a tomato on her plate and kept her fork in it and with the tomato acting as a broom head she pushed her salad in circles around her plate.

"My name is Anthony. I sit in a chair. I punch small square keys on a keyboard and try to find meaning."

"Does it pay?" she asked.

"It depends on the weather."

I could tell by the way his left leg was shaking and the number of times he'd taken a drink of nothing from his empty water glass that the gossip blogger next to her was getting a little antsy. This Amy was a truly lovely piece of Texas, the main bed partner, I assumed, for the freelance gossip blogger. Twenty-eight years old, probably a year out of grad school. By the length of her upper torso and the bit of leg I could see that wasn't hidden under the table I guessed she was five feet ten. Her natural blond hair was full, with a flip and bounce on the ends. She had those Texas blue eyes that make one think of hunting and roasting wild boar on the back forty, feeding the family, and then fucking for the next ten hours of one's life.

"Sweetheart," the gossip blogger said, "you really need to eat. You know what happens when you don't eat and you have a few drinks."

"I become a total irredeemable bitch?"

"I didn't say that."

"But last night you used that phrase."

I extracted myself from earshot of the quarrel and said hello to the young woman at my left. Young girl, I thought. She looked about sixteen, strawberry-blond hair, wide sweet smile, blue jeans and a flower-print blouse. I wondered if her father was one of the injured men among us. I looked for him.

She said to me, "I served as a private in the 82nd Airborne Military Police." She lifted her right leg and with her knuckles pounded on it. The sound was of titanium. "Guess how they got me? You don't have to guess. IED."

It was the first time that day that I'd found myself speechless. This girl, this woman, who looked as though this very morning her mother had made her scrambled eggs and rushed her off to homeroom, was living the pain of war right here next to me while at the same table a pair of ill-fit lovers quarreled stupidly about nothing.

I thought I'd been handling the carnage fairly well: the ruined mother holding the clippings from her son's newspaper story, the Bolivian sergeant with his grandma and niece, Colon with his lessons in cunnilingus. None of it had been pretty but it had all been tolerable. In advance of this trip I'd prepared psychic shelves for these brands of trauma.

The injured young female private had drilled this war too deep.

Our salad plates were replaced with entrées, steak.

"Hello, Private," I said. "I was in the Marine Corps during the first Gulf War. But I'm out now. How is your treatment?"

"Mostly good, sir. It's a long process, you know. The barracks are kind of cruddy, worst I've ever had. Food tastes like shit; that's why I come to these as often as possible. That, and I got an autograph from Tiger Woods for my dad a couple months ago. And I get to see Fernando." She motioned to her left. A young kid sat up straight in his chair, chewing steak, Army cap with sergeant stripes pulled down tough over his forehead, black silk Army jacket, alert eyes. Fernando nodded slowly at me, every move tentative with pain.

"The Army doesn't want us together because he's a sergeant and all, but we're both getting out; he broke his back when his Bradley flipped, so we're getting out. But they can't stop us here. They can't keep us from these dinners."

On my other side, from Amy and her man, I heard the low-voiced, choking hatred of two people who are no longer in love. They'd traveled shockingly far from the early romantic terrain where you buy each other used copies of your favorite books and spend whole weekends fucking and drinking Bloody Marys or margaritas, depending on the weather, and nothing on Earth strikes you as more romantic or fulfilling than the relationship that is a slowly closing noose around your neck.

I had no appetite. I nodded at the private and her illicit sergeant boyfriend and excused myself to the terrace. Here, mostly male soldiers and marines stood or leaned and smoked. I'd never smoked, I'd never had a cigarette in my life, but I asked a young marine with a high and tight haircut if he could spare one.

"Sure thing, dude," he said. He'd flared *dude* into a sharp and shrill California beach cliché. His buddies loved it.

My hair wasn't long, but it was longer than any military guy's. I tried to fake the carriage of a US Marine, especially around this crowd, but my hair read Slimy Civilian and so did those extra pounds and my suit. I noticed myself looking at the men, grading their appearance and behavior for military bearing and discipline. How absurd. The marine lit my cigarette for me and I inhaled deeply and coughed. The smoke was bitter and burned. I threw the thing into a planter that was being used as an ashtray. This drew a chorus of laughs.

"Damn, where'd you learn to smoke?" the kid who'd given me the cigarette asked. "You owe me like a dollar, man."

"I'll smoke it." And someone else picked up my waste and lit it.

"That was my first one ever. And my last," I said.

"If that's the case," the kid said, "could you go on a beer run?"

"What are you guys drinking?"

"Beer." The huddle of smokers laughed.

I counted eight of them. "Eight beers."

"Make it sixteen," one of them chortled.

"I'll see what I can do."

Inside, waiters set dessert in front of diners and at the stage a country band made ready for its show. I asked the bartender for sixteen beers. He didn't want to give them to me.

He said, "We can't get these kids too wasted. Some bad shit has gone down in the past. Who knows what meds they're on."

I pulled a fifty out of my wallet and handed it to him, and he put sixteen beers in a wine box.

On the terrace I put the beer at the feet of the smokers and they all exclaimed and whistled and clapped their hands, as though I'd handed them the spigot from the fountain of life.

"Those bastards will never give us more than one beer per person. They think we're going to get drunk and get in a fight back at the barracks, a bunch of gimps beating the shit out of each other with crutches and canes."

"No, they're worried that we'll skip out on the bus and go to a bar and beat the shit out of some civilians."

"All I want to do is get drunk. I don't give no fuck about the senator's son and I don't give no fuck about you gimps."

"It's *a* fuck. I don't give *a* fuck, not *no* fuck."

"He learned to cuss in the Air Force. They use proper grammar when telling you to go fuck your mother."

"How'd you get sixteen beers out of that guy?"

"I pulled rank," I said.

Back at my table the staff sergeant and Colon seemed to be making exemplary progress with the two ladies from the nonprofits. Maybe for these girls tonight there would be true profit in veteran advocacy.

Amy and her man were still engaged in clenched-mouth carpet-bombing of each other's character. The private and the sergeant had disappeared, likely to a broom closet or toilet stall, I assumed. I tried to figure out how a guy with a broken back and a woman with a prosthetic leg would fuck in a toilet stall. There had to be a joke in there somewhere, but I could not locate it.

I ate my spongy mousse cake in peace and solitude.

Amy put her hand on my leg and said, "We have something else to get to, a bar birthday for one of his friends. But here's my card. And I'd love to get your information in case I'm—in case we're in New York sometime we can all get together."

The gossip man and I exchanged nothing, not a look or a handshake or a business card.

They left.

I read her card. I flipped it over and on the back she'd written the name of a bar and cross streets and the joyous greeting: SEE YOU IN AN HOUR OR SO.

The country music band was turning the volume way up, which meant it was time for me to go. I thought I'd leave the business card on the table and let someone else meet her in an hour or so. Blondes in the lobbying game weren't my ambition. I thought about it long and hard, and I decided it had been at least ten years since I'd slept with a blonde. It wasn't yet ten o'clock. I could push it hard and be home by two in the morning. I could call Ava and she would be in my bed when I got to Manhattan. After a day like this I needed a body in bed and I needed to fuck. I couldn't sleep alone tonight. But the question was whether or not I wanted to drive four hours or a few miles to not sleep alone tonight.

I decided to save the gas.

I wished everyone at the table a good night and told Colon and the staff sergeant that I planned to see them the next time I came to town.

I DROVE TO Georgetown and found the bar, somewhere off of Wisconsin. I assumed that I'd show up to the gossip blogger's friend's party and that it might take me hours to peel the lobbyist away from her crowd, or that I had completely misread her intentions or that she was playing a game with me. All of these possibilities swirled in my head. There are only three things a man enjoys more than sleeping with a woman within hours of meeting her. And at this moment I couldn't remember what those things might be.

Dance music thumped, people spilled and drank drinks,

bartenders poured more, a pushing match broke out between two heavily muscled kids in polo shirts, and I spotted Amy in the back of the bar. She sat alone.

"Where is the rest of our party?" I asked.

"I'm a party of one," she said.

I retrieved whiskeys from the bar.

"So what are you doing, research for another book?"

"Book?"

"Those marines told me you're a writer. They think you're spying on them. They think you're trying to do an exposé on Bethesda."

"If I'd seen poor care or dirty conditions I would write about it. But that place runs pretty tight, as far as I can tell. I was only on the ward for ninety minutes, but I sensed that the care is expert. A naval hospital is different from an Army hospital, in that there are no members of the Army running the show."

"Of course. Even the old marine loves the Navy. All this services pride is such bullshit."

"Maybe so. Maybe not. They found rat shit all over Walter Reed, right? My Polish cleaning lady would have been impressed with the spit shine on that ward. As they say, Joseph's baby mama could've eaten off of that floor."

"So tell me, who the fuck are you?" she said.

"I'm just a guy drinking whiskey with a stranger in a strange town. I should've driven home hours ago."

"Girlfriend?"

There was no need to lie. "Depending on the week and which lies we are telling one another. I believe that for most of this week I had a girlfriend. But I can never tell. Where is your boyfriend?"

"That guy? He was a one-night stand that turned into

something it should never have. A wasted year. Still some nights he comes around. Did you sleep with this woman the first night you met her?"

"Two days later. She had a live-in boyfriend in Brooklyn. I lived in Oakland and had a girlfriend in Manhattan. It was messy. It still is."

"Aren't you too old for that?"

"Someday I hope to be too old for it. But right now I am not."

"Neither am I," she said.

The bar had filled with more young drunk people. I wondered where they had all come from. They were so goddamn happy and carefree. I thought about the marines I'd scored the beer for earlier that night, sleeping on bunks now, listening to the nightmare confusion of one another, fighting their way through the long war.

I smelled burned sand and scorched asphalt.

Someone spilled a drink on Amy's leg. I wiped her leg with napkins. She asked me to kiss her and I did and then she asked me back to her apartment.

The sex from a one-night stand is never spectacular, it rarely breaks land speed records, but with Amy it was great. She was under thirty but she knew her body and was proud of it. She wanted me to want her and I did. We continued to drink whiskey, a not-very-good Canadian whiskey, as I recall, and we were still awake and talking when the sun came up.

"So if you weren't there to report about Bethesda, why were you there?"

"I am often asked about the wars. And I say that the wars are a waste of human life on both sides and a deep strategic blunder. But I had never sat in a room with a wounded marine. And I needed to do that. But I am no clearer on what the wars mean."

"Do they have to mean anything? Can't they just be a show of American force and power in a region full of Islamists and enemies of freedom?"

"Wars mean something whether the wagers of the war want them to or not. Vietnam is still being fought here in DC. Kerry lost in 2004 because of the swiftboaters; Bush won in 2004 because he was a crafty and ardent draft dodger and thirty-plus years later he stuck to his story: 'Oh, yeah, I forgot I was supposed to be flying planes in the National Guard. Sorry guys.'"

"I just fucked a liberal," she said. "My father will kill me. Aren't you a marine? Like, don't marines want to go to war and kill? Jesus. I haven't fucked a liberal since freshman year."

"You are the first conservative I have ever fucked. We might as well do it again."

WE WERE UP front about never needing to contact each other again unless one of us was in the other's town and wanted sex.

I HURRIED BACK to Manhattan. Ava and I were throwing a dinner party that night at my apartment. I still needed to shop. I'd make roasted leg of lamb, pierced with anchovy and slivers of garlic and sprigs of rosemary.

I drove I-95 back to the city. I took it slower than I had on my way down. Mostly I went the speed limit. I listened to NPR. I smelled burned sand and scorched asphalt.

7

Welcome to Fabulous Las Vegas

Before heading to Iraq again my friend Sammy threw himself a going-away party in Vegas. I'd had a strict twelve-hour rule for Vegas: land at six p.m., fly out by six a.m. the next day. Any more time in that town is completely ruinous to one's cash flow and sanity. But Sammy talked me into a long weekend, Friday morning through Sunday night, and I hadn't seen him for a while, and Ava and I had just broken up for the twentieth time and she was in the UK fucking some puffer with bad teeth and I needed to get out of Manhattan.

Sammy knew some guy who knew some guy who had gotten us into a club with five-hundred-dollar bottle service, but before that we were eating the subpar food at the attached restaurant, a Manhattan import that had done ten cycles of anabolic steroids before being dropped down on the Strip. A couple of Sammy's marines were along with us, senior enlisted guys who'd seen the same shit as Sammy in western Iraq. In this town, this club, this bar with all these dolls and all these straight guys wearing corset T-shirts and waxed eyebrows and Botoxed faces, the marines' hostility was apparent: their hair was short and so were their tempers. They looked around the room as though choosing targets for an easy hundred-yard shoot. Their targets: anyone who might get in the way of their mission, and the mission, clearly, was women.

I remember dancing and doing watermelon shots with a gaggle of Filipina girls from San Diego. It crossed my mind that a thirty-six-year-old man might spend his time in more sober or age-appropriate pursuits: say, whiskey and bull-riding. But it is hard to argue against the beauty of a twenty-five-year-old Filipina doing watermelon shots on a dance floor. I couldn't decide if I looked like a pervert or like a cohort or simply lost.

A few bottles later, it was late, and the attrition rate for our evening was high: Sammy and I were the only ones left. While barely five-four and not much over 120 pounds, Sammy had been drinking like a pro all night, downing shots, beers, cocktails, whatever made its way in front of him. He had a war to get to but first he needed to drink.

I would have been drinking the same way had I been on my way to or from Iraq. The first time he'd gotten back he'd been a little jumpy and had been smart enough to go to the base doc for some help. But all the pills did was keep him from getting hard and he couldn't have that so he flushed them down the toilet. He downplayed what he'd done and seen but I knew whatever it had been, it had been enough. No one ever wants more war. But Sammy was going back. He didn't have to go back. After twelve years in the Marine Corps he'd resigned his commission and matriculated in a graduate writing program. We'd talked about it and it seemed like the right thing to do. Certainly his mother agreed.

And then one day he called me: the commandant of the

Marine Corps had signed his resignation, but Sammy couldn't say goodbye to the Corps. That afternoon, observing the marines he'd been training for six months, it hit him like a roadside bomb—he knew he couldn't send them back over alone. He'd rescinded his resignation, and that is why we were wasted in Vegas.

I looked up from our booth and a meaningless conversation with someone and saw that three bouncers, three huge bouncers, had cornered Sammy by an elevator bank. Together they probably weighed ten times as much as he did.

He was smiling, that big huge dumb marine smile, the smile that says, "Come on, fellas, let's have a dance."

I rushed over.

One of the bouncers said, "Is he your boy? You better get him the fuck outta here if he's your boy."

I said, "He's cool, man. He's a crazy-ass marine, and he's going over to Iraq again. Give him some leash."

"He's wasted, you gotta get him out of here or we'll send him down the trash chute."

I talked Sammy into the elevator and, stumbling, we made it back to our room. I delivered him to the shower, where he stripped and cold-showered himself.

It was late, but it wasn't yet daylight, which meant I still had time. I'd gotten a local girl's number back at the club. Wanda. She had drugs and she came to my room. In the suite, sunk down into the couch, with this girl I'd just met, I did drugs until noon. She had a story, and that's why I sat doing drugs with her. She was completely gone, but she had a story.

Earlier that night she'd stolen her boyfriend's Yukon and driven in from the suburbs and she wanted to party. She'd left her kid at her mom's house and she was going to party all weekend, because she'd found out her boyfriend was sleeping with one of her friends, because that is how you teach a man who is treacherous with your heart: you steal his SUV and drugs and you go off and play with strangers.

I don't know why I loved her story so much, the bleakness of it, the raw fact of people fucking each other over, the totally ballsy act of this petite woman stealing her thuggish boyfriend's car (and his drugs) on a Saturday night and going into the city for a party, so clearly a death wish that it must have resounded with me. I knew all about the pleasures of the death wish. Here I sat in the middle of my own, blowing my brains out with cheap drugs.

Of course, this was neither the first nor the last time I'd done drugs with a stranger in a hotel room.

I JEOPARDIZED SAMMY that night. If the girl's boyfriend had somehow found us, if hotel security had gotten a tip that two people were doing blow in a large suite on the thirty-fifth floor, who knows what could have happened, and Sammy would have been implicated despite being passed out in the shower, and I would have ruined his career. I hadn't given Sammy enough thought, and in retrospect I'm ashamed. A marine always looks out for his platoon. How had I forgotten?

And I was too wasted for sex. I'd wanted nothing more than to get a screw on with a sexy black girl from the Las Vegas suburbs, but we just sat there all morning talking about what a crazy place Vegas was and how you had to be an animal to live there.

SAMMY HAD ANOTHER friend who knew a guy who knew a guy, and we got some choice real estate at a pool party. The scene at the pool party replicated the scene from the night before except everyone wore fewer clothes. I was neither tan nor in very good shape, and so I stood in a corner of the pool drinking beer and not chatting with anyone.

Sammy attracted an unending parade of girls, and I talked to some of them, and they all seemed the same: attractive, in very good shape, possibly fake breasts; mostly they lived in LA or New York and they worked in film or real estate. We talked a lot about TV shows I'd never seen but had heard of, a particular show from that series, the amazing second season of that series.

We met a couple, Claire and Tony, from Long Island. They were on vacation with their parents. She was a nurse and he ran an auto body shop. They were great people, the kind of people I had grown up with and never met in New York City. He talked vaguely about being a criminal as a kid, and she laughed and rolled her eyes. And we drank.

I had a flight out at two but I changed it to three, and then to four, and then to five. I was supposed to fly to LA to see a woman I'd met on the East Coast a few weeks earlier. I didn't want to see her: making the plan had merely been a function of boredom.

I've wasted tens of thousands of dollars on flights booked late at night, out of boredom: meet me in London, meet me in Baden-Baden, meet me in Seattle, meet me in Rome; I'll fly you to Tokyo, I'll fly you to Paris; I'll fly you anywhere but here.

I finally stopped calling the airline to change the flight and instead I started calling around town for a new room. I wasn't sure how many days, at least three or four, I told reception at every place I called. I finally found a room at the Wynn, in the tower suites, for five hundred dollars a night.

*　　　*　　　*

THE ROOM WAS twice as big as my apartment; the bath could hold three people. I settled in for a bath. I was sunburned now, and kind of drunk. I'd been ignoring my phone, ignoring the thought of Ava in London, or wherever she was, fucking someone else. I dialed her and hung up. I sat in the bath, reading *In Cold Blood*.

I stayed in the suite a week.

8

Freddy Business

Freddy drove a different car every time and he'd meet me anywhere in Manhattan. He didn't go to Brooklyn, only punks dumb enough to drive miles for a single deal did that, and the drivers in Brooklyn were shit crazy out of their minds, worse than Chinatown. Freddy said he'd be there in twenty minutes but then he took an hour. It was a smart tactic for a drug dealer, always keep them guessing, always keep those dumb rich white motherfuckers wanting more, sitting around in their dumb rich white bars paying ten dollars for a beer. And the next time he told me an hour he was there in five minutes, texting, "WTF? There are f'ing cops all up in this place."

It was Manhattan, so of course there were cops everywhere. But it was below Ninety-Sixth Street and above Canal so the cops didn't do much but try to get laid.

Sometimes it didn't matter how long Freddy Business took because I was already high, because someone had copped so much the night before that, despite our having been awake until noon, there were still a few bags going around, and it seemed like the party would never end and that the cops were after me no matter what I did so why not do a shit-ton of drugs?

Freddy pulled up in his car in front of the Swan on Twentieth Street. One of my friends was doing yoga on the sidewalk and another was talking to an NYU coed who was reading *Sophie's Choice* at the dim light of the bar. But I was buying tonight so I jumped in Freddy's car. Freddy never drove; big enormous black guy who would either break your neck or shoot you if you did some stupid shit always drove and he never said a word, but he looked at me and nodded and I thought, *He must think I am one stupid white boy.*

Freddy didn't like this block so his driver drove east and then south on Park, west on Sixteenth to Sixth Avenue, and then up to Twenty-Sixth and east again. Pulled up in front of 15 West Twenty-Sixth Street, where I'd once had an office. What did I do there? Nothing. What did this mean? It meant nothing, it was simply a place to pull over, but it made me nervous. It made no sense, it made no sense at all, but why would a twelve-hundred-dollar drug deal make any sense wherever the dealer parked? Across the street people were paying astronomical prices for Texas BBQ and beer. Who would spend so much money on BBQ? Some nights I would, but not tonight, tonight I'll eat nothing, I'll barely eat anything for three days.

I was buying for three and for the weekend so I told Freddy I'd go big, and I pulled the cash out of my pockets; I hadn't even counted, eight hundred of it was mine, four hundred cobbled together by friends, and Freddy counted it and said it was a thousand, but maybe I didn't give a fuck because it was Thursday night and Freddy had the drugs packed like jewels in his glove compartment.

My father once told me: always carry hundreds and fifties. It is proof you go face-to-face with a banker. If you walk around with a bunch of twenties in your wallet you look just like all the other assholes who use the ATM, so I handed Freddy hundreds.

Freddy was jumpy tonight, and he kept counting the money again and again, coming up with different numbers, saying now it was seven hundred, telling his guy to drive around the block again, down Broadway now, past Madison Square Park.

"Dumbass white motherfuckers in line for two hours for a ten-fucking-dollar cheeseburger," Freddy says. "Let's call it a thousand," Freddy says.

Now I'm nervous, now I want out of the car, I want my money back and never want to do drugs again: *Go back in the Swan and flush the drugs you have down the toilet*, I think. *Tell those assholes you're doing drugs with to fuck off.*

"Naw," Freddy says. "It's nine hundred. I'll give you a shitload for nine hundred."

Can I argue with a lying drug dealer named Freddy Business who has all the drugs and all the money and all the guns? Not really.

But I do.

"Freddy Business," I say. "There is more than a thousand there, man. There's twelve hundred. I know there is twelve hundred. I fucking counted it."

The driver looks over his shoulder at me. A threat?

"Maybe it's twelve. Yeah, it's twelve. I can give you four large and four small, a little extra for your trouble and continued patronage."

Yes it's a sign of trouble when the drug dealer gives you a deal. But who ever sees the signs until it is too late?

I never do.

Freddy drops me off in front of Pete's Tavern on Irving and I call my friends and tell them to meet me there, and they will because I just spent all their money on drugs. My pockets are literally bulging with drugs.

This allows me time to consider how I got to this place, how I got to Sixteenth and Irving in Manhattan with twelve hundred dollars' worth of cocaine in my pockets, enough drugs to send me to prison for a fair stretch of time; even though it's not crack and I'm white, I could still spend a lot of time in jail for the drugs in my pocket. I couldn't just explain it away.

"I pulled on someone else's jeans this morning, Officer."

But I don't have the answer to how I got here. I don't even know where I am. Once I was married, once I lived in a beautiful house in Iowa City and I was married to a beautiful woman and then we lived together in a beautiful house in Portland, and then I fucked that all up, destroyed it, and I hate myself, and rather than think about that I go downstairs at Pete's Tavern, the Place O. Henry Made Famous (how did he do that, by doing blow in the bathroom?), and I do some more drugs because it's easier, so much easier to do drugs than to think about my old life, that old good life I ruined.

But I think about it. No matter how hard I try to blow my brains out, I think about it. I think about the various good lives I have lived, how long these periods usually last, and I wonder why, now, in the richest city in the world, in the loveliest city in the world with the most beautiful women in the world and the best food and some of the best architecture and the best art and the best parks, and the most money that I have ever had in my bank account and a piece of real estate in this rich city and five hundred bottles of wine in my cellar, why, of all the cities on Earth, I am here now fucked up on drugs and deeply depressed in this great shining city on the island?

I come back from the bathroom and some blue shirts have taken my place at the bar, so I leave. I tell my friends to return to the Swan but they never left, so I walk there.

One friend is still doing yoga on the sidewalk. The other friend is mumbling into his own hands at the bar. And I talk to the girl reading *Sophie's Choice*, and she tells me her name is Sophie but I assume this is a lie.

The drugs are passed around and Sophie joins. She says she never does this stuff, just maybe sometimes on weekends and holidays or when her mother is in town.

Much later Sophie comes home with me. I do drugs with her all night and read Styron aloud, and I'm in bed with her and during sex breaks I read more Styron. We spend the morning taking turns reading the entirety of *Darkness Visible* aloud, and I wonder if Styron would get a kick out of this, a writer in bed with a twenty-year-old, high on cocaine, reading aloud Styron's book about the crippling effects of his depression and his years of self-medicating.

9

Genesis: an Imagining

For a not-wealthy man of twenty he wears a fine new suit. It is not borrowed. The suit is black, and a thin gray tie parts the white sea of his shirt. The young man is handsome, and if he were smiling the smile would be large and welcoming, a bit crooked to the left, and his teeth would be in perfect shape, a gap between the front two. His white skin is lightly tanned; this is not a laborer's tan but neither is it a banker's. His nose is thin at the bridge and widens considerably at the nostrils. His blue eyes look like jewels. Beneath the hat his hair is thick, dark, and wavy. Sweat has begun to darken his collar. He stands with other similarly attired and sweating men. The women wear black dresses and cool themselves with silk fans but the women do not sweat.

His wife died a few days earlier. And here we join him at her graveside. The graveyard is the Old Auburn Graveyard in Auburn, Alabama, for whites only. It is July 24, 1941.

The man's thoughts are a swirl of hatred for God, forgiveness for God, guilt and shame, and love for his newborn son. He does not hear a word the Southern Baptist preacher says, but later at the reception at his in-laws' home the guests will tell him it was a spirited sermon and that for certain her soul left her body at the end of it, rising to the great heavens above.

The man shovels dirt onto his young wife's casket. The sound is hollow, a fist of knuckles against pine. He buries the spade in the pile of dirt and balances himself with the handle. He looks at the gathered crowd: his wife's mother, her sisters and brothers, a smattering of nieces and nephews, a few of her dead father's colleagues from the university. The man is poor and these people are not. He suspects they have designs on his baby son. He has sent word back to west Georgia that a cousin should come fetch him sometime in the next week so that he can return to Georgia with the baby boy.

He thinks, "Lord, God, our eternal savior, take from us now the soul of Annie Swofford. She is yours. Her body belongs now to the earth. She died with the love of Christ in her heart. She will be renewed in your Kingdom of Heaven. Amen."

John Columbus Swofford walks through the streets of Auburn in the procession mourning his wife, Annie Swofford. The sweat on his body feels like devil spit. He wants a shower. He wants to put on a pair of work trousers and boots and a white cotton undershirt, and he wants to go out to the woods and chop down an acre of pine. But he must go home and take care of his month-old son.

JOHN COLUMBUS SWOFFORD first met Annie Howard when she stopped by the little gas and sundries station he owned and ran out by Ridge Grove. To say he owned it gave him pride but it wasn't exactly true. He'd worked there a year for Mr. Shanker, and then Mr. Shanker died and his widow told John Columbus to take it over and give her 10 percent of the monthly. And so he did. But he felt like an owner, kept the books, ordered the gasoline and the Coca-Cola and the ice cream and the hard and soft candy and work gloves, fan belts, and motor oil and tires.

Mr. Shanker had had a side business of moonshine, doing his part to whet and supply appetites in this dry county, but after taking over the station John Columbus lined those thirty liquor bottles up at the edge of the wood behind the store and plinked them one by one with his .22 rifle. He'd left one standing and named it Temptation but in a year he'd never given in.

When a man asked for moonshine John Columbus said, "Plumb out, fella."

And when Adolphus Rickman came by each month with a new supply John Columbus said, "Mr. Rickman, with all respect, we don't traffic 'shine no more."

John Columbus considered affixing a name to the station, J. C. Swofford's, something of the like, but the store had never had a name, it had always simply been "the station at Ridge Grove," and the old-timers might not think it right if a name were attached.

One afternoon John Columbus sat in his stoop chair, shading himself from the sun, thinking about the future, thinking about a chain of J. C. Swofford's stores, and a trucking company, because he had the sensation that the roadways were gonna be big. He had plans.

A Ford coupe pulled up and out jumped a girl of about seventeen. The car pulled off and left the girl in a cloud of dust. All the girls he'd ever seen around there were in Opelika or Auburn. Other than stocky old Miss Shanker he'd never seen a woman at Ridge Grove, except maybe in the backseat of her daddy's car. He'd never seen a girl in a pretty white dress *standing* in the middle of his gravel driveway.

"Sir," she said.

He stared, dumb.

"Sir?"

He stood. His deep baritone boomed, "Yes, ma'am?"

"I got me a flat tire driving my car back to town. I was coming in from Slaughters, where my cousins live. Ain't this a gasoline station? Ain't you a mechanic?"

He said without really thinking about it, "I'm the owner, not a mechanic, but I know a thing or two about changing a wheel."

He pointed to his dilapidated flatbed Ford. He opened the passenger door for her. Inside the cab of the Ford it looked as if two raccoons had gotten into a fistfight. Only the faintest rumor of upholstery remained on the seats, and the floorboards were even less of a rumor.

"Hold yourself a moment," he said, and ran inside the store and grabbed a package of clean white shop towels.

He covered the passenger seat with the towels and ushered the frightened girl in.

"There ain't hardly no floor," she said. "Where do I put my feet?"

"On the edges," he said. Rust-chewed floorboards accessorized every vehicle he'd ever driven and he knew that this girl had never seen such a thing.

His tires tore the gravel as he pulled onto the hardtop.

"May I ask why that gentleman in the Ford didn't help you?"

"He was a salesman of some sort, Bibles, maybe, brushes, I don't know. But he said he was already late to Opelika by an hour but he'd drop me to your station. The car ain't but around the turn up here. It's a, what they call it? A Cadillac."

"Your daddy's?" he asked, with hope.

"It is."

"He let you drive that big car all the way to Slaughters and back?"

"Ain't that far. But he don't know I'm gone. He's with the university choir on a competition down Montgomery. And my mama never notice nothing."

"Your daddy sing in the university choir?"

She laughed. "No. 'Course not. He's a professor of musicology. He lead 'em. He writes hymns and they sing 'em."

"You sing in the choir?"

"Not in the university. At the church. Opelika First Baptist."

John Columbus had been to First Baptist to hear the preacher a few times. He'd left unimpressed. After two years in town he was still preacher-shopping. He'd never paid much attention to any choir. But now he would.

Off to the opposite side of the road was a black 1938 Cadillac.

He pointed at the Cadillac. "That your daddy's?"

"Yes it is."

He drove past it and then flipped a U-turn and pulled up behind the gleaming Caddy. He knew this car. He loved this car. It was a 1938 Sixty-Special. That first year it had outsold every other Cadillac on the market. John Columbus thought the car a bit daring for a university man, but quiet men often took dares with their automobiles.

He'd pumped gas into a Sixty-Special before, but no man driving a Caddy would let a redneck grease monkey play around with his car at backward Ridge Grove—*A rich man more likely to push his fancy car all the way to a proper mechanic in Auburn than allow me to fool around it*, John Columbus thought.

Once he'd nicked an owner's manual from the glove compartment of a Sixty-Special while the man used the toilet.

John Columbus sat up at night reading that manual, memorizing it and hoping the man would come back someday so he could return the manual, but that had never happened. And last night, after reading the Bible for an hour, he'd glanced through the manual and had in fact been studying the whereabouts and the functionality of the jack, and the location of the spare tire. It was as though a divine intervention had occurred and here was the result: a pretty girl in a white dress with a flat tire on her daddy's Cadillac and no one in ten miles to fix the flat but him.

She didn't know his name because he hadn't offered it nor had he inquired of hers. She stood near the right front wheel of his falling-apart hauling truck, her arms crossed, and she watched the man work. He removed his checked button-up and set the shirt on the backseat of her daddy's car. His brown cotton work pants were clean and the white undershirt fit his body tight. She wondered if he had a woman, a mother or sister, who took care of him, or if he was a wanderer, a Southern vagabond of the type her father had told her to stay away from.

"Beware the man with a big smile and a box of tools and no home address," her father had once said.

This man beneath her daddy's car seemed unschooled but overtly and severely polite.

He jacked up her daddy's car. The muscles in his forearms rippled with each heavy turn of the crank, and the monstrous car slowly lifted from the earth. She smelled the dirt and the pine from the woods and she thought she might smell her own body. On the ride from Slaughters she'd sweat a thunderstorm; the sun had beat from the west into the back window, the car had become an oven. Or maybe she'd already been burning up for this blue-eyed man before meeting him. She stared at him and enjoyed the effect, a rugged handsome face: long nose thin at the bridge but widening at the nostrils, wide strong forehead, sharp chin, sly smile of white teeth. His body lengthy and fit.

He stopped cranking the jack and looked at her, pleased with his work, shot her that smile, and stood.

"Well, miss." He stopped. "I do believe I've failed to properly introduce myself. I'm John Columbus Swofford. And you are?"

He stepped forward, offered a slight, awkward bow. No man had ever bowed to her. She didn't know how to respond. She curtseyed, and flirted with her eyes.

"Mr. Swofford, my name is Annie Laurie Howard, of Auburn, Alabama. I'm pleased to meet you."

"The pleasure is mine, Miss Annie Laurie. If you've got ten more minutes to spare I'll have you on the road back to Auburn and let's hope you beat your daddy home from that singin' competition in Montgomery."

"Well, sir, the car don't look a bit movable right now, so I'll give you ten minutes or twenty if you need 'em. But I do must beat my daddy home, if you can be of any help."

He moved quickly, assured of every action, not stopping to chat nor waiting for comment from her. He lowered the car back to the turf, stowed the jack in the trunk. He leaned against the open trunk, his right arm wide and high above her, holding the flat in the other hand.

"Miss Annie Laurie," he said, "you've got a predicament. Now if I place this ruined tire back in that side panel, one day your daddy is gone be driving and get a flat, and go for his spare, and find his spare is also flat. Not just flat, but looks to me like you

195

run on it a few miles at least, it's got teeth marks of a hyena all over it. Every man I know stay attuned to the whys and hows of his vehicle, and your father would, I'm guessing, find this mangled spare a queer event, not to mention a major inconvenience."

"What do I do?"

He knew. He'd been thinking it with every crank of the jack. But he paused; he knew not to seem too eager. He looked to the woods. He looked to the ground. He played his chin with his fingers.

"I think I got it. Figuring two days from now is Sunday, and you'll be at Opelika First Baptist with your family, what I could do is drive down tomorrow, get a proper Caddy tire on this wheel, and while you are in church with your family on Sunday, I'll return it."

"That seems like a perfect idea, Mr. Swofford. You'd do that for me? But I'm a stranger. Oh, my daddy would be on fire, as much fire as he ever get, if he knew I'd took his car out to Slaughters. You'd save me an awful lot of trouble."

"Consider it done. How early your family gets to church?"

"Bible study starts at ten and the service at eleven. We try to get there by nine forty-five."

"Well then, I think you're ready to get on home."

"How will I know you've replaced the tire?"

"If you see me in the pews, listenin' to you singin' to the Lord, you'll know."

He slammed the trunk shut and leaned the wheel against his truck. He grabbed his shirt from the backseat of the Sixty-Special, and opening the front door waved Miss Annie Laurie toward the driver's seat.

She sat down with a flourish, a bit of pomp, and he closed the door.

Through the open window he watched her start the car, and heard the beautiful purring of the V-8.

"You drive safe now," he said.

"What I owe you?" she asked.

"Nothing just yet."

She smiled and headed home.

JOHN COLUMBUS SLEPT in the tiny storeroom at the back of the station. His sole belongings: a camp cot and linens, a lantern, a Bible, ten undershirts, ten button-ups, three pairs of work trousers, a pair of dress trousers and almost-matching sport coat, two ties, one pair of black wing tips that he kept in a paper sack, and the owner's manual to a 1938 Cadillac Sixty-Special. He did not have to live this way but chose to. Back in Lafayette, Georgia, his parents lived in a big country house. They were not wealthy people but they were "of means," as would be said.

John Columbus felt he should strike out on his own when he reached eighteen. He sent small amounts of money home when he could. He'd wanted to design airplanes but didn't have the schooling and didn't have the patience to get the schooling.

He'd spent a year doing highway work for Georgia, and then at the state line he took over work for Alabama, and the road crews pushed their way west, eventually to settle on the outskirts of Auburn, near the train tracks, waiting for work.

After a month he grew tired of the tent city where the road authority housed him, grew tired of the drinking and whoring and gambling that most of his cohorts took to as a profession, and he left the camp, and after a few days of wandering around, sleeping in let rooms, and asking questions of anyone who might listen, he ended up spending the night in the let room of a Mr. Shanker. Didn't take long for the men to hammer out the details of his new employment.

And now here he was.

Tonight he'd give the Lord a rest. Every page of his Bible marginalia and eraser smudges evinced a man working hard for the Lord. John Columbus never proselytized but he knew his Bible better than most men. But tonight he'd spend more time with the Sixty-Special.

SATURDAY AFTERNOON HE pulled up to the Cadillac dealership in Auburn. The manager's face broadcast his horror: what redneck in his shit-jalopy Ford truck just pulled into my lot?

John Columbus wore his church clothes.

"Hey, partner," he said to the manager. "Blew this tire out on my Sixty-Special. What it take to get me a new one?"

The salesman looked at John Columbus, and to his truck and back, and said, "I know every man who bought a Sixty-Special over the last three years within a hundred miles of here, and I know you ain't one of 'em."

"That's 'cause I bought mine up in Atlanta, sir. And good to meet you, too, my name is John Columbus Swofford."

The salesman uneasily shook his hand.

"Well, sorry about that, on account of your truck and them 'Bama plates I assumed you was from around here."

"Can't a man buy a car in one state and drive it to another? I know the answer to that. So what's it gonna set me back?"

The salesman inspected the wheel and tire.

"You just sit in the waiting room. I'll get the mechanic to take a look. And, pardon, but do you mind wheeling that truck behind the building? Don't look quite right up against all my Caddies. I'm trying to sell cars here."

"You just find me when it's all done."

Before pulling around back he walked among the half-dozen Cadillacs, sat down in one or two, smelled the new-car drug.

He was napping when the salesman rapped on the hood of his truck.

"Hey, buddy," the man said. "I got you road-ready. That'll be six dollars."

John Columbus had planned on paying two dollars but he couldn't really argue with the man now. He pulled the cash from his pocket and paid. For the next few days he'd be eating canned food out of the store—chili, franks, green beans. No bacon breakfasts at Mama's Roadside and no chicken-fried steak dinners down at Earl's. These were lean times until the end of the month.

SUNDAY MORNING HE drove slowly through the gravel parking lot of Opelika First Baptist, keeping his eyes out for the Sixty-Special. He felt like a thief when in fact he was the opposite of a thief, but he imagined it could go either way if someone saw him with the side panel of Mr. Howard's car swung open and a wrench in his hand.

There sat a black Sixty-Special, but he'd remembered the plate number, 488-531 D, and this wasn't it. In a lane opposite he spotted the car, parked between a Packard and an older-model Cadillac, the style he didn't know offhand, but it paled next to the Series Sixty. He parked a few spots away. It was fifteen past ten and the Sunday schoolers were deep in their Bibles by now, and he had plenty of time before the rest of the congregation arrived for the service. The coast looked clear.

He used a shop towel to carry the wheel and the tire iron he'd use to screw the wheel back in place. He wanted Miss Annie Howard to appreciate this gesture, to recognize him as a gentleman, and to say yes when he asked her out for a walk downtown after the service, maybe a Coca-Cola at the fountain. He hadn't been on a date with a girl since leaving home almost two years before. That foolish bow he'd offered her the other day still haunted him. What kind of imbecile *bows* to a woman? Next time politely shake her hand.

He slithered up to the passenger side of Mr. Howard's car. He easily unlatched the spare compartment, a revolutionary design a few years earlier. He swung open the panel, and to his surprise there was a spare already affixed. He looked around, confused. He squeezed the tire, it had air. He checked the plates and confirmed that this was the right car. He started to sweat. Had he been set up? If so, for what? Set up to do a good deed? He had no choice but to get the heck out of there.

He'd wasted a week's salary on a Cadillac tire for no one, for nothing. There would be no date with Annie Laurie. He couldn't walk into that church and sit through a service. He didn't like the preacher's way with the Bible. What a way to spend a Sunday morning. He felt the pressures of class, he felt money laughing at him; he knew his jacket did not perfectly match his trousers, that anyone could see that.

He started to latch the spare compartment when he heard the crunch of shoes against gravel.

"Hey there, son," he heard a man shout. "What exactly do you think you're doing with my Cadillac?"

He turned to see two men in their fifties approaching quickly. They both wore fine linen suits and straw hats. He'd seen clothes like these in the windows of the finest men's shops in Atlanta.

He noticed one of the men, the manager from the car dealership the day before.

"You must be John Columbus Swofford," the man on the left said. "I'm Mr. Howard, father of Annie Laurie. This here is my good friend Tad Williams, who sold me my car a few years back."

John Columbus nodded. "I am J. C. Swofford, and I'm acquainted with Mr. Williams."

Williams gave him a wicked smile.

Howard said, "Well, son, I hear my daughter Annie Laurie got into a little bit of trouble and roped you into it. It sure was kind of you to replace my tire. A seventeen-year-old girl does generally find herself in a mess of trouble once she starts fooling with her daddy's car."

"Yes, sir," John Columbus said.

"And sometimes a twenty-year-old boy finds himself in a mess of trouble when he starts doing favors for a seventeen-year-old girl."

"Yes, sir," John Columbus said.

"We got a preacher in there can *preach*. Why don't you join us?"

AFTER THE SERVICE John took Annie for that walk he had been planning on. He got on well with the family. His lack of learning was evident to a painful degree to everyone, but his Bible knowledge could not be challenged by anyone at any table, not even Mr. Howard, who taught choral singing and hymn-writing at Auburn. In fact, more than once the professor had pulled the mechanic aside and asked for a critique of a hymn or some advice on biblical fact.

John and Annie were married in the summer and a few years later she was pregnant before Halloween, or possibly on Halloween. For a while the couple called the unborn baby Jack-o'-Lantern. Eventually they settled on John Howard.

Annie gave birth to my father and a month later she died.

10

Atlanta to Austin, Dead Swoffords, August 2010

I didn't socialize much while living in Mount Tremper. One night I landed at a birthday party at a bar in Kingston and later that evening ended up in bed with a woman, but I forget her name and never saw her again.

Occasionally I traveled down to the city for sex.

There was the Budding Comedian: mostly she had a serious pill problem, which worked well for me given my state of mind. We chomped a lot of pills and snorted cocaine and ended each night in her bed, fucking and watching reruns of *Celebrity Rehab*. To watch *Celebrity Rehab* while totally high as a kite on pills and cocaine is one of life's finer pleasures.

One Monday July afternoon I stumbled out of the Comedian's apartment and on to the Bowery. I found the nearby International Bar and fortified myself with bourbon. I was not yet ready to return to my cabin in Mount Tremper, so I contacted a former fiancée of mine, the Boho Artist, and luckily she was free for dinner. I dumped my bag off at a friend's house, and the former fiancée and I had a great dinner at one of our old romantic spots on the Lower East Side and then we went to her apartment and had sex and watched *Charlie Rose*.

The next morning, after she confessed to being involved with someone else, I returned to Mount Tremper. That night I sat on the couch for eight hours thinking about killing myself. I had the rope and the sturdy beam, or any one of thousands of trees to choose from. But I chose to live.

LATER THAT SAME week the Boho Artist was visiting friends in Kingston one afternoon and I picked her up. She had recently become a devotee of the teachings of Gurdjieff. I assumed that the man she was involved with was also a devotee or even a Gurdjieff Guru. Gurus get tons of ass.

I am not opposed to anyone's spiritual development but I did some reading on this Gurdjieff and he seemed to me a positively masterful con artist. I'd been reading a biography of the young Joseph Stalin, and Gurdjieff might easily have traded places with him. Perhaps in two thousand years Gurdjieff would be the new Buddha, but it seemed unlikely.

The Boho Artist and I talked about our past and the possibility of starting anew. We had once been engaged and then that hadn't worked out, and the resultant mess still caused a bit of anxiety and animosity between us. It hadn't worked out because I'd called it off. But still during the following two years we had had a lot of sex and had seen each other regularly. I thought we might work things out but I did have a serious problem with the fact that she had a boyfriend.

We had sex. I grilled steaks. We drank a 1999 Volnay. We had sex again, and again in the morning, and I took her to the bus station. At the bus station we talked about her boyfriend, how she had broken up with him for the week and he was waiting to hear from her a verdict. She asked me to come down and see her later in the week.

I had been down this road before, sexual relations with a boy-friended woman, and I did not like the feeling one bit. In the past there had been jerks who fucked my girlfriend, and I had been a jerk and fucked people's girlfriends, and generally I frowned on the act. It was, as they say in the South, a messy affair.

Later in the week I did visit her. We ordered in, at her apartment on the Lower East Side. We had sex before and after dinner. She told me that she was still in contact with the Gurdjieffian but that she had not been able to come to a conclusion about the affairs, or which affair to end and which to continue. I finished my wine and left and never saw her again. She occasionally sent me nasty text messages but I never responded.

IT WAS LATE July 2010 and I was officially out of women to have hassle-free sex with in New York State. A novel I was working on had stalled. I'd grown tired of the beauty of the Catskills. I planned another RV trip with my father. This time I agreed to meet him in Atlanta and travel west with him as far as I could handle. Also, this time I would figure him out; I would crack the code on John Howard Swofford and thus crack the code on myself.

WE DROVE FROM one small west Georgia town to another and wandered around the cemeteries looking for Swofford headstones. Or, rather, I wandered around the cemeteries looking for dead Swoffords because my dad's lungs were in such bad shape that he couldn't get out of the RV. My dad knew these towns from his youth and he knew that people we were related to were buried all over these cemeteries, and for a reason I could not extract from him he wanted photos of their headstones. He'd pull the RV into a town, find the cemetery, and send me out.

"Who are these people, Dad?"

"I don't know for certain. I musta known some of 'em. My old blind aunt. Um. You know, hell, Tone. They are your kin, Swoffords! Just go on now, take me some pictures."

And that is what I did, in Villa Rica, Temple, Mount Zion, Bremen, Carrollton and Whitesburg, and other towns, at the little church cemeteries.

I remembered the Whitesburg cemetery from drives with Iris when my brother was dying.

It was one of those hot Georgia August days when you look into the sky and expect to see birds stuck in mid-flight, so muggy and thick is the air.

We relaxed in the RV and looked through photos on the camera.

"Yep." He pointed at the screen. "That there, in Bremen. That is cousins of my aunt. So what does that make them to you?"

"Dead cousins of your dead aunt?"

"This is family history."

I didn't see it as family history. I saw it as my father bringing to life the dead Swoffords whom he knew he would be joining very soon. It didn't really matter what their names were or how they were related or even if they were related. He wanted to jam his digital camera with as many Swofford headstones as possible. If here, now, decades after these forgotten people had died, an old man wandered around their old tired towns and cemeteries and instructed his son to take photos of their headstones, they were not forgotten, and thus he must believe that someday decades from now another man might do the same. In 2070 a man might drive his son around west Georgia and instruct him to take photos of Swofford headstones, and one of those dead Swoffords would be a John Howard Swofford. And the living men would not have known him but they would have taken the photo of his headstone and thus brought him back to life in 2070.

The next afternoon we pulled into Auburn, Alabama. The university town's streets were tight and narrow. When oxygen-depleted, my father was unable sometimes to remember the names of his own brothers and sisters, unable to recall what year he'd lived in Seville or Tokyo, but with ease he glided his massive RV to the old whites-only cemetery in Auburn. I had been here many times as a boy and the place had always scared me. It was out of a movie set, an old white Southern graveyard, the stench of history so heavy about the place.

"This here is my mama's grave," my dad said.

"I know that."

"Just so you know the importance. This ain't like those anonymous Swoffords yesterday."

"I understand. Do you want to give it a shot? Want to try to make it to her graveside?"

"Don't think I can make it, Tone."

"Do you know where it is?"

He hopped down to the curb and pointed toward a massive oak. "Right around there. Right near that big oak. One way or the other from it. Probably this way from it."

I grabbed his camera from his hand and headed toward the oak. I walked with my head down. I was not here to read the names of other dead Southerners. I was here only to make it to my paternal grandmother's grave and snap a picture. Once my father died, there would be no reason for me to truck around the South. I'd probably never be back. I knelt at the grave, a very simple stone marked with her name and the dates 1921–1941. I realized that if she had lived I would probably not exist. What did this mean? Nothing. The life of the animals. But I grieved for my father. I grieved for that cute little chubby boy who never knew his mother. He sat one hundred yards away from me in his RV and the wounds from July 1941 burned still today.

Back at the RV my father stared at the digital photo of his mother's grave marker.

"Same as I remember it," he said. "I'm gonna be buried here, Tone. There's still a few spots in the plot, you probably seen. My cousin is looking into it. Looks like I probably got rights to it."

"It's probably the place for you," I said, without knowing whether I believed this or not.

THE NEXT DAY we drove along the Gulf Coast. When my grandfather returned from World War II the family moved to Biloxi. I knew that my father's years in Biloxi had been the happiest of his boyhood. We drove up and down the coastal strip in Biloxi for hours and my father looked for the ghost of the little boy John Howard. We also drove by the VA old soldiers' home. It was one of my dad's favorite cracks, to say he wanted to retire to an old soldiers' home. We pulled up to the gates but they wouldn't let us in. The compound had been destroyed by Katrina.

"You OK with me setting up in an old soldier's home, Tone?"

I knew that what he wanted me to say was "No, I'm not OK with that. Come live with me."

"I'll visit you here in Biloxi," I said. "I like the weather and the oyster po' boys."

NEAR HOUSTON WE saw a fuel tanker catch fire on the roadside. The flames shot a hundred feet in the air. We pulled into a road-side hotel and my father slept in his rig and I got a room for the night.

In the morning while my father took his medications I went for a long run. It was a hundred degrees and I was out of shape, and about three miles out, down a long flat road, I was pretty certain that I'd initiated a cataclysmic cardiac event. I thought: *Jesus Christ, my sick old dad is in his RV sucking meds for his failing lungs and I'm going to have a fucking heart attack on the side of the road and die a week before I turn forty, in the middle of nowhere, in Texas, with an unfinished novel languishing on my laptop.* There along the deserted road in Texas I swore off drugs of all kinds.

An old lady in a powder-blue Cadillac stopped and asked me if I needed a ride and I took her up on it: I swear she looked something like Jesus. The air-conditioning in her car was the best I'd ever experienced in my life.

Over a lunch of canned soup, my father said, "Can you help me out with something I been trying to figure out?"

"I'll give it a shot."

"I don't understand why you rented out that fancy New York City apartment and moved up to the woods to live in a shack."

I'd been lying to my father. I'd told him that I was renting my Chelsea apartment to a friend and that I'd decided to move to the woods to escape the city for a while.

"I mean," he said, "I seen photos of that Manhattan

apartment, and I seen photos of that shack, and I don't see why any young single man would choose to move to the woods when he got that bachelor pad in the city. Ain't all the women in the city?"

"I can confirm that most of the women are in the city. But I'm not young. I'll be forty next week."

"It's a private writer's retreat, or something like that? I just don't get it, Tone. Don't make a lick of sense to me."

I could not keep the lie going any longer.

I said, "In that letter you sent me a few years back you said that someday you would see me on my way down. Well, here I am, Pops. I'm on my way down. You got what you wanted. I'm in total and complete financial ruin. I had to sell my apartment to scratch up some cash to live on. I live in a shack in the Catskills because it's all I can afford right now."

"I never wanted you to fail," he said. "I just wanted to point out to you that sometimes people make money and it changes them. And then they turn around, and they have nothing. Not money. Not family. Money don't mean shit. You always got family if you don't alienate them."

I left the RV and went to the hotel pool. By now it must have been over 110 degrees out. There were no vehicles other than my father's RV in the parking lot, and I assumed no employees would leave the air-conditioned comfort of the hotel. I took off my clothes and stepped into the pool. I floated belly-up for as long as I could take the sun burning my body.

I thought, *So that's it? I have assumed for all these years that my father wanted me to fail, but in fact he did not want me to fail? And so now I have failed, in order to give him what he wanted, but it is not what he wanted?*

From the pool I watched my father moving around in his RV. He lived alone in Fairfield and he mostly traveled alone in the RV. I knew that this solitary life he had created for himself fit in well with his fantasies of being a Clint Eastwood character from a western—the epic wanderer, the stoic, the man who lives on canned beans and shoe leather and the hard-bought realities of the road. But wouldn't my father have been happier if he were in love with a woman and living in a clean and tidy house? I loved my father, and I understood the allure of this iconic western fantasy, but the possibility that I might end up like my father—old, alone, and dying—scared the shit out of me as I floated naked on my back in the hotel pool west of Houston.

It frightened me so intensely that back in the RV I told my father that I needed to return to New York ASAP to take care of some things. We made it to Lockhart that afternoon and ate BBQ at Kreuz Market. We made it into Austin and drank a few beers at a bar and my father glared with passion at the college girls who served us. So did I. In the morning I flew home.

11

The Girl from Tarawa Terrace II

I don't remember much of August. Friends in the city threw a party for my fortieth birthday.

And then it was September. I counted my money. I thought of moving to Los Angeles, where a friend was shooting a movie, or to Phnom Penh, where from god knew I'd never return.

I DIDN'T WANT to go to the reading in Rhinecliff. I wanted to spend my Sunday afternoon watching NFL football in Phoenicia with construction workers and bikers. But a good friend of mine was reading from some anthology or another, and my landlords, old-time country musicians, happened to be the band for the occasion, and I lived upstate and I had no social life other than driving down to Phoenicia and watching NFL football with construction workers and bikers and eating a burger and drinking a few beers. In other words, I needed to get out.

I drove across the river to Rhinecliff from Mount Tremper. I stopped somewhere along the way and checked the score. The Jets were up. I arrived early for the reading.

I drank a few glasses of cheap white wine and ran into Betsy, an acquaintance from the city. She was cute, and used to work for a nonprofit but had recently moved upstate to find meaning or find a project, or find a man, who knew.

She answered me the same way I answered people who asked me why I'd moved upstate, evasively and with a bit of cunning: I needed a change; it's just for the summer; I love the Catskills, it was either the Hudson or the Amazon.

For me this would have been the only true answer: After seven years of a completely deviant and ridiculously expensive life in Manhattan I ran out of money and nerves, at about the same moment. I didn't have the balls to move to Cambodia or Ecuador so I took the baby step up the Hudson, incubator for lost city souls. When I figure out what I want to do with my life, I will move somewhere else. The only thing I really want to do with my life is write books and fall in love with a talented and beautiful woman, but how realistic is that? And I want to hold on to her, and make a life with her, have a family. This is no midlife crisis: I have already plowed through women and wrecked a sports car. This is the reverse midlife crisis: I want a wife and a family and a station wagon.

When Betsy asked me why I had moved up from the city, I said: I needed a change; it's just for the summer; I love the Catskills, it was either the Hudson or the Mekong; I feel a strong magnetic pull from these mountains.

She didn't believe any of it and that was the point.

After the reading we exchanged numbers and said goodbye and I assumed I'd never see her again, or I'd see her in another five years at a horrible party in the city.

And then a week later she called and said, "You should meet my friend and me for dinner tonight. She's up from Brooklyn. I think you will like her."

We met at the cheap Mexican place in Tivoli. I hadn't been since my unfortunate evening involving the police nearly four years earlier. Just as then, the chicken something I ordered was so-so and the margarita was weak, but when I first met Christa I knew that she would be in my life for a long time, perhaps forever.

She wore a short skirt and a flirty, blowsy top and cowboy boots. Here at the end of summer she was dark but I could tell that in winter her skin would turn a luxurious white. She said funny, unflattering things about hippies and monks and yoga masters, and every time she had a chance she showed off her legs or her brilliant smile. Occasionally she played with her dark hair.

She'd gone to Bard in the late nineties and one semester she'd worked at this Mexican restaurant. When she said this I must have stared at her both stupidly and longingly: after a decade of dating and once marrying and twice engaging and unengaging myself to women who were doctors or lawyers or the daughters of doctors or lawyers or academics or wealthy bankers I'd decided earlier in the summer that the next woman I was with would need to have been a waitress at some point in her life, not for "fun and experience" but in order to make the rent, or if she hadn't been a waitress her mother needed to have been one in order to feed and clothe her children.

Not only had Christa been a waitress at this Mexican restaurant, her mother had once been a waitress at the Officers' Club on Marine Corps Base Camp Lejeune. And as a child she'd lived on Camp Lejeune, in base housing in a development called Tarawa Terrace II. Tarawa was the bloodiest battle of World War II. Upon my joining the Marine Corps twenty-two years earlier this fact had been drilled into my head. Some nights I still had nightmares wherein a drill instructor yelled to a room of recruits, *Tarawa!* And the recruits, me included, standing and straining in some stress position or another involving a rifle and a heavy ruck-sack, replied, *Sir! Tarawa, bloodiest battle of World War Two, sir!*

This smart and engaging and beautiful woman had heard of Tarawa, a small and now inconsequential island in the Pacific that in my mind was still soaked with the sanctified blood of marines. Most beautiful women from New York City would have guessed that Tarawa was a kind of chutney or a new method for removing pubic hair.

She'd been student council president at her school in Tarawa Terrace II in Camp Lejeune, and each morning she and the sec-retary were responsible for running the US and Marine Corps flags up the flagpole and then announcing over the PA system the names of the children bound for detention that afternoon.

She hinted at an adult darkness: a car wreck or two, some off-prescription dabbling in psychotropics, a failed early marriage that had infidelity written all over it, a recently terminated vola-tile relationship with a Viagra-popping old man.

But she'd spent this summer alone in the woods writing a book and taking pictures and meditating at a Zen monastery that happened to be on my road in Mount Tremper: the days of wild-haired glory and abandon were over, it was time for her to settle down, or so she said.

She asked me why all my most important belongings, my library and my kitchen, were in storage in Brooklyn, and why I lived alone in a cabin in the woods. I answered stoically, I looked away, I said I'd had work to do, that Manhattan and its people had begun to bore and depress me: the bubble city had become difficult to breathe in.

She knew that what I meant was: *That place nearly killed me; it was a children's zoo and play park and I had had many a turn on all the rides, and there was no longer any joy in standing in line with a bunch of morons waiting to spend many hundreds of dollars on dinner and oblivion every night of the week.* What I was saying was: *I need to build a nest and I need a lover who won't drive me crazy.*

Betsy sat at the table with us but she wasn't really there, or rather, Christa and I paid her no mind: she was the fairy dust that had brought us together but otherwise totally irrelevant.

We talked about Christa's photography and the novel I was working on, and we talked about the weather, and the best swimming holes in the Catskills, and the best pancakes, and we talked about traveling to foreign countries, and slow-cooking short ribs in red wine and braising leeks and preparing salmon poached in champagne, but really, what we were asking each other was: *Are you possibly the one or is this all another hoax?*

Betsy ended the dinner abruptly and awkwardly with an urgent outburst about needing to feed her cat. I wanted to ask Christa if she would travel across the river and have a drink with me and then stay awhile. But of course I didn't. We hugged and said goodbye.

There are many moments that I could point to in our quick courtship and say, *That is when I knew she was good.* But the first moment occurred when we said goodbye that night on the sidewalk in Tivoli: she nearly jumped as she hugged me, and she wrapped her arms all the way around my neck and she hung from me for the briefest moment; she hung from me and we floated together in space; with her body she said, *I already trust you, please do not injure my heart,* and she squeezed me deep and hard with her thin little bird arms and I knew she was good.

On my drive home I realized that I hadn't even asked for her last name.

IT HAPPENS A few times in a man's life that as soon as he meets a woman and shakes her hand an electric current rushes through his body that sends the signal: someday soon, possibly even within hours, you will sleep with this woman. If I were to be honest I would say that that electrical current had coursed through my body about a dozen times in my life, but it had always settled in my crotch and stayed there. It is, indeed, an enjoyable sensation, full of the promise and potential of one's manhood and the easy procurement of sex with attractive women. I have never ingested a drug that produced anything nearly as satisfying.

But with Christa the sensation bounced around my head for a few hours, and then a few days: I saw her visiting me in my cabin; I saw us on the rocks at the Big Blue swimming hole; I saw us eating a meal I'd prepared, perhaps those slow-cooked short ribs with a Volnay to wash it all down. Yes, I saw sex, I saw us giving each other our bodies without remorse or keeping score.

This was a crazy, sexy, perhaps irresponsible waking dream: I began to see her next to me in our family car, and the blurry outline of a child in the backseat and then another. And I saw sports games and badly performed children's plays and hiking in the woods, and family dinners, holidays, the wonder.

We did not waste any time falling in love. We had one date in the city and one in the country, and then we were never apart. We walked into each other so completely it was as if we'd known each other for decades. And really, we had. I knew that if I was ever going to be in a relationship that lasted it would have to be with a woman who didn't care about my past, who wouldn't ask me how many women I'd slept with, and who didn't care because she was so totally confident in herself and the love she was capable of giving and receiving.

The woman would also have to be otherworldly talented. I'd tried dating a few bad artists and dilettantes and it was worse than being with a woman who was bad in bed.

By November we were engaged and living between her Fort Greene apartment and Mount Tremper.

I guess word spread. The Rich Girl/BoHo Artist texted me: *I hear you are engaged! You move fast!* I never responded.

The Hedge-Funder texted me: *You ruined my life!* I never responded.

The Physician e-mailed me: *Anthony, please can we have dinner?* I responded: *I'm getting married.* I never heard back.

We decided to get married at City Hall when my friend Oren and her friend Amanda were both in New York. We chose the twenty-seventh of December.

A few days before Christmas I was wandering around the East Village after taking a steam at the Turkish and Russian Baths on Tenth Street. I bought Christa a Christmas present at a dressmaker on Seventh Street near Cooper Square. I popped in next door at McSorley's for a burger and a beer.

It took me a while to realize that I had trouble in mind.

I had lived in Chelsea for years but a majority of my debauchery had gone down in the East Village and the Lower East Side. I knew three drug dealers within a five-minute walk of where I stood. There were a dozen women I'd slept with a hop, a skip, and a buzzer away. The sun had set.

Christa was out with friends and didn't expect me back in Brooklyn for many hours, midnight or later, whenever. I felt the old twinge, the cheater's twinge and the casual drug user's twinge. Christa would not tolerate cheating or drug use. But those phone calls are so easy to make.

I walked to First Avenue and stepped into Tile Bar. I knew she'd be there: the Comedian. On a stool. She jumped up and gave me a hug. She was high as a kite. And she looked good.

She said, "You shopping for me?"

"Of course," I said. I hugged her close and I thought I could smell the drugs sweating out of her body.

"I heard you were, like, getting married?"

"Maybe." I smiled and sat down and ordered a double bourbon.

She rubbed my leg. "Oh, Tony. You're back! I'm so happy!"

She handed me a few pills in the sly practiced way of someone who passes and receives illicit drugs all day. And I took them with the same sly expertise.

She said, "Let's buy some coke. My guy can be here in twenty minutes. Let's go back to my apartment and get high and fuck and watch *Celebrity Rehab*!"

She turned to her friend at the bar, some wasted chick she must have been passing pills to all day, or all week. I drank my bourbon. I thought about the dozens, no, the hundreds of times I'd cheated on women with this exact protocol. I knew how to do it without getting caught. I was so fucking *good* at it. Who on Earth could fly two women to the same hotel in Tokyo, from two different continents, and have sex with them both for an entire week without getting caught? I could! I had done that! Who could go out at midnight in Madrid while his girlfriend was asleep in their hotel room and meet a British girl in a bar and take her back to the same hotel and get blown in a broom closet?

I could! I was a Zen master of infidelity. I was untouchable. I spoke a language no one else had ever even heard of.

I drank my bourbon. I was about to get married, but I wasn't married yet. The pills were beginning to melt in my hand. I needed to swallow them and get this thing rolling. The Comedian's friend was pretty and thin. I could have them both. Isn't that the way to go out just before getting married? I'd have my own private bachelor party with two women and pills and blow, and Christa would never know.

I thought of Christa. I thought of the family we talked about raising one day. I thought about my children respecting their father.

I ordered an ice water.

I dropped the pills on the floor and crushed them with my boot. I crushed them and crushed with them everything I hated about my past and myself.

I said to the Comedian, "I'll be back in fifteen. Gotta run an errand."

CHRISTA'S FRIENDS HAD canceled on her and she was home. We talked about our marriage plans. We trimmed our Christmas tree and talked about the rest of our lives together.

A MASSIVE SNOWSTORM hit the night of the twenty-sixth and shut much of the city down. But Mayor Bloomberg knew that marriage was good revenue for the city and the show at the Marriage Bureau went on on the morning of the twenty-seventh.

I wore a black pin-striped suit, a white shirt, and a pink tie. Christa wore a cream dress and she looked like a fierce pale bird. When I said yes, I knew that I would be married to this woman forever. We were married. We had a wedding lunch at Lupa with friends and family. We walked around the West Village together in the snow. We bought champagne on Seventh Avenue and walked around the city, drinking champagne from the bottle, married.

It is that simple.

FOUR DAYS LATER, on New Year's Eve, up in the cabin in Mount Tremper, I made short ribs for dinner. A little before midnight I stepped out to grab some firewood and to pull in a bottle of champagne that I'd buried in the snow. When I reentered the cabin, Christa was sitting on the couch. She had a surprised and delighted and terrified look on her face. She stood up and walked toward me, holding what looked like a thermometer in one hand.

She said, "Sweetheart, I think I'm pregnant."

I said, no; I screamed, "Amazing!"

She began to cry sweetly and she fell into my arms and she said, "Oh my god, baby, we are going to be parents. We're going to have a beautiful baby."

My body shook, my entire body shook, and I held Christa close, and I said, "You will be a beautiful mommy. You will be the best mommy in the world. That will be our lucky baby."

THE NEXT DAY we went to see a movie. We were still in shock, but after having tried three more tests the night before, we were pretty certain that she was pregnant. But just in case, Christa took another one in the bathroom at the theater. It, too, was positive. We watched *The Fighter*.

12

Fairfield to Aspen, Getting the Venom Out, March 2011

My father's home is a mess, not in terms of clutter or food waste, or dust, for he has a cleaning lady he employs occasionally to bring the place up to an acceptable level of cleanliness and even neatness. The home is a structural mess. It is a ranch home from the 1960s, and he bought it for less than one hundred thousand dollars in the nineties, and at the zenith of the 2000s housing bubble bankers and appraisers told him that it was worth many times what he paid for it, and he borrowed their money on that lie, and he kept borrowing, the way many people did back then. But what made my father a special case was that he was convinced he would never live to pay the money back. He considered these offers free money, and really, that's exactly what they should have been to a man in his mid-sixties with chronic lung failure who could not walk more than ten feet without using an oxygen tank. If the banks had been paying attention to the people they were loaning money to they would have looked at my father and said, "Wait, this man will never live to pay us back." But the beauty and stupidity of that money meant they did not look at dying men prior to loaning them large unrecoverable sums.

I'm certain my father intended to perform repairs on his

house with the proceeds from those loans. One night over Mexican food he drew on his napkin plans for attaching a second story, a penthouse of sorts that he planned to rent to businessmen. I'd grown up hearing my father's remodeling and adding-on fantasies, and sometimes they came true: on Vale Drive in Carmichael he added fifteen hundred square feet to the house one year—two bedrooms, a bathroom, and a family room. My mother dubbed our home in Tachikawa, Japan, the Winchester Mystery House: every few months my father would knock down a wall and build out another room or hallway. But usually his large-format plans remained mere fantasy.

Here in Fairfield he had replaced a toilet in the spare bathroom, and he ripped up the bathroom floor and he paid some day laborers to install a new bath and shower stall and a vanity.

A few moments after I arrived for this visit I made the mistake of stepping into the second bathroom to take a leak and I almost fell through the framing to the earth below. I looked at the disused bathroom, the manufacturer's labels still attached to the toilet and the vanity and the shower kit. My father had told me about this remodel months before. It's the kind of project that, when I was a kid, he would have banged out over a weekend.

On a Friday night he said to my mother, "Hey, Momma, how about we redo the kids' bathroom?" After *Dallas* he retreated to his office and drew plans. I helped out with some measurements. He awoke me early in the morning and I joined him on the materials run to Lumberjack.

The wet, woodsy, and thick smell of lumber and the pungent metallic bouquet of a box of nails will always bring forth for me the image of my father with a hammer in his hand, ready to build.

We bought everything he needed to redo the entire bathroom:

toilet, vanity, shower kit, tile and grout, mirror, and medicine chest. We ripped the bathroom apart with hammers and crowbars and then began the rebirth. By noon on Sunday my father was on his hands and knees, installing the tile. It was beautiful tile, Moorish in design. He skipped dinner. By the time Andy Rooney wrapped up *60 Minutes* my father had completed the bathroom redo. He was a master craftsman. That bathroom is where a few years later I would hide the major volumes of my pornography stash and do most of the masturbating of my teen years. I can never look at Moorish tile and not think of that bathroom and the thousands of hours I spent on my back on that cold tile floor masturbating to Ginger Lynn and cheerleaders and other girls I'd never have.

And here in Fairfield his bathroom had no floor. That my master-craftsman father had neither the strength nor the desire to finish the job distressed me. In fact it shamed me. Shouldn't I complete the work for him? I am the son that the master craftsman raised—shouldn't I have the skills to pick up my father's tools and finish the job? I am nearly the same age he was the weekend he refinished my boyhood bathroom. If I were a complete man, I'd pick up my father's tools and finish the job for him. But I am not a complete man. Once I sanded and painted a café tabletop two feet in diameter for the small terrace of my Manhattan apartment. That is the extent of my building experience in the past few decades.

I say to my father, "Dad, do you need a hand finishing up that bathroom? We have a few days before we leave for Aspen. If you've got the energy, you can supervise and I'll do the work."

He looks at me and laughs. "Ah, Tone, you used to be my best helper when you were a boy. But you got those soft writer hands now. I'll pick up some guys at the Home Depot and have them finish the job."

I wanted nothing more than to help my father finish his bathroom remodel. But I didn't push the issue.

My father had no energy for dinner out so I left him alone at his kitchen table and he listened to KGO on the radio.

There was not much to do in Fairfield. I went to a coffee shop and got online and tracked down a high school buddy who had been living nearby in Alameda for a few years. I finagled an invitation for tacos with his family that night.

I knew the East Bay freeways like the back of my hand. When I'd lived in Oakland for a lonely year after my divorce I spent many nights driving the 580 and the 880. There were two women I regularly slept with, Marin County and the counter girl from my optician, freeway-close the both of them. The Mercedes 320 had been an old man's car but still sleek and fast enough as I raced my libido around the East Bay trying to forget Sarah.

I PULLED UP to Danny's house in Alameda. Christa was home in New York, fourteen weeks pregnant, and Danny, a kid I had looked up to and admired all through high school, greeted me at the door, his wife and two daughters behind him, smiling.

Their condominium was piled high with the matériel of raising children: plastic jungle gym and play kitchen and bouncy chairs, dolls and books and dolls and toys that made noise. Danny opened his arms and took me in for a big hug—he was a heavyweight wrestler in high school, I wrestled 154s. He might have crushed a few of my ribs, but that was fine.

I had last seen him a few years before in LA. He'd drunk ginger ale and taken me around to music venues and later for chicken and waffles at Roscoe's. I'd met his wife briefly, but never his two daughters.

Danny prepared the taco meat and I drained a few beers while his daughters worked on homework at the dining table. I was forty years old and most of my cohorts had been at this parenthood game for a number of years, but my new wife was pregnant with our first child. This life Danny lived seemed like a television show I'd seen dozens of times, reels from a lifestyle I might never attain: *Lifestyles of the Happy and Stable.*

As Danny cut and then cooked steak he fielded his daughters' questions on California history and math. He interrogated them. A teacher himself, he wasn't about to feed the answers to the kids, no matter how sweetly they asked. A few important homework matters were settled, and we sat for dinner.

I remember that his girls were polite at the table, and that there was much laughter, and a lightheartedness that my childhood family table rarely achieved. Mother and father kidding with the children, the children kidding back. None of this was a show for me, the stranger. I ate too many tacos. I didn't want the fun to end. The girls were sent off to ready themselves for bed, and Danny and I headed out for a drink.

For Danny and his family I'd joined them for Tuesday Taco Night, no big deal, tacos, homework, and baths, but to me their routine resonated: *This happy life is possible.*

At the bar in town Danny had a ginger ale and I took a Manhattan. He was excited about the imminent birth of my daughter.

I said, "You have a beautiful family."

He said, "Growing up my family life was kind of a mess. I thought happy families happened elsewhere. But they happen wherever people want them to happen. My wife and I, we want a happy family, so we will have it, at all costs."

"It can't be that simple," I said.

"Dude. Christa will have your baby and then you will have the knowledge. Capital *K*. You will see that baby girl and you will understand. Capital *U*. And you will know it is that simple. You know how men fuck up their families? With their dicks! You've had your fun, motherfucker! Where'd it get you? Last summer you were living alone in a cabin in the Catskills!"

"That was my choice," I said.

"Don't tell me you wanted to be there."

"I needed to live there. I nearly killed myself in the city."

"You spent nearly an entire decade living the life!"

"You flatter me. You don't want to know how many nights I spent alone, and how many mornings I awoke, staring at the Empire State Building from my bed, thinking about what an awesome height that would be from which to jump."

"But you didn't jump! You wanted a wife to love and a baby. And you found the right woman. Just in time. She will have your baby daughter and you will have the knowledge. Someday you'll tell me I was right about how simple it all became."

I dropped Danny at home and headed back toward my father's house in Fairfield. I got lost trying to find my way out of Alameda, and before finding the freeway I drove around the island for twenty minutes, at the posted speed limit of twenty-five. I inspected the neighborhoods. Many of the homes were grand, and if they were not grand they were modest in an orderly and respectable way. A man raising his family here in Alameda would feel safe and responsible. Simply driving the roads made me feel like a respected member of society.

IN THE MORNING I awoke on my father's couch with an aching back and the unshakable need to hold my wife. She'd flown home from

227

our LA vacation four days earlier. Since our third date we'd never spent more than a few nights apart. I felt like a schoolboy separated from his summer camp love. In every other relationship I'd ever been in, other than my first marriage, this kind of distance and time away from the lover would have meant that I would be waking up with some other woman and telling the girlfriend lies about where I was and where I was going, what that noise in the background was, and even which continent I'd called from.

What a pleasure to wake up at seven a.m., sober, and to call my wife in New York and tell her *Hello*, and *Good morning*, and *I love you*, and to tell her that my back hurt from sleeping on my dad's shitty couch. We checked in about our day, the POD, we called it, military jargon, the Plan of the Day. I told her that today finally my father and I planned to depart. He'd put our departure date off a few times, but the day before, his fresh oxygen supply had arrived and he had no more excuses. And if we didn't leave sometime today I'd have to cancel the driving portion of the trip altogether and fly to Aspen alone in order to attend the disabled veterans' sports clinic.

We talked about the baby in her womb. We'd been calling her the Baby Animal. The Baby Animal is hungry. The Baby Animal wants to disco. The Baby Animal wants to hear her favorite Wallace Stevens poems before she goes to bed.

I said, "I love you, sweetheart, and I love the Baby Animal. I'll call you from the road. Goodbye."

THE OTHER BIG RV trips had ended with me seriously considering patricide. Why on Earth would this trip be any different? The elevation? Why another trip at all? It was true I needed to be in Aspen to teach a writing class to injured veterans, but I could've flown. None of the other RV trips had accomplished what they were supposed to: the Reconciliation—an unbreakable bond between father and son, bygones becoming bygones. The stakes were higher than during last year's trip because with my father the stakes increased every day his lung capacity decreased.

He always played his medical cards close to his chest, but with enough reading about his disease, and the right laser-accurate questions, I surmised that his lungs were at 20 to 25 percent capacity, meaning that while most healthy breathers inspired and expired 150 milliliters of air per breath, what is called tidal volume, my father subsisted on about thirty milliliters. If my father challenged an Olympic sprinter to a fifty-yard dash it would be like a drag race between a 1970 riding lawn mower and a 2011 Ferrari.

My father sat at his dining room table and tuned up his lungs: the terrible coughing, the inhaled medicines, the gurgling and spitting, the very prolonged and agonizing sound of his lungs opening for partial business.

I loaded the RV with my suitcase and his clothing, and some of the prepared foods he subsists on: microwavable food-like items such as shells and cheese, and chili, and dry items like crackers with peanut butter paste and sweet buns. What exactly are sweet buns? I wondered. After reading the ingredients I decided it's better not to know.

As befits a former Southern Baptist turned lapsed Catholic, my father liked his rituals. He also respected machines and the process of prepping the machine. This machine, this massive Winnebago, needed a lot of mojo, and oil and fuel, and as far as I could tell from the trips I'd taken with him, an infusion of good luck.

My father would not allow his Winnebago to budge an inch without preventive maintenance.

I knew that it drove my father crazy that I was not as attuned as he to the finer mechanical details of the vehicle. He thought of the Winnebago as his castle. After logging in my two thousand plus miles I considered it a dilapidated blue tarp on the fringe of a homeless encampment. It's true that the beast had cost nearly two hundred thousand dollars. But to me the RV trips seemed like very expensive camping excursions. I'd done the math and we'd have been financially better off in a Prius, stopping every night at a roadside budget motel for a shower and some actual sleep. We could have bunked in the occasional Four Seasons or Ritz and still maintained a tighter budget. But RVs and boats share this: only the owner of the vessel can truly understand its beauty and perfection. And RVs, just like boats, are always breaking down.

But I needed this trip. I wanted something: I wanted that Reconciliation.

I began to think of the RV as a truth machine, a narrative machine, like a photo booth but better—a story booth. The story of my father. And I realized that he, too, must feel this way: story equals truth and truth equals forgiveness. Driving along America's roads on each trip we talked, and our mouths were spades, digging toward truth. He wanted me to forgive him and he wanted to go back to the beginning of time. It was naïve of me not to have recognized that part of my father's RV dream, his desire for constant motion, was the wish to slow life down inside that machine, to stop time, to stop the decline of his health, to stop his aging, even to stop his own death and the death of his family.

"Drive faster, drive farther, and you will cure all that ails you," I can hear him telling himself. And "You might even bring Jeff back to life."

He handed me the maintenance list:

Install and secure oxygen tanks.
Check engine oil.
Check coolant level.
Check transmission fluid level.
Check water level on house batteries.
Check house water (shower and toilet).
Check generator oil (vehicle must be level).
Install and secure oxygen tanks.

My father didn't notice that he'd listed the oxygen tanks twice. If I had needed those things in order to breathe I'd have listed them three times.

I performed the duties mostly as directed and a few hours later we hit the road. We decided to take the southern route because a storm was heading straight toward the Sierras.

There is much American romance made of the Road. And I have driven much of that romanticized American Road and I'd say that if you are not on coastal Highway 1 in California, or certain blank desert stretches of Utah, or a length of coast along Biloxi, or certain mountain roads in Colorado and Montana, most of what greets you on American roads is intended to bore you with mind-crushing familiarity.

Other than about twenty miles of the Tehachapi Pass, where the southern Sierras and the Tehachapi Mountains meet, the distance of road on the southern route between Fairfield, California, and Las Vegas, Nevada, is so boring you must bang your head against your steering wheel in order to remain awake.

We left Fairfield so late that we arrived at the Tehachapi Pass in darkness. I knew that beyond the windows existed a rather awesome landscape that I'd miss on this trip.

I was tired, and I said to my father, "I need some jalapeños."

"Some what?"

"If you want me to keep driving I'm going to need some jalapeños to stay awake."

"That's just plain crazy, Tone. Whatever happened to a cup of coffee?"

"Coffee won't do it. And I'm nostalgic. It's how I used to stay awake when heading back to base late at night on a Sunday from a long weekend in Los Angeles."

"Well, let's load up on fuel and jalapeños," he said.

We did just that and pushed toward Vegas.

MANY HOURS LATER as we drove through town and saw the city throwing its garish light against the sky, my dad said, "Vegas. That's a place where a man can find some trouble."

I nodded while doing my best to keep our massive metal coffin on the road. I thought of my week in the hotel suite and the various kinds of trouble and destruction I had invited along for the party. I shuddered.

I said, "I came very close to killing myself there once or twice."

"How's that, Tone?" he asked, and sat up in his seat. My father was always game for a good self-destruction story, especially if the self was mine.

"You don't need to know. In the same way that I never needed to know about your sexual exploits in Vietnam and Taiwan, you don't need to know about my adventures in Vegas."

"Goddamn, Tone, you brought it up. My son says he almost killed himself somewhere I want to know the story. Ain't that fair?"

"I have no idea what is fair and what is not. I don't care about fair. Fair means nothing."

"Hell, what's the wrong with me trying to live vicariously through my own son? I don't got the plumbing anymore. You do. You can screw all the gals you want."

"No I can't. Nor do I want to. I'm married."

"You got a nice wife, Tone. But you can at least tell your papa some of your old carousing stories. Someday you'll want to relive them."

"You're wrong. That's the difference between the two of us."

"You like to talk about our differences, don't you?" he said.

From the tone of his voice I knew I'd hurt him, and a part of me enjoyed it. I couldn't beat the old man with my fists but I could rough him up with words.

He said, "Look in the mirror, Son. There are very few differences between us."

"Sometimes all I see is differences. It's hard not to."

"You were a dirty dog, Tone. I was a dirty dog. You got it from me. I'm not ashamed to say it."

I thought of what Danny had said in Alameda the night before.

"Let me tell you one difference between us. You got married young and you were unfaithful to your wife and thus your young children and the life of your family. I did all of my fucking around in my thirties, without a wife or child. It wasn't even fucking around. I was living the life of a man in a large city inhabited by many beautiful women. The numbers were in my favor. But I'm married now. In six months my wife is having our first baby. I'm a different man than you. I'll respect my wife and the life and sanctity of my family. I'm not so stupid as to fuck it all up with my zipper."

At this point my rage and derision for my father were so heightened that I thought I just might run us off the road. But I couldn't think of what this kind of death would be called. Death by misadventure? That's how dear old drunk Malcolm Lowry went. But no, on the contrary, this would be pure adventure. I supposed they'd have to call it a homicide/suicide by Winnebago. Right here in Vegas, a Winnebago homicide/suicide. They might talk about that one for a while, at least until an escort went missing in the desert.

"I can't talk to you when you're like this," my father said. "You're totally unreasonable."

He had a point. I was, after all, considering ending his life and mine by running our tin can off the road. It didn't matter that while growing up he was the most unreasonable person I knew and I'd been forced to live with him for nearly two decades. Why was I still unable to get over events like him shoving my face in dog shit? Or, in his version, *toward* dog shit? What is the difference, in terms of the psychic wound, in shoving a small boy's face *toward* rather than *in* dog shit? I'd say the difference is nil.

I ran atop some of the road Braille and it made the staccato sound of gunfire.

He said, "Please drive safely."

From the freeway I noticed the signage for a famous strip club.

I pointed and said, "One night I spent five thousand dollars at that strip club."

"That's more money than most folks make in a month. We all know where that got you, smart guy."

Any time I mentioned my profligate spending he turned quiet with rage. I wanted him to shut up for the next thousand miles or so and this might do the trick.

Moab was about five hundred miles away and I knew that the sooner we made it there the sooner we'd make it to Aspen and I could escape this RV and check in to my hotel, and shower, and drink some bourbon with my veteran friends and relax.

I was aware that I'd started the journey with my father only about eight hours ago, and that the journey is supposed to be the point, and that I had things I wanted to extract from my father during this trip—I wanted him to apologize for not attending my brother's funeral, but at this point I couldn't stand the man. The hatred I felt for my father at this moment rivaled the hatred I'd felt for Ava at the worst of our relationship, when she called me from a hotel in Miami, high on cocaine, to tell me she was about to sleep with a man she'd just met.

Maybe it sounds strange to compare a father to a lover, but it isn't, really. All family love is also a romance, and every romance suffers. And my romance with my father had been suffering greatly since approximately the day my brother had been buried thirteen years earlier and my father had decided not to show up. Goddamn, I hated the man for that. That is a long time to hate your father. To stomach this hate any longer just might kill me, I knew. But parts of me loved the hate.

I needed to calm down. I felt the stress coursing through my neck and across my shoulders and down my spine. It felt as if my spine were in a vise, and with each mile we traveled the vise tightened.

I said, "How far do you want to make it tonight?"

"As far as you can go, Tone."

"Why don't I try to make it all the way to Moab? We can check out the Arches first thing in the morning."

"Damn, Tone. That's near eight more hours down the road. You can make that? Don't kill us."

"I'll see what I can do."

"Maybe you need some more of them jalapeños?"

I did not need jalapeños. The adrenaline that my rage at my father produced might keep me awake for days.

He said, "I think I'll try for some shut-eye if you don't mind."

"Not a bit, Dad. I'll see you in the morning."

He stood and steadied himself. The RV shook and rattled. My father's oxygen cord hung and swung in unison with my rhythm on the road. The noise the oxygen tank produced always haunted me, the mechanical breath it forced down into my father's lungs sounded like a tire slowly deflating. He retired to the back cabin.

I drove on through the desert. Occasionally I passed a big rig. I blasted through the desert like a massive comet rumbling toward the Earth. My father never allowed me to take the RV up over sixty-five without a stern admonition about safety and gas mileage. But now he was asleep in the back and the road and the desert and the RV were all mine. I felt like a teenager. I thought of the night I took out his 1970 Impala, a monster of a car with a sickeningly fast engine for its time. I picked up two friends and we drag-raced all over the suburban sprawl where we lived. I beat a Mustang and a Camaro and I lost to a Corvette. When I pulled into the driveway at five a.m. I ran over our mailbox. That one had been difficult to explain.

But here in the desert my father was in the back cabin and there was no one to explain anything to. I hadn't driven over one hundred miles per hour since I'd busted up my BMW in Germantown. The beastly RV was no one's idea of a race car, but one hundred miles per hour felt the same in your stomach whether you did it on a motorcycle, in a BMW, or from the command post of an RV. Any slight wrong move and it was all over. I saw visions of the RV busting into thousands of pieces all over the desert. They'd need the NTSB to figure out what the hell had happened.

I slammed the accelerator to the floor. The V-12 engine screamed and whined, and our massive tin shell hurtled across the desert. The turtle and his son are on the move.

Everything in the rig shook and rattled: I thought the TV above my head was going to fall out of its carousel. This was the earthquake I wanted. I heard my father's metal oxygen canisters rubbing up against one another, a shrill, nervous sound. The refrigerator door slammed open and food spilled all over the floor. I knew that in the back of the cabin my father was being thrown all over the bed like a cowboy riding the fiercest bull at the county fair. I was the fiercest bull. I made it to ninety-five miles per hour. The big beast disappointed me and refused to be pushed faster. I kept it at ninety-five for twenty miles.

I blew by big rigs and minivans and a yellow Porsche. The Porsche driver must have felt emasculated because a few minutes later he tore past me like a rocket; he must have hit 130. How I wished I were driving that Porsche.

I PULLED INTO Moab at about seven in the morning and my father continued to sleep. I parked at a gas station. The cabin of the RV was a total mess: tools and boxes of food and oxygen tanks were strewn all over the floor. I'd clean it later.

I stepped out. My road exhaustion heightened all my senses. The smell of a desert town early in the morning is unlike any other—damp smoky earth and history and the mountains on fire from the sun. I'm rarely up this early. It made me feel that I was a part of society.

I stepped across the street to support the local economy by purchasing a cup of coffee and a breakfast burrito at a café. The clientele were a mix of tough construction workers wearing Carhartt, tar, and mud, and young carefree outdoorsy people in neon fleece and hemp products. I wore flip-flops, food-stained jeans, and a red-and-blue plaid flannel shirt I'd bought for three dollars at a truck stop a few hours before. A handful of swishy elderly British men sporting brand-new walking shoes and smart sweaters snickered and judged us all for our sartorial calamities.

I entered the RV and my father was bent over the sink, taking one of his inhalers, doing the morning routine of tuning up the lungs. He looked at me as though I were an intruder. He was in white briefs and a white T-shirt, his Uniform of the Day. He'd worn this ensemble every morning of his adult life. His white hair looked Einsteinian. His blue eyes shone wild. He could not speak during the administration of this medicine. He wanted so badly to speak. He held up a finger in the air, telling me to wait. I knew this gesture from my childhood. It meant "Stand by for your punishment."

He gestured around the room at the mess that my racing had caused, and shrugged his shoulders and frowned. I liked this game. I shrugged back and moved to the front of the cab and sat down to call Christa.

We talked about the Baby Animal. Christa had never been to Utah. I described to her the beautiful landscape and the sensation that one was not only in another state but also on another planet. I promised to take photos at the park.

My father said, "What the hell kind of mess is this, Tone? It looks like we got robbed."

"I hit some rough road last night, Pops."

"That wasn't just rough road. Utah's got good road. How the hell fast were you going? You damn near knocked me out of bed."

"I got her up to seventy-five," I said.

"I think you're lying to me, Son. How goddamn fast did you go? Jesus, my oxygen canisters all came loose. You coulda blown us sky-high."

"Eighty, Pops. That's all she'd go."

"Can you clean it up? I thought you said seventy-five?"

It took me about half an hour to tighten and tidy the place. I went back across the street and bought my dad a burrito. And finally we headed to Arches National Park.

I admired how much a fan of national parks my father was. He aimed to see as many of them as possible before he died. When I was a kid our road trips always included a national park or two. I'd always thought it was because my dad was too cheap to pay for other family entertainment—sporting events, a deep-sea fishing trip, a house on the beach for a week. And money might have been a part of his motivation. But later I realized what a fine education in the natural riches of the country we'd received on trips to the parks. It was also for my father a point of patriotism: *Look at what belongs to our country.* At a visceral level, as a veteran of a foreign war, he felt a bit of personal ownership of these parks: *I fought for this, I saw men die for this.*

I dropped my dad in front of the visitor center and parked the RV out by the big rigs. Moab was at four thousand feet and I noticed the elevation already affecting him. Once we got to Aspen we'd be near eight thousand.

The desert sun beat down hard on my face as I walked through the parking lot. My dad had not made it far, only about fifteen feet toward the door. He leaned against a bronze sculpture of a bighorn sheep.

"Goddamn, Tone," he said, shaking his head. "Lord, what I'd do for a new set of lungs."

Seeing my father incapacitated out in the world was a totally different experience from seeing him stuck in his RV. In his RV he ran the show—all his meds, his oxygen, his timers, his potions, his magic, were available, and the disease seemed manageable. But under the intense winter desert sun, in front of the visitor center, he looked weak and small. I wanted my father the mountain cat to take down that bighorn sheep, but all he could do was lean against the bronze sculpture and pray to the Lord for a different set of lungs.

My rage at my father melted.

Strangers stared at my father and his oxygen contraption. I hated the strangers for staring. And I'll admit I was ashamed of his disease, the stupidest disease a man could possibly come down with, COPD. It could have been the flight line chemicals he spent decades around, but most likely he did it to himself by smoking for forty-five years. What a stupid goddamn disease and what a stupid man. My father was sixty-nine years old, and other than his failing lungs, the man was an ox. With healthy lungs he would have lived to be a hundred.

We drove north through the park, up Park Avenue, and

frightened other road warriors with our bulk. At every viewing point we pulled the beast over and I got out of the rig and hiked as near as I could to a rock formation and took pictures. I snapped the Organ and the Three Gossips and the Tower of Babel. Snapped the Petrified Dunes and Ham Rock and Balanced Rock and the Garden of Eden.

At the Windows Section I had to take a proper hike to make it to the sights. It was hot enough that I took a bottle of water with me.

"Be safe, Tone," my father said.

I walked out into the desert because my father could not. I looked at the groups of friends and families on their way back to their vehicles, laughing and carrying on as friends and families do. I felt robbed. In my twenties, before my brother died and while my father and I still enjoyed a loving relationship, I had dreamed someday of family vacations like this—a healthy group of Swoffords heading to a splendid sight in Yosemite or Yellowstone, my father hiking with my family and me.

But at the Arches I walked alone. Christa sat at home in Brooklyn writing her own book about her own dysfunctional family, and my father sat in his RV, a half mile away from me, taking his meds and asking the Lord for a new set of lungs.

The Windows are an impressive rock formation. I took some snaps. I walked as far from the crowd as I could and looked out on the desert. In the end, the Windows and the Tower of Babel and all the rest of them are just rocks. Someday gravity and erosion will do their work and these massive formations, too, will be dust. But the desert will remain a large expanse of nothingness and everything.

I took my time walking back to the RV. My father's illness had transformed him from a man of constant action and movement into a man who might die from too much action and movement.

"How's it look?" he asked.

"Looks like a rock with massive holes. Good stuff."

To our west was another formation, and I decided that we must have at least a few photos with my father and me present. I stood my father up against an old ranch fence and took his picture with a beautiful expanse of desert and towering massive red rocks in the background. I ordered him to smile, and he did offer a big smile. His oxygen tube was wrapped around his face, and his Einstein hair blew wildly in the wind and he looked happy. My old sick father leaning against the wooden ranch fence with towering massive red rocks in the background looked handsome and even beautiful. I switched spots with him and he snapped my picture. I suppose I could have used the timer and taken a shot with us both in it but it didn't cross my mind. I'm sure that someday I'll regret that.

We made our way out of the park to grab lunch in Moab. By the time we hit the road it was almost six. I knew a storm would hit Aspen overnight and I wanted to arrive by midnight so I could get the keys to my room. My friend Dan, who had my keys, would be crashed out if I arrived any later. I hadn't showered since we left Fairfield. I wanted a shower and a fire in a fireplace and a few shots of bourbon. And none of those things were available in the RV.

AN HOUR OR SO out of Moab my father said, "We need to empty the septic. If we get on up that mountain and all that shit freezes it'll be a goddamn nightmare. You want your old man to shit in an icebox?"

"Shit freezes?" I asked. "When was the last time you emptied that thing?" I'd been careful to take toilet breaks on land.

"Hell, Tone. I don't know the last time I emptied it. Three or four months ago? Not since your mom and I went to Mexico. We gotta empty it. It'll ramp up our gas mileage heading up the mountain."

Outside Grand Junction my dad saw a sign denoting a septic dump at the next rest stop.

We pulled into the stop. Some weekend ATVers were dumping from their small camper trailer. It was a man and his young son. The kid must have been ten or twelve and the guy was my age. I watched as the man instructed the son on how to pull the septic tube from the rear bumper of the trailer and then do the dump.

They pulled away and I pulled our rig into the spot.

My father said, "I think I need to get out for this, Tone."

"Are you serious? Dad, I'm mildly educated. I can figure out how to dump the shit out of your RV. It can't be rocket science."

"I have my system. If you don't follow my system this time then next time the system will be totally fucked."

"The system is called gravity. Your septic system is above the dump. I attach the tube and open the lever and God or whatever you want to call it does the rest. If a twelve-year-old kid can do it, so can I."

"That was a very rudimentary system they were running on that rig. You see that thing? That was from the eighties at the earliest."

"Gravity barely changed from the eighties to today."

"I've got my system, Tone. I'd appreciate it if you follow it."

This displeased me greatly. It would take my father twenty

minutes just to walk around to the other side of the RV, and then if I was dumping the shit at his slow and meticulous pace, this could take us hours. The storm was coming and the last thing I wanted to do was spend another night in this RV, or even at a Motel 6 in Glenwood Springs at the bottom of the mountain.

It turned out that my father's septic system was slightly more complex than what the ATVers before us had sported. There was a red tube for evacuating the system, a black tube for washing the system out, and a white tube for refilling the entire system with new water. My father directed me throughout. I had flashbacks to my boyhood and receiving instruction from my father on how to change the oil on a car or how to roof a house or how to run a hot wire from a breaker box. I suppose these are skills that a boy should learn from his father, but ultimately my father's lesson plans included a major dose of his anger and my humiliation when I didn't complete a task exactly as he'd detailed.

In order to stay sane while following my father's directions for flushing the septic system, I fantasized Jack Rebney of *Winnebago Man* fame. Rebney became known for the profanity-laden outtakes from a 1980s Winnebago instructional video he'd recorded. I turned my father's directions into Rebneyesque insanity:

What you've got here, you fucking fuck, is your basic septic fucking system that moves your sick shit from your asshole down into the toilet on this piece-of-shit fucking Winnebago. See those goddamn flies? The flies are here because you are a lazy fucking prick and you waited four months to empty your fucking feces from the goddamn Winnebago. The issue here is not the fucking Winnebago but you, the asshole who drives the Winnebago and thinks he can shit in it endlessly, as though this is a goddamn toilet at Yankee fucking Stadium. Your fucking Winnebago, I see you got the thirty-four-footer because you didn't have the fucking balls to buy a forty-footer, so your fucking thirty-four-footer won't carry as much of your putrid shit so now you must ask me, Jack Rebney, the Winnebago Man, how to empty your shit store, right? Well, what the fuck do you want from me? Do you want me to get down on my fucking hands and knees here in Grand fucking Junction, Colorado, and empty your shit for you? I guess you do, you lazy fucking prick. So here we go: the 2008 Winnebago has a holding tank that holds what we call the fucking gray water, which comes from your kitchen, where you wash your dishes, and from your sinks and shower, when by some fucking chance you wash your rotten fucking ass. There is also the black water, which, no shit, is the water in which your shit and piss are held. It is important to never cross-contaminate the hoses. If you do this you are a stupid fuck and you deserve dysentery or whatever fucked-up third-world disease you get because you are fucking stupid. So now you have emptied the gray and the black water and you, fucking numbnuts, have managed to spill some shit and piss on the sleeve of your flannel, and how does that feel to have your parents' shit and piss spilled on your flannel fucking shirt? That's payback for all the times you shot shit and piss out of your goddamn diaper and all over your loving parents when your numbnuts were the size of fucking raisins. Now you attach the fucking white hose to the tank and fill it up with non-potable water. *Non-potable* means you cannot fucking drink it, so don't be a dumbass and drink from the fucking sink in your fucking thirty-four-foot Winnebago. Don't even use that water to brush your fucking crooked and rotten teeth. So now that this bullshit took you almost an hour, you better hurry the fuck up or that storm is going to catch your stupid ass and you'll be sitting at the bottom of the mountain sleeping in this fucking piece-of-shit recreational vehicle while all your friends relax in their very nice ski condominiums. So don't be an asshole. Get the fuck out of my face.

WE PULLED INTO the village at Snowmass, above Aspen, around two in the morning. My friend Dan was incommunicado, so that meant I'd be spending one more night in the RV with my father.

We found a good parking spot in the rodeo grounds parking lot. I made a few bags of microwave popcorn and my father and I sat at the kitchenette table and drank beer.

Snow began to fall in big clumps. At eight thousand feet my father had serious trouble breathing. He could speak only a few dozen or so words before needing to catch his breath.

He asked me, "I gotta know, Tone. How long is it gonna be before you get this venom out? This is our third trip. That's a lot of goddamn gas. And you still seem pissed off at me. I don't know what you want."

"I want to know what happened in Vietnam. I want to know why you cheated on my mother. I want to know why you didn't go to Jeff's funeral."

"My answers are never good enough for you, Tone."

"How many times did you cheat on my mother?"

"I don't know."

"Ten?"

"I have no idea."

"Twenty?"

"I have no idea."

"Thirty?"

My father shook his head. He pounded his arm, karate-chop style, against the table. "You sound like a fucking lawyer. 'Would it be between five and ten, or ten and fifteen?' Does Vietnam count?"

"Vietnam doesn't count," I said.

"Vietnam don't count." He chopped at the table. "Does Taiwan count?"

"No."

"Taiwan don't count. Does Texas count?"

"Texas counts," I said.

He frowned. "Texas counts. Does Spain count?"

"Spain counts."

"Spain counts. Does Germany count?"

"Germany counts."

"Does Copenhagen count?"

"No."

"Copenhagen doesn't count." This pleased my father.

He twirled his oxygen line and thought about Copenhagen. With the backs of his fingers he scratched the beard on his neck in an upward sweeping motion exactly the way I do. He must have appreciated the freebie I'd given him. His marine brother was dying in a hospital in Copenhagen when he visited. That means while his brother died in a nearby hospital and his wife and two infant children were alone in Seville my father was in his hotel room banging some girl he met in a Copenhagen bar.

"Does Japan count?" he asked, somewhat hopefully, I could tell.

"Yes."

"Japan counts." He exhaled heavily, defeated. I could see him in some dim Shinjuku sex parlor. Who knows, he might have taken me with him and had the mama-san watch over me while he took care of business in the back. I wouldn't put it past him.

He asked, "Does Guam count?"

"No."

"Does Okinawa count?"

"No."

"I don't understand your logic, Tone. No on Copenhagen but yes on Tokyo?"

"Combat deployments don't count and cities where your brother is dying don't count. I assume you went through Guam and Okinawa on your way to Vietnam."

"That's correct. Does Hawaii count?"

This was a tough one. My father took leave from Vietnam in Hawaii and my mother met him there. I was conceived on this trip.

"Yes, Hawaii counts."

"OK. I don't remember anything."

"That's good work, Dad. I think it qualifies you as a pussy hound."

He paused. He let my compliment soak in. He glanced at me and looked away. Now he wasn't certain whether it was a compliment or not. He took the barrel-chest pose, hands on his knees, attempting to open up his chest as wide as possible. Physiologically this did nothing, but it must have helped psychologically: *If I open my chest as wide as possible to the world, the world will offer more oxygen.*

He said, "When I was stationed there in Moses Lake, Washington, we'd head to Spokane on weekends." He chopped at the table a few times. "That university there, Gonzales?"

"Gonzaga."

"Gonzaga. It was a good pussy town, Spokane was. We'd go down to the lakes. That's where the girls hung out. This was before I married your mother. We met a lot of girls. Back on base one Monday morning, I worked for two German civilians on a roofing crew. I pulled into the warehouse where we worked. One of the old Germans pointed at me and then pointed at my car and he said, 'You are *Scheidenjäger.*' And I said, 'What?' And he pointed at my car. 'There are panties hanging from your bumper. *Scheidenjäger.* You are pussy hunter.' From then on I was known as the Pussy Hunter."

That was my father's explanation for decades of infidelity: *I am pussy hunter.*

I won't lie. A part of me liked this characterization. Virility is intoxicating, and virility in one's father means the gene has been passed down. My father was a very handsome young man, and I like to think of him scoring women all over the world, why not? But he was also a married man and my mother's husband, and a cheating bastard.

I looked out the window. Over a foot of snow had fallen and I couldn't see five feet beyond the RV. On the radio they said we might get eight feet overnight.

"I don't know what to say, Dad. You lived an amorous life that some would envy and others would despise. It's hard to listen to one's pussy-hunter father detail his worldwide pussy-hunting exploits. I don't know what to do with it."

"I always loved your mother. This was never about you kids

or your mother. The world was different back then. Men were different. What qualified as acceptable behavior was different."

"Maybe I've wanted to know too much."

"Then it's my turn, there are some things I want to know, too. Like why all you want to do is talk about our differences. Makes me think you are afraid of our likenesses. Look in the mirror. Look at your nose and your chin. Your eyes. Look at your hairline. You are Swofford. You got Swofford blood, boy. You can't change that. You ran all around the world and fucked all the girls you wanted, just like your old man."

"I wasn't married."

"OK. Next question. Why did you ignore your Granny when she wanted to give you a medal from the Daughters of the Confederacy?"

"This again? Give it up."

"You got your questions, I got mine. Now answer me. I'm genuinely interested to know."

"I didn't want a medal from a neo-racist organization. Fuck the Daughters of the Confederacy. I did not grow up in the South. I don't care about the DOC. It's a bunch of old racist white ladies holding on to bullshit ideas about why the South got their asses kicked in the war."

"Now you not only disrespect your Southern heritage but you disrespect your blood."

"I have no emotional link to the old dead Swofford Confederates whose gravestones Granny shines."

"You're pushing me, Son. You got Swofford blood. My great-great-grandfather Solomon Willis Swofford fought for the Confederacy. You got linkage whether you like it or not."

I thought, *You want me to push you, old man?*

I said, "You care more about those Swofford Confederate gravestones than you do about Jeff's. You didn't attend your own son's funeral. You disgraced yourself and your entire family."

My father and I have been having this fight off and on since shortly after Jeff died. I'm like a pack of hyenas at a felled buffalo. And when I'm done with that I want another. And now give me another.

I say, "What happens if I die tomorrow? Will you show up? Or will you stay home and get drunk alone and cry in the corner rather than show your face? Is that how you'll show your love?"

When my father is extremely angry, at his angriest, he gets very quiet, deathly quiet, and his face looks ghost-white, and the anger sparks off his face like micro-explosions. I know that if he were capable he would try to beat me physically right now. I know that he would like to beat me down into the ground with the same force and remorselessness with which I would like to ruin him.

He cleared his throat. "You will never understand what it was like for me to lose my firstborn son. There are no words. You will never understand. I couldn't handle it. And I won't apologize for how I behaved. It was all I could do. Goddamn, Son, how many times I have to tell you? Wait until Christa has your baby. Then ask me that question again."

"All you could do after your thirty-five-year-old son died was drive around to the same shitty GI bars in Fairfield where you'd been drinking for thirty years? Did those people offer you solace? Where are they now that you can barely breathe or walk? You think they care about you? What did they offer you then? A couple of free rounds because your son died? Your family was there in Georgia, in your hometown, grieving for your son. I was there. Kim and Tami were there. We grieved for our brother. All of your brothers and sisters were there grieving for their nephew. Mom was there. Mom. The woman who gave birth to him. You want to pull some hierarchy of grieving bullshit? OK. The woman who gave birth to Jeff sat in the room with him the night he died. She read his Bible to him and she listened to him expel his last breath. And she attended his funeral. You lose."

I knocked the bowl of popcorn and the two empty beer cans off the table.

"You cheated on your wife, you mentally and occasionally physically abused your children. One of your sons died and you didn't go to his funeral. You can't guarantee that you'd go to my funeral. I know your mother died when you were a month old, and I know that fucking sucked, Dad, I can't think of a sadder way to grow up than carrying that horrible knowledge with you. And I know your half brother died. And I know you watched people die heinous deaths in Vietnam. And I know that Jeff died. That is one shitstorm after another, but it gave you no excuse to treat your children the way you did."

My father was scared. I knew it. And I liked it. He looked anxious and he could barely breathe, the elevation had nearly knocked him out.

He said, "I need a Xanax, Tone. Can you hand me my meds?"

I handed him his meds backpack overflowing with medications. He shook while he looked through the bag for the right bottle. He shook one out and took it down with a gulp of water.

"The elevation. I didn't think about the elevation. I can barely breathe. Goddamn, Tone. I need those new lungs."

"I need an apology."

"I won't apologize no more, Tone. I'm done. I apologized a couple years ago about my behavior. I'm done. I don't know what else to tell you. I want to help you get the venom out. It'll kill you, Son."

"You never really apologized. You said that you understand that the way you treated us kids then would today be considered child abuse. That is not an apology. That is a finely crafted disavowal of responsibility."

I stood over my father now. He could barely breathe.

He said, "Get the venom out. Do you want to beat me? Do you want to kick my ass the way I once kicked your ass? Will that help? You can do it, if that'll help."

I ignored my father and walked to the back of the cabin. Yes, I did want to beat him; I wanted to grab him by his neck and shove his face in a pile of dog shit and tell him he was stupid and tell him he would never amount to shit, and I wanted to beat his face in, and bloody it, and I wanted to make him weep and cower the way he had once made me weep and cower. I felt sick to my stomach. I lay back on the bed and closed my eyes. I thought of Christa and the Baby Animal. I thought about the life we would live and the loving home we would build for the Baby Animal, without rancor, without violence, without hatred. But still I wanted to go to the front of the rig and beat my father.

And then the rig started to move. I looked out the window, and yes, we were on the move. My father had started to drive. The snow was up at about five feet now, it was deep, and it was four in the morning. I walked to the front of the cab.

I said to my father, "Where are you going?"

"I can't handle you anymore. I'm dropping you off. There is a bus stop down the road. You're such a big man. You can take your suitcase and get out of my rig. I can't be treated like this anymore. I can't help you. You can take your venom with you."

My father drove wildly through the massive and empty parking lot. He didn't know where he was going; he could barely see and he certainly couldn't see his way out.

"Goddamn it, Tone, how do I get out of here? Where is the exit?"

I stood above him, he in the captain's chair, speeding in circles around the huge snowy parking lot. The lot was the width of two football fields and he drove it like a madman, looking for an exit, but the lot hadn't been plowed and there was no way out. Cabinets banged open and food and tools flew about the back of the cabin in a reprisal of my show from the night before.

"Tell me how to get out. I want you out of my rig."

"You're going to kick me out of your RV at four in the morning in the middle of a blizzard? You do this and you might never see me again and you'll never see my daughter."

"You're a big man, Tone. You don't need your pop. You don't even like me."

He gunned it on a straightaway. Our tracks in the parking lot made it look as if we had our own little ice car race going on. When my father said that I didn't like him it was one of the worst things anyone had ever said to me. Because I did like him. Sometimes I didn't love him, and sometimes I hated him, but he was an immensely likable fellow, with a charming Southern accent and whiskey barrels full of engrossing and engaging stories, some of them far too bawdy for him to have told his son, but still, he had the stories and he had the charm and everyone loved my father. And I loved him and I even liked him. I didn't want to be him. I didn't want to be the kind of father that he had been. I hated him for not being a good role model. I hated him for not giving me a happy family history to tell. If I want to tell a story of longevity, and commitment, and happiness, I will have to make it my own. As he sped around the parking lot trying to find a way to evict me during the snowstorm, I loved my father more than I ever had before. I loved him for standing up to me and telling me to get rid of my venom. I loved him for showing me what kind of father not to be.

"Stop," I said. "Just stop the RV. You can't get out of the parking lot. If you want me out of here I'll walk up the hill. It's a mile to the lodge. I know where I am."

My father stopped the vehicle and slumped over the wheel.

"Goddamn, Son," he said. "I was not a perfect father. I am not a perfect man. But cut me some slack. I love you. I love your company. I love your fellowship. You are my son and I love you."

I dropped to my knees at my father's side and I put my hand on his back. I rubbed his back. I looked out the massive RV windshield and saw nothing but a thick white snowfall, a blanket of white. A purity and newness I'd never seen before.

"I'm not a perfect son. I love you, Dad. And I like your company, too. Let's get some sleep. Let's get over this."

WE SLEPT TOGETHER in the back of his RV in the queen-size bed. I hadn't slept in the same bed with my father since I was three or four years old. It took me a while to fall asleep. I was exhausted from fighting with my father and driving twelve hundred miles in a day and a half.

My father slept next to me in a deep quiet. The only sound in the world was his oxygen machine feeding him what he needed in order to live. The workings of the machine sounded like the distant whine of an airplane engine.

I thought of one of the few Vietnam stories my father ever told me. His unit was assigned to go deep in the bush and build landing strips for C-130 cargo planes. The planes were to land empty and leave full of evacuated villagers and the few belongings they could carry in their bare hands. It was a classic and totally absurd Vietnam tactic: if you bomb the entire infiltrated village to high heavens then there will no longer be a village for the Viet Cong to control. On one of these missions the timing was super tight. They had twenty minutes to evacuate the village and take off before the bombers arrived overhead to drop their loads.

They hustled the civilians onto the plane. The GIs were tense. There were probably VC among the villagers, there might be a guy with a grenade buried in his armpit, and the bombers might arrive early and blow them up, too. My father was at the rear of the plane, helping the last few villagers embark as the plane began to pull away. He got them all on and he hopped on the tongue. The sound of the engines was loud and violent. An old lady holding a scrawny chicken under each arm, everything in the world that she now owned, lurched as though she wanted to run back for something else. A photo of a child or a husband? It didn't matter; she couldn't go back. My father grabbed her around the waist and held her tight as the plane picked up speed, bouncing over the landing strip he'd built the day before. She screamed an animal scream and dug her old lady elbows into my father's ribs and her chickens made a racket and my father held tight as the plane gained altitude and the bombers began to drop their loads. My father and the woman watched as her village and her home were destroyed.

13

Oh Josephine

Christa and I wanted to bring our baby home to a stress-free environment. The stretch of Washington Avenue where we lived in Brooklyn did not qualify as such. I called it Little Kandahar. Most nights there were fistfights on the street; the occasional gunfight erupted nearby; once a car careened into the building; from the apartment window I'd witnessed a hit-and-run; and there were at least two men who patrolled the block in wheelchairs and aggressively panhandled and cursed and threatened physical violence against anyone who didn't hand over money.

A block away one might eat at one of the better Italian restaurants in the city and pay twenty-five dollars for a plate of pasta. This neighborhood was wildly popular with art students and kids just out of college working their first shitty jobs before they had to depart the city for Montgomery or wherever they'd come from. Also there were a lot of white creative types in their thirties and forties who had for a number of years reportedly been civilizing the place with their wit and vigor and children. I saw no indication of this.

I admitted that my years in Chelsea had blinded me to the

harsher realities of the outer boroughs and the inanities of the white creative class.

In early summer we moved full-time to Woodstock.

We spent the summer nesting. I painted the baby's room Persian Violet and we acquired all of the matériel required for the first six months of her life. We hiked and hung out at swimming holes that only locals knew. We made fun of the hipsters who visited the Catskills on the weekends.

In early September Christa's due date passed and we began to panic. She'd had a healthy pregnancy. Nothing indicated a problem birth, but her doctor talked about inducing her if she made it to a week past. Christa wanted a natural birth but she'd grown tired of pregnancy.

She said to her doctor, "Please get this baby out of me."

The doctor said, "We'll talk next week."

We continued to nest: now we painted the large main room of the house. I went to the gym twice a day. I cleaned out the gutters on the house. I swept the chimney. We walked the three-mile route along Upper Byrdcliffe Road where we lived. The baby sat on Christa's bladder like a queen on a throne, and our walks aggravated the situation. Christa learned how to squat at the side of the road and pretend to admire flowers when actually she was taking a pee.

We considered driving fifteen hundred miles to Tennessee so she'd be certain to have the baby naturally at The Farm, the birthplace of contemporary American midwifery. But we realized we'd have to drive home that same fifteen hundred miles with a newborn and that seemed cruel to everyone involved.

There had been talk of castor oil to induce a natural labor, an old trick of the midwives. All tricks have believers and naysayers:

the believers said, *Go for it*, while the naysayers said, *Enjoy sitting on your toilet for a day or two.*

We'd heard of a restaurant in Georgia where they guaranteed that at your due date or beyond you'd go into labor within twenty-four hours of eating their eggplant Parmesan. Christa wanted a dozen servings delivered express.

One afternoon I stopped by the butcher and decided that for dinner we must eat a massive three-pound porterhouse.

At home I dropped it on the kitchen table and dubbed it the Labor Steak.

Christa said, "God, I'll do anything to get this baby out of me."

And I knew she meant it.

"The Labor Steak will do it, sweetheart. A steak must work better than eggplant Parmesan."

In the early evening I returned again from the gym and found Christa reclining on the couch, a glass of syrupy pink liquid in front of her.

She said, "God, this tastes awful."

"What is it?"

"Fruit juice and castor oil."

"Where did you get castor oil?"

She laughed. "I bought it weeks ago."

"How much did you take?"

"A teaspoon."

"That's child's play. You need at least two tablespoons or it won't work," I said with the certainty borne of a Google search. I fixed Christa a higher dose.

It was the chilliest night since we'd moved to Woodstock,

and we decided to have our first fireplace fire. Castor oil. Labor Steak. Romantic fire. We couldn't go wrong.

Christa loved eating a steak so nearly raw you'd think it still had a pulse. Like a good husband I'd refused to allow her a rare steak throughout her pregnancy, but at nearly a week past her due date I decided she'd earned a steak at whatever temperature she desired. Outside on the deck I prepared the charcoal.

Inside, the fireplace spat out flames and Christa set the table. I stared at her through the window. She was my extremely beautiful and massively pregnant and petite wife and I knew that very soon, possibly within hours, our lives would change forever.

Like every other night we ate late. It was almost ten when I threw the meat on the grill. The woods that surrounded our home were dark and quiet.

The beastly three-pound porterhouse crawled off the grill and onto a serving platter after a few minutes of cooking.

We sat down for dinner, and the shadows from the fire licked our freshly painted walls and we ate our steak there in our charmingly rustic family home. All we were missing was that darn baby.

We'd each had a few bites of the steak. I wanted to ask about the castor oil but also I didn't want to ask about the castor oil. I knew that during her pregnancy she'd spared me the details of a number of the bodily mortifications she'd suffered. I assumed that if the castor oil experiment failed she'd keep the results to herself. I didn't mind this.

Christa looked at me and her large doe eyes grew wider and she said, "Oh. Jesus. I think I need to spend a lot of time alone on the toilet." She looked bashfully at the floor and pushed her plate away.

I said, "I'm sorry. This isn't going to be fun, is it?"

"I'm sorry to ruin our dinner," she said.

"Don't be silly."

Her eyes grew wider and she said, "Wait. I think my water broke?"

"How do you know?" I stupidly asked.

She reached down between her legs and said, "I know."

She grabbed her phone and called the hospital.

I used the fireplace tongs to throw the burning logs into a large copper cauldron and dragged the cauldron outside and onto the deck. If my wife hadn't needed to rush to the hospital I would have paused to admire the awesome sight of flames shooting five feet high into the dark night. But I doused the logs with a hose, and by the time I made it back inside Christa was already out front waiting in the car. The birthing center in Rhinebeck was forty minutes away.

She said, "Speed, speed, speed. I'm going to have this baby in the car!"

I have never regularly obeyed speed limits and the slightest encouragement from a passenger will always cause me to slam down the gas pedal. But this night, with the most important life at risk, I refused to speed.

"It will take longer if I get pulled over," I said.

"You speed on this road every fucking day, like three times a fucking day. Are you kidding me?"

"I'm not kidding. Delivery is a long way off."

I'd read the books for expectant fathers. They were all very clear that the father shouldn't speed toward the hospital. They also advised that when your partner no longer thinks your jokes are funny she is definitely in labor. We drove by the bar in Woodstock where my old landlord from Mount Tremper played bluegrass every Thursday night.

I motioned toward the Wok 'n Roll and said, "Want to hear some live music?"

She did not laugh.

"Let me drive," she said. "I'll speed."

I refused to relinquish the wheel. We arrived in Rhinebeck without birthing the baby in the car.

We settled in the room. Christa had hired the help of a doula, a woman named Mary. Mary had about her the old mountain wisdom and also, I'd thought, a whiff of the hippie grifter.

My main job was to play the *Josephine Birth Mix* from my laptop. Over the summer Mary had urged us to forgo the usual birthing classes, and when Christa asked about breathing techniques Mary said, "You are alive. You already know how to breathe. You were born for this. When the time comes just relax and have your baby. She'll tell you when she's ready."

Which is what happened.

I won't say that I did nothing. I'd like to think that I was a calm and supportive presence for my wife during one of the most intense physical and psychological moments of her life. This might be true. I played the Black Crowes' song "Oh Josephine" on repeat for about an hour around three-thirty in the morning. At about five I played "Into the Mystic" on repeat. I held the oxygen to Christa's mouth when Mary told me to.

I repeated, "You are an amazing woman and you are giving birth to our beautiful baby and we will both love you forever."

But mostly I watched four women—Christa, Mary the doula, the nurse, and the midwife—take part in the craziest thing I'd ever seen in my life. I'd been shot at during war and I'd seen what American-made five-hundred-pound bombs do to the human body, but nothing I'd witnessed compared to the intensity and immensity of my wife giving birth.

I watched these women take part in the natural birth of Josephine and I realized men could never accomplish this: four men trying to bring life into the world? Two would be engaged in a fistfight, one would be doing whiskey shots in the corner, and the other would be on the floor in a fetal position, weeping.

Josephine did tell us when she was ready for the world, at exactly 5:22 a.m. I caught her, as they say. She was a small bundle of loose limbs and of vernix, crying a beautiful cry. Her head looked like a collapsed hothouse tomato. I wondered if it would ever regain human shape, but I didn't betray my alarm to Christa.

I moved Josephine to her mother's chest, and I said, "Oh, Josephine, welcome to the family. We've been waiting so long to meet you."

She latched on to Christa's breast and we both held her little body. We were a family.

At first Josephine looked like every other baby, and then she began to fill out. There were days when I glanced at her and she looked like a complete stranger. And other days she looked just like Jeff. She usually looked like Jeff in the mornings, for some reason. I could see him in her brow and eyes and dear sweet smile. Around this time one of my aunts happened to send me a package with dozens of photos, many of them from the years when my parents lived in Spain and Jeff was an infant. And these photos confirmed for me Josephine's resemblance to her uncle Jeff.

ON THE LAST weekend of October we're warned to prepare for the biggest and earliest snow in New York State in decades. In a matter of hours the mountain we live on in Woodstock has turned from leaf-peeping ideal to deep winter landscape. The tourists who booked up the hotels months ago for the last look at red and yellow leaves descending from oak and poplar must change their plans. The leaves and trails are now frozen, which means no rigorous hikes up Overlook Mountain this weekend. Perhaps they might drive down to Kingston and purchase a sled at a sporting goods store and sled-race down the hills, or buy bourbon at a liquor store and submit to the baser instincts during a storm: get drunk and stay warm.

The tourists will be smart to learn from the twenty-two-year-old hiker Ryan Owens, who managed to get lost hiking near Moon Haw Road in the Slide Mountain Wilderness on Friday afternoon. He and his friend's dog Maggie spent the evening in a cave, and in the morning, as the big snow began to drop, they covered seven miles through rugged mountain terrain before finding civilization. Ryan had with him only Maggie and a bottle of water and he wore a long-sleeved thermal T-shirt.

Just over a year ago, had I been this Mr. Owens, I would have welcomed the snow and the fury of this freak early storm, and I might have stayed in the cave to die.

Tonight Josephine has been fussy, something new for us. My mother is visiting from California but she offers no baby-calming advice, and we appreciate this. After all, I am the last infant she took care of, forty-one years ago. The techniques have changed and this she must be aware of. And if my mother offers advice, I can counter with the knowledge that she smoked while pregnant with me and continued to smoke in my presence until the day I left home for the Marines. I often joke with her and claim that her in utero and secondhand smoke caused both my bad eyesight and my slow times in the forty-yard dash, and that if not for her smoking I might have been a fighter pilot or a football star or both.

Some truth and rage course through the nuances of my joke. I still blame my mother for some of the hurt and fear I suffered throughout my childhood: *Why did you not protect me from your secondhand carcinogenic smoke, and why did you not protect me from my father? You must have known that both were toxic.*

The snow falls steadily and Christa worries that we will lose power. We lost power for a week during Hurricane Irene and were lucky to retreat to a friend's vacation cottage in Maine during that time. A lengthy power outage with the baby in the house might be enough to scare us off the mountain and back to New York City.

Christa says, "If we lose power again, I'll tell Byrdcliffe we just can't take these risks with the baby. I'll kick the renters out of the Washington Avenue apartment and we'll be home in Brooklyn for Christmas."

Here in Woodstock we rent an idyllic converted barn from the Byrdcliffe Artists Colony. It is a wonderful place to have brought the baby home but we are ready for a return to city living. The mountains are too slow. The power outage flirts with our city dreams, and the lights flutter off and on throughout the evening, but the power remains on. We both want the power to fail and to have to head to the Thruway and get a few rooms at the Holiday Inn and use this as the ammo for breaking our lease. Dragging your baby to a Holiday Inn so she doesn't freeze to death is reason enough to break a lease, right?

This evening my mother cooked dinner. She made the enchiladas I grew up eating. I've been talking up these enchiladas to

Christa since our first date. I remember from my boyhood only a few good feelings as constant and certain as the news that my mother planned enchiladas for dinner.

Tonight the enchiladas disappoint with a surprising blandness, and my mother knows it and I know it and Christa knows it, but we tell my mother that the enchiladas are great and we both take seconds because this is what you tell your sixty-eight-year-old mother. Growing up I loved my mother's cooking, but now I am a rather accomplished self-taught home cook, and I can cook smoke rings around my mother, but no one needs to say it. And it doesn't matter.

Yesterday I took my mother to the grocery store and she bought the same canned enchilada sauce she has used for decades. I wanted to tell her that she could make her own sauce from scratch, that it would be very easy in fact to make from scratch a flavorful and robust red enchilada sauce, and that in our pantry we had everything she would need for this tasty sauce, but I bit my tongue. Sometimes food is not about the flavor but the gesture. My mother made dinner for me and my wife and my newborn baby daughter. That is more important than the flavor of the meal, isn't it? Someday when my mother has passed I will remember the night in Woodstock when I left my foodie pretensions in the canned food aisle of the supermarket and my mother cooked the enchiladas of my childhood for my wife and daughter. I will not remember that the enchiladas tasted bland. I will cherish the fact that as a winter storm streaked the Catskills with flashes of freezing snow, my mother labored in my kitchen and after the meal we were all full and we were happy. And by that time I will even forget that as a boy my mother failed to protect me from my bully father and that she smoked Pall Malls and ruined my speed in the forty-yard dash. Won't I? Mothers are immensely forgivable creatures.

For the fussy baby, Christa and I have tried all the tricks we know as new parents: slings and swings and lullabies and Van Morrison and college football. Neither of us says so, but we are both thinking the same thing: *Some ingredient from the canned enchilada sauce has entered into Christa's breast milk and turned our baby into a monster!* I watch a close football game and bounce the baby on my knee while Christa scans a number of child-rearing books trying to locate the exact cause of our daughter's sleeplessness and distress. We count the diapers Josephine soiled today, we count the feedings, and we count her farts. We add the values and divide by our anxiety squared. Baby sleep is a science and we are both humanists, total failures at science.

I say to my mother, feeling guilty about something, "JoJo never does this. It's midnight. She's usually asleep by nine."

And my mother says, "Sometimes babies don't sleep."

This is the wisdom from a mother of four children. It is basic and it is true tonight just as it was forty-one years ago: sometimes babies don't sleep.

You need not blame yourself or your mother's canned enchilada sauce.

Christa is tired and I have work to do, and I say to her, as though I am now an expert, "Sweetheart, sometimes babies don't sleep. Go to bed; I'll work with her on my chest."

A friend who had a baby a few weeks before we did sent me an e-mail one night that said only: "Skin-to-skin solves everything."

I took off my shirt and unclothed the baby and I slung her tight to my chest. I walked around the warm main room of our house and I sang her Van Morrison tunes, and I looked outside at the thick white blanket of snow on the ground and the tree branches weighted with snow.

At first the weathermen said the storm might drop eighteen inches, and then they revised that down to twelve, but it looks to me as if so far we took on eight inches at the top end, if the snow on my picnic table is any fair measure. But eight inches is a good snow for late October, a real snow.

It is only one in the morning, and we might still lose power. That is the measure of a proper storm. Some people must die: there must be danger. A storm also measures the man: will you protect your family when the storm shows? In the life of a family many storms threaten and some arrive full force. I'll pass this first test. I will pass them all, I tell myself.

Josephine sleeps against my chest. Some of her slobber has dripped down into my chest hair. I find this charming and beautiful. I find everything about my daughter charming and beautiful. Someday this will probably change. For instance, she will steal money from my wallet for beer and cigarettes. Hell, I will find this charming, too.

I will make enchilada sauce from scratch but my baby will not care; all she will want and need from me is guidance. She will need my sure and steady voice. During storms and during calm, she will long for my sure and steady voice, she will say, "That is my father, that is his sure and steady voice." And I will calm her.

I walk the house and I think about Mr. Owens spending the night in the cave last night. I wonder how or if his parents slept knowing their son was lost in the wilderness with his friend's dog. I can't imagine sleeping in such a situation. Sometimes I can't imagine sleeping ever if I do not know exactly where my baby daughter is sleeping.

I think of my father out in California, in his house, his cave, the place where he rests each night, oxygen mask tied to his face, knowing that if somehow he loses that oxygen overnight his life will end. For my father a power outage really could be a matter of life and death. I think of my mother sleeping upstairs in my home. I haven't slept under the same roof with my mother in at least twenty years. I like having her here. I wish my father were here, too. I know that he is alone in bed in Fairfield struggling to breathe. I hope that tonight he thinks of me, his son, holding his newest granddaughter to my chest.

I join Christa in bed. The baby makes some of her snorting noises and then settles back to sleep. The spotlight in the back of the house is on and I can see snow falling and I can hear the calm nothingness of the night, the quiet eternity of an evening with my family.

The baby warms my chest, and we sweat on each other. I feel JoJo's life against my chest, an inferno. I hear next to me my wife snoring. I hear the snowfall. I hear the baby breathing and I feel the baby's life burning against my chest and I am on fire and I am in love with my wife and my daughter. I am a husband and I am a father. This is my life now and this is how I live.

Postscript

My father's death clock had been ticking for over a decade, but since Josephine's birth the thrum and thunder of the clock had increased so much so that when my father and I spoke on the phone I could barely hear our conversation—I heard only one recurring thought: *He is dying, he is dying; bring your daughter to meet him.*

It was warm in Fairfield when we arrived. It is a town where people wear the warmth with pride the same way old soldiers wear their worthless and tattered ribbons.

My father greeted us standing in his driveway. Usually he wore a white T-shirt and briefs but now he sported a western suit and shirt with a bolo tie we had sent him for Christmas. He wore his black leather zip-up boots I had admired as a teenager because they looked like something Johnny Cash might wear.

I carried Josephine toward him. He also wore his oxygen tube stuck into his nostrils. She wore a pretty pink dress I had picked out.

He held her close to his chest and said, "Hello, Miss Josephine. I am your grandpa John."

She cooed when he kissed her cheek.

He seemed to strain under the weight of my fifteen-pound daughter. He stared at her. She had his blue eyes and his forehead and his ears. He must have noticed the glimmers of Jeff. I watched my father staring at my daughter and I finally understood the life-shattering loss that he'd suffered when Jeff died. I would never again challenge him on his behavior surrounding Jeff's death.

He said, "Take her back, Tone. I don't want to drop the beauty. I'm weak."

Christa greeted and kissed my father and we all entered his home.

We sat in his living room and he presented to us some things of his mother's that he wanted us to give to Josephine when she got older—her wedding and engagement rings, her watch still in the case, and her cedar keepsake chest.

Christa fed Josephine.

My father asked me to do him a favor by installing a motion-activated spotlight over his driveway.

"Thieves," he said. "They are everywhere. Gotta scare 'em off."

As his sickness worsened my father's paranoia increased. It was as though he waited every evening for an ambush. I did not point out to him that not many thieves would want to make off with his 1970s-era reel-to-reel stereo system unless they were throwback hi-fi aficionados.

It had been years since I had used my father's tools but I knew where to find everything. I needed a ladder and a drill and bits and the fixture itself. The sun shined bright and hot on me while I worked, and sweat stung my eyes.

I'd been at the work for a few minutes when my father appeared at the side of the house. He'd crept up silently enough that I hadn't seen him until he was ten feet away. He was bent at the waist.

"Hey, Dad, need a hand?" I said.

He pointed an index finger skyward, the John Howard Swofford sign that he was catching his breath.

I assumed that he'd appeared in order to micromanage my work on the spotlight. My father would never change. I readied myself for a tense scene like when I'd emptied the septic system on the RV. I thought, *Jesus, Old Man, give it a break.*

He propped himself up against the ladder I was standing on and took a few deep breaths.

He said, "You know, I've been talking about being buried in Opelika next to my mother for so long. I checked it all out, and it's a done deal if that's what I want."

I said, "I always liked the idea of you being buried next to her."

"The thing is, I ain't Southern, Tone. I left the South when I was seventeen. Ain't nothing but ghosts there. I'm a Californian. I love this state. I want to be buried over there at Dixon at the national cemetery next to all them other dead GIs."

"Whatever you want."

"Will you visit me there?"

"Of course."

He shuffled slowly back into the house and I returned to my work on the fixture.

I thought about my father and Christa and Josephine inside and of the spotlight I was installing and how it might scare off a thief but I hoped that what it would do was help my father to *see.*

I wanted him to see that whatever kind of father he had been to me I would become a very different father to Josephine. I knew that he must want that, too. For many years I had considered combat the only test of a man's greatness, but I'd begun to understand that for me fatherhood would be the real measure.

I wanted my father to look at his only surviving son and say to himself, *That is a man I admire, that is a father I admire; I wish I had been more like him, everything in this life can be new.*

When we left, he kissed Josephine goodbye and she cooed some more. We made plans to see him the following day.

As we pulled away from his home it was just becoming dusk. The spotlight shined upon my father and he waved.

Acknowledgments

I must first thank my agent Sloan Harris for his unyielding support and generous spirit, on the page and beyond the page. Sloan, thanks for kicking me in the teeth when I needed it and talking me back from a number of ledges.

Thank you, Cary Goldstein, at Twelve. You wielded the book and deduced where I'd been hiding and the corridors I'd yet to search. Your comradeship proved invaluable throughout. Brian McLendon: thank you for your hard work. It is a treat to have one's book in passionate hands. Libby Burton: thanks for your assistance in moving the manuscript along. Mari Okuda and S. B. Kleinman: thank you for tending to the copyediting and pointing out the corrections I'd missed. Catherine Casalino: you nailed the cover.

Kristyn Keene at ICM is a rock star and I thank her for all she does. And my thanks to Shira Schindel at ICM.

Thanks to C.H. for his friendship and discussing and dissecting my father over burgers and beers in dive bars throughout the city. To my numerous other male friends for the talks we had about those unyielding beasts, our fathers, thank you. You know who you are. I'll never tell your fathers what you said about them.

Dan Clare and Rob Lewis are true heroes for the work they

do at Disabled American Veterans. I appreciate their bringing me into the fold and introducing me to dozens of remarkable young injured men and women, veterans of the wars in Iraq and Afghanistan.

The Movermans: you are my family. Father: thank you for all your flaws and your beauty and your tragedy.

I should note that I borrow my book title from the first line of a James Tate poem called "The Private Intrigue of Melancholy."

My wife Christa is a brilliant writer and artist and a loving mother and the most amazing partner a lumpfish like me could possibly hope for. Every day with her is a splendid gift. She read this manuscript more times than is healthy for a spouse and she made me make it better when I was lazy or dumb or wanted only to walk in the woods with her and our beautiful daughter. Thank you, sweetheart, and our dear daughter, Josephine Clementine, joy of our lives.

About the Author

ANTHONY SWOFFORD is the author of the memoir *Jarhead* and the novel *Exit A*. He lives in the Hudson Valley in New York with his wife and daughter.

ABOUT TWELVE

TWELVE

TWELVE was established in August 2005 with the objective of publishing no more than twelve books each year. We strive to publish the singular book, by authors who have a unique perspective and compelling authority. Works that explain our culture; that illuminate, inspire, provoke, and entertain. We seek to establish communities of conversation surrounding our books. Talented authors deserve attention not only from publishers, but from readers as well. To sell the book is only the beginning of our mission. To build avid audiences of readers who are enriched by these works—that is our ultimate purpose.

For more information about forthcoming TWELVE books, please go to www.twelvebooks.com.